Drawing on Religion

T0355401

Drawing on Religion

Reading and the Moral Imagination in Comics and Graphic Novels

Ken Koltun-Fromm

The Pennsylvania State University Press
University Park, Pennsylvania

Library of Congress Cataloging-in-
Publication Data

Names: Koltun-Fromm, Ken, author.
Title: Drawing on religion : reading and
    the moral imagination in comics and
    graphic novels / Ken Koltun-Fromm.
Description: University Park, Pennsylvania
    : The Pennsylvania State University
    Press, [2020] | Includes bibliographical
    references and index.
Summary: "Develops a critical reading of
    comic religious narratives to engage
    moral sources that both expand and
    limit our ethical worlds"—Provided by
    publisher.
Identifiers: LCCN 2020035745 |
    ISBN 9780271087757 (paperback)
Subjects: LCSH: Comic books, strips,
    etc.—Religious aspects. | Comic books,
    strips, etc.—Moral and ethical aspects.
    | Comic books, strips, etc.—Criticism
    and interpretation.
Classification: LCC PN6712 .K65 2020 |
    DDC 741.5/382—dc23
LC record available at https://lccn.loc.gov
    /2020035745

It is the policy of The Pennsylvania State
University Press to use acid-free paper.
Publications on uncoated stock satisfy
the minimum requirements of American
National Standard for Information
Sciences—Permanence of Paper for Printed
Library Material, ANSI z39.48–1992.

To my students at Haverford College

Contents

Illustrations

Acknowledgments

I argue in this book that lingering in unease, in spaces and with images that make us uncomfortable, is a productive way to expand our moral imaginations. So too is listening to others and quieting oneself to create pathways of dialogue and discernment. All this can be difficult and sometimes painful; learning can be challenging, uprooting, and ongoing. Haverford College, where I teach, offers one of those lingering spaces for us to collectively learn with one another. Acknowledging this college as my home is more than descriptive of some twenty years of teaching and researching; it also recognizes the space of my discomfort, the context of my learning, the community of my fellow educational travelers, and the impact of this institution on my moral imagination.

My colleagues in the religion department at Haverford—Molly Farneth, Pika Ghosh, Guangtian Ha, Naomi Koltun-Fromm, Anne McGuire, and Terrance Wiley—have all been part of my educational journey and growth, and working with them is inspirational and humbling. Those colleagues who have moved on—David Dawson, Tracey Hucks, Terrance Johnson, Brett Krutzsch, Michael Sells, and Travis Zadeh—still linger in the college halls and certainly in the deep recesses of my mind. I do hope that the kindnesses of all these colleagues find their echoes in this book.

Haverford is, as we like to say, a small liberal arts college, and so reaching out to colleagues here and beyond is as necessary as it is rewarding. Lou Charkoudian, Robert Fairman, Andrew Friedman, Barbara Hall, Aryeh Kosman, Ben Le, Laura McGrane, John Muse, Deborah Roberts, Jeff Tecosky-Feldman, David Harrington Watt, and Joel Yurdin here at Haverford have been formative in my thinking about our ethical worlds, but they have also provided friendship and companionship when I needed it most. Laura Levitt, J. T. Waldman, and Steve Weitzman, three colleagues in the Philadelphia area, are all brilliant scholars and close friends, and I am fortunate to call them neighbors. Indeed, the Religious Studies Consortium here in Philadelphia has grounded me in a broader circle of religious scholars who, like me, thrive in the context of collegiality. I am especially indebted to my Swarthmore colleague Yvonne Chireau, with whom I taught a course on comics and from whom I have learned so much about visual representation and race.

To my cherished "Uneasy Objects" friends, a motley crew of dedicated scholars in the field of Jewish studies—Samantha Baskind, Jonathan Boyarin,

Zachary Braiterman, Leonard Kaplan, Laura Levitt, and Elissa Sampson: I am grateful for our friendship and community, and I look forward to many more summer gatherings. And I am deeply appreciative for David Morgan's and A. David Lewis's close readings of this manuscript and helpful suggestions for improvement.

These people and many others have made spaces open to moral imaginings; also important, however, is the practical but all-too-necessary financial support I have received from Haverford College and the National Endowment for the Humanities for my research. I am also grateful to the University of Mississippi Press for allowing me to republish in chapter 1 of this book portions of my cowritten essay (with Madeline Backus), "Writing the Sacred in Craig Thompson's *Habibi*," in *Comics and Sacred Texts: Reimagining Religion and Graphic Narratives*, ed. Assaf Gamzou and Ken Koltun-Fromm (Jackson: University of Mississippi Press, 2018), 5–24.

Finally, and in many ways most crucially, I want to thank my students at Haverford College, especially Shayleah Jenkins and Paige Walton, who dedicated a summer to reading, critiquing, and engaging this work; Madeline Backus, who helped me to see the pedagogical beauty and challenges of comics; and my Chesick students, who have transformed how I think about and account for my education. I have been radically challenged and moved by your presence and commitment to justice and inclusion. I dedicate this book to all of you, and to the many other Haverford students whom I am privileged to teach, with deep gratitude and recognition. My moral imagination, however tenuous and suspect, has been that much more expansive and enduring because of your presence here at Haverford.

KEN KOLTUN-FROMM
Haverford College

Introduction

The Ethics of Representation

The attack on the French satirical weekly *Charlie Hebdo* on January 7, 2015, was more than a vengeful murder for perceived blasphemous depictions of Islam and the prophet Muhammad. Even as the two brothers gunned down eleven employees, shouting in Arabic, according to some reports, "We have avenged the Prophet Muhammad,"[1] their attack revealed to the world that comic representation is anything but comic. To be sure, *Charlie Hebdo* was no stranger to religious controversy, and the newspaper featured cartoons mocking religious practices and beliefs of all faiths. The weekly had taken to ridiculing religious traditions that appeared too comfortable with the sacred character of religious images. In these parodies, *Charlie Hebdo* presented more than a caricature of identity; the magazine sought to expose, and so open to critique, what religious persons take to be their most sacred beliefs and practices. Opening ourselves in this way requires a vulnerability and a willingness to reconsider our most revered convictions, and it cultivates a moral imagination that travels beyond the safety of our familiar truths. Being porous and open also means cultivating fragility as we negotiate unfamiliar modes of being in the world. The two gunmen on January 7 sought to impair that world, and that moral imagination, in a violent act of destruction. This book voices a response to that repressive silence by expanding our moral imaginations through readings of graphic religious narratives. As *Charlie Hebdo* made clear, comics are a powerful medium of communication and iconic representation. The ethical import of these storied images is the subject of this book.

Drawing on Religion: Reading and the Moral Imagination in Comics and Graphic Novels is a work about visual representation and the ethical presentation of self, community, and religious practice. Throughout this work I appeal to the collective responsibility of all of us readers, practitioners, and creative thinkers—indeed all persons—to consider what it means to imagine both expansive and repressive moral lives. When I write "we" and "us," I suggest we are all called on to do this kind of ethical work, and I invite you to join me in that struggle. This book develops a critical reading of comic religious narratives to engage moral sources that both expand and limit our ethical worlds. Representing religion is dangerous and powerful, and one need not even recall the *Charlie Hebdo* attack to understand this. Exodus 20 warns its readers not to carve or make images in any likeness of God, and though ambiguous in meaning, this text still generates interpretive concerns about iconic representation and idol worship. There remains a profound sense here that religious adepts *should not* represent God, much less idolize false deities. This is true as well for God's chosen representatives on earth. Although not all Muslim communities refuse to depict Muhammad's countenance, paintings exist in which his face is literally scraped away. In Hindu traditions, the significance of *darshan*—the very act of seeing, and being seen by, the gods—reveals the potency of the divine gaze.[2] Depicting gods or religious acts, to be sure, functions as a mode of world maintenance and religious order, as scholar David Morgan often describes this visual piety.[3] But the comic texts discussed in this book show how ocular moments can also severely disrupt, engender, and create religious anxiety and ethical perplexity. *How* texts represent religion is an ethical issue, I argue in this book, because images, and especially comic images, provoke imaginative portrayals of the sacred, and in so doing they introduce but also blind us to new and unfamiliar possibilities of human existence. In the very act of representing divinity, comics also display oppressive images that value some identities more than others. In all this, comics open us to unexpected, provocative, and harmful states of being. One feature of the critical reading practices developed in this book is the recognition of how comics both cultivate and hinder our moral resources to imagine unfamiliar religious worlds.

In some sense, all religious iconography can do this kind of imaginative work. But graphic religious narratives face a particularly challenging problem in the ethics of representation: comics traffic in stereotypes.[4] For the influential Will Eisner, "the stereotype is a fact of life in the comics medium. It is an accursed necessity—a tool of communication that is an inescapable ingredient in most cartoons."[5] In many ways comic stereotyping is a function of what Scott McCloud calls "amplification through simplification," where "we're not so much **eliminating** details as we are **focusing** on **specific details**."[6] Yet as "an idea or character that is standardized in a conventional form," the stereotype can cause harm or offense and, as Eisner admits, can even be used "as a weapon of propaganda or racism." Comics appeal to our common perceptions of characters and experiences, and they deploy stereotypes to do this easily and quickly.[7] Eisner believed we could critically distinguish "good" from "bad" stereotypes by addressing authorial intent and the artist's recognition of social judgment.[8] But as Jeremy Dauber makes clear in his fine article on Eisner's life and work, Eisner's intent—whatever that might have been—does not absolve him of the blatantly racist and sexist depictions of his characters.[9] Neither does it absolve us, as readers, from critically engaging *how* religious representation works in the comic form. Recovering authorial intent, even if one could do so, can explain only why an author makes certain artistic choices; it does not relieve us of our own moral obligations to imagine new ways of being in the world.

Stereotyping is a risk for those artists who work within the comic medium because readers could always get it wrong: one might read racial profiling, unconsciously accept ethnic slurs, or absorb gendered hierarchies when authors never intended such readings. Tahneer Oksman's thoughtful book on Jewish female graphic memoirs, *"How Come Boys Get to Keep Their Noses?,"*[10] brings these challenges to the fore, even if she ultimately does not resolve the ethical dilemma posed by them. In her chapter on Aline Kominsky Crumb, Oksman contends that readers can reconstruct how an author uses stereotypes to undermine common perceptions of self: "By favoring a seemingly unself-conscious portrayal of how conventional notions of the self and of communal identities continue to define the way she depicts herself and others, Kominsky Crumb risks being misread as an amateur artist confirming these stereotypes even as she distorts and dislodges them. Her postwar autobiographical comics present the potential of stereotype as a means of representation that, through dynamic reconstruction, can lead to new ways of seeing and understanding the self, although these new ways of seeing are also always connected to a limiting and destructive past."[11] What might seem like an unselfconscious use of stereotypes (the word "seemingly" suggests that Kominsky Crumb only appears to dabble in the practice) is actually a move to undermine them (she distorts and dislodges them). But only "through dynamic reconstruction" can such "new ways of seeing and understanding the self" be found, and here Oksman appeals to her own expertise to uncover Kominsky Crumb's authorial intent. But neither Kominsky Crumb nor Oksman takes responsibility for those who "misread [Kominsky Crumb] as an amateur artist confirming these stereotypes." Only if we understand Kominsky Crumb's intent and the way she employs stereotypes can we see how she reimagines identity.[12]

Oksman shares this appeal to interpretive reconstruction with many other readers of graphic narratives. Jared Gardner's thoughtful piece on stereotypes in comics argues that "sequential comics" can destabilize stereotypes and caricatures we often find in single-panel cartoons. He believes the work that readers do in the "gutter" between those panels becomes a "more complicated and unruly enterprise" that "disables stereotype and the easy readings of the hegemonic gaze."[13] But the ethical quandary of visual representation does not disappear with authorial intent or reading it right, in the gutters or elsewhere. Trafficking in stereotypes is always a visual risk because readers, especially comic readers, invest their own imaginations, as Gardner suggests, in the creation of the narrative story. Indeed, some scholars believe that this readerly investment defines what is unique about the comic book genre.[14] Yet comics cannot "force" their readers to do the progressive work that Gardner hopes they will do. Even if Kominsky Crumb wishes to undermine those stereotypical fantasies, readers might very well decide to live by them. Misreading authorial intent, even in sequential comics, is what we do as readers, and comic stereotypes enable misreadings because they traffic in misrepresentation.

So if comics work in caricature and stereotype, how do they enable reflective, ethical critique of their artistic medium? Although I do not know whether Art Spiegelman ever intended such a reading, his magisterial *Maus* at one point engages this ethical concern. Upon entering his father's house to interview Vladek, Artie confronts a crying Mala complaining about her husband (who is also Artie's father). "**Pragmatic? Cheap!!**" she screams in bold script to Artie. "**It causes him physical pain to part with even a nickel.**" A pensive, somewhat depressed Artie responds, "It's something that worries me about the book I'm doing about him . . . In some ways he's just like the racist caricature of the miserly old Jew." Rather than sympathize with Artie's anxiety, Mala confirms the caricature as true representation. "**Hah!**" she bellows. "You can say **that** again!"[15] Now, one could read this interaction in a number of compelling ways: (1) perhaps Artie comes to understand, finally, something true about his father; or (2) Artie cares more for his artistic craft than he does for his father's cheap habits; but conceivably (3) Artie now accepts that he works in stereotypes and so is responsible for those images before his readers. I imagine these and other readings could produce vibrant accounts of this image-text. But in the context of my own concerns with ethical representation—and here I self-consciously swerve my misreading from any authorial intent—Mala and Artie raise the stereotype as an ethical problem for comic images. Not just the belief in but the very use of stereotype becomes a suspect form of *doing* comics.

Here in this precarious zone of ambivalence, ethical reflection can be most productive and powerful. How *should* stereotypes function in comics? How might we begin to see differently through them? The point here is that we can access new, imaginative possibilities of being in the world when we encounter the stereotype as problematic image. Eisner might be right that comics necessarily traffic in stereotypes, but our ethical work begins rather than ends there. We want to understand what stereotypes do and how particularly religious stereotypes function in comics in ways that might expand or diminish our imaginative worlds.

I understand comics as a kind of cultural and ethical practice; I am interested in what they do—how they enact, enable, or hinder moral reflection—and how they deploy images and texts to provoke this kind of ethical reasoning. I find it far less fruitful to define comics or to present robust theories of graphic narratives within the field of visual studies. Scott McCloud is perhaps the most influential of those theorists who believe that we must define the field before engaging in it. But his thoughtful account of comics as "juxtaposed pictorial and other images in deliberate sequence, intended to convey information and/or to produce an aesthetic response in the viewer" encounters two immediate problems: (1) a focus on sequence leads McCloud to emphasize a unity of comic grammar, such that the sequential images present an "overriding identity," thereby "forcing" a reader to consider the images "as a whole," and (2) by attending to the "aesthetic response in the viewer," McCloud sidesteps the ethical and religious dimensions (among others) that are critical features of the comics discussed in this study.[16] To be sure, viewers do things to comics, as McCloud makes clear in his account of closure, in which readers stitch together visual and textual unity in the empty spaces between and among images. The gutter—this empty space of readerly involvement and creativity—invites that kind of participation but neither forces it nor always enables a wholistic or singular reading and viewing.

Comics and their readers do many different kinds of interpretive acts, and we will see in this book how divergent and often subversive those acts can be. Images do not arrive clean, as it were, as though they are transparent in meaning. So it is simply not true that pictures are, according to McCloud, "**received** information" in which "the message is *instantaneous*." As I hope this book reveals quite clearly, images do not work that way, in comics or in other visual media. David Freedberg notes, in the very title of his work *The Power of Images*, that pictures themselves leverage a certain kind of authority: "We must consider not only beholders' symptoms and behavior, but also the effectiveness, efficacy, and vitality of images themselves; not only what beholders do, but also what images appear to do."[17] Images work on us as we work on them. There is labor involved, but much of what viewers do with images is learned from their surroundings. Indeed, stereotypes work precisely because they draw on recognizable cultural and religious codes, and comic authors expect familiarity with those codes. If McCloud is right that "we need no formal education to 'get the message,'"[18] then this means only we have not done enough imaginative work to unpack the labor involved in the ethics of representation.

To engage in what images do, comics entail more than "a system of signification."[19] They certainly do signify and point to meanings, but they are also more than "a collection of codes"[20] or a language game that can be addressed only "through the lens of semiotics theory."[21] Graphic narratives conjure up imaginative worlds, they play with emotions and bodily responses, they suggest absence of meaning, and they are in many important ways material objects that traffic in economic and cultural zones. Jean-Paul Gabilliet's material history of comics focuses on cultural production, and so his definition offers something very different from McCloud's. Rather than examining the conceptual understanding of comics (as McCloud does) through ancient engravings, or the Bayeux Tapestry's depiction of the 1066 Norman invasion of England, or even William Hogarth's eighteenth-century caricatures, Gabilliet turns to the Swiss storyteller Rudolphe Töpffer (1799–1846) and his "picture stories" because he "adapted them to the era of mass publishing." For Gabilliet, "comic art is the form taken by stories in images in an age of mass publishing that started in the nineteenth century."[22] The material features of comics as pulp magazines produced on cheap paper[23] enabled their mass publishing, but those features also highlighted their "visual narrative form," as Thierry Groensteen labels this graphic labor,[24] and these "stories in images" tethered meaning to what images do.[25] That visual leverage also invites a reader to construct graphic tempo because a comic, "in displaying intervals . . . rhythmically distributes the tale that is entrusted to it" and motivates a "cadenced reading" as a kind of "breathing aroused."[26] Hillary Chute and Patrick Jagoda even describe the power of comics "to derive movement from stillness."[27] These concerns with rhythm, bodily comportment, readerly motivation, the material features of production, and visual materiality all work against "reading" comics as a system of meaningful codes. It is not only about "getting the message," as McCloud has it, but also about stimulating a reflective aesthetics of the moral imagination.

Instead of decoding hidden meanings in comics, I think we should imagine them as visual stimuli for judging, expanding, and critically assessing our ethical and religious borders. Judgment in religious ethics begins, in my view, with a porous imagination in which alternative modes of being in the world become real possibilities for a good life. This can sometimes mean exposure and openness to radically new configurations of living, even if those new configurations are not ones we would choose for ourselves or for those we love. It is something close to what Robert Orsi calls a "suspensive" ethic, in which we should all honor our "commitment to examining the variety of human experience and to making contact across boundaries—cultural, psychological, spiritual, existential."[28] This is what the two brothers wanted to prevent in their attack on *Charlie Hebdo*, and this is what this book seeks to accomplish by exposing graphic narratives to our ethical imaginations.

But such ethical exposure of one's own worlds in communicative openness can also bear witness to fundamentally mundane, everyday occurrences that too often go unnoticed—as if their very commonality blinds us to their revelatory potential. Part of what I find so important about Michael Taussig's account of drawing in his *I Swear I Saw This* is his appeal to the everyday sacred. As an extended meditation on his fieldwork drawing of two people near a freeway tunnel in Medellin, Colombia, in 2006, *I Swear I Saw This* poses this extraordinary account of bearing witness: "The real shock—if that is the word—now seems to me to be that we so easily accept scenes like the one of the people by the tunnel. In the blink of an eye they pass into oblivion. The real shock is their passing from horror to banality. The real shock is that fleeting moment of awareness as to the normality of the abnormal, which, as with a wound, soon covers itself over with scar tissue. . . . To witness, therefore, is that which refuses, if only for an instant, to blink an eye."[29] Taussig believes that drawing is a kind of "shadow text" to the diary entry as it captures the fleeting sense of the extraordinary—a moment of the everyday sacred that linguistic script too often misses. The "terror of writing" is "this sinking feeling that the reality depicted recedes, that the writing is actually pushing reality off the page." The drawing, though, pays "homage to the marvelous" in which "a little bit of everyday hell is given its due." This is Taussig's point about his drawing of the people by the tunnel, that it "emits power as image because it suggests secrets and, on occasion, unusual insights into the human condition."[30] Bearing witness means, in this sense, to recognize an everyday event as wonder and as tragic beauty. To witness is to reveal sublime modes of being human in the world.

Drawing does not get at the really real, even though Taussig does suggest that it touches on something distinctly human. Instead, drawing opens up imaginative possibilities, and Taussig's meditative writing mimics well this sense of playful but serious openness. In revealing these subtler modes of human expression, drawing demands a physical interaction with the drawn object: "To draw is to move my hand in keeping with what I am drawing, and as the hand moves, so does the body, which tenses and keeps changing the angle of vision." Taussig compares this movement to dance and to a form of sympathetic magic. It is a kind of engaged corporeality "in which an image of something provides the image-maker bodily access to its being."[31] This equivocal sense of "its being" (for whose "being" is referenced here?) witnesses to a refusal of distance: the image-maker and the material object, like sympathetic magic, traverse the boundaries of subject and object *through* the image. For Taussig, drawing opens up the revelatory potential of the other to transform one's very self.

Assaf Gamzou and I have tried to get at this extraordinary potential of the everyday to enliven moral resources in our coedited volume, *Comics and Sacred Texts* (2018). We devoted an entire section of that book to "The Everyday Sacred in Comics," for we believe that graphic narratives expose "holy presence in the mundane, common, and often overlooked features of familiar existence." This is a new visual learning, much like Taussig's form of witnessing, in which "the pedestrian and local can become windows to revelational encounter."[32] One sees this clearly in Shiamin Kwa's beautiful reading of Kevin Huizenga's *Walkin'*, where she argues that "this comic continuously reminds readers of the strangeness of the common, a strangeness that should give them pause."[33] I will take up this notion of pausing in the conclusion to this work when I explore the pleasures of lingering in comic spaces. But here I want to point out Kwa's focus on moments of the inexplicable and encounters of oddity that Taussig marks as revelatory for understanding the human condition. We must learn to see comics as iconic windows into new moral worlds that demand imaginative responses from their readers.

This is how Taussig wishes us to bear witness through drawing, and this too is how I seek ethical reflection through religious representation in North American graphic narratives.[34] The comics discussed in this book bear witness to the ethical imagination and to the possibilities of traversing religious landscapes but also to the problematic status of racial, classed, and gendered stereotypes of religious persons. I want to see drawing in comics as opportunities for ethical reflection and discernment about what religion looks like, about how one comes to recognize the religious *as* religious, about how stereotypes often limit ethical boundaries, and about how we might expand our ethical horizons to see other modes of living well in the world. This is less a comparative project than a concentrated, belabored one in the American comic tradition, and this explains why most of the comics in this book focus on popular American religious traditions. The labor involves an acute focus on image-texts that bear witness to the religious imagination in all its revelatory beauty and horror. Some of the image-texts discussed in this book are remarkably closed to the kind of imaginative ethics I call for here; others, as we shall see, divulge a keen sensitivity to the visionary. *Drawing on Religion* is really a work about the graphic imagination and about how seeing is a form of visual judgment. Bearing witness to the unfamiliar familiar is not exotic travel. One should not see the other only to discern something true about where one stands. Religious graphic narratives open us to the kaleidoscopic possibilities of being in the world and move us to expand our ethical imagina-tions. We may decide not to live in those other worlds, but they can transform our own world when we recognize them as good ways of living. In this sense, although I might continue to stand right here, the place where I stand is no longer the same place. That is the risk and beauty of the moral imagination and the ethics of representation.

Drawing on Religion explores how comic graphic representations expand and contract ethical worlds, ethical possibilities, and moral imaginations. Each chapter focuses on a particular feature of graphic narratives and its capacity to develop and narrow the moral religious imagination. Chapter 1, "Stereotypes and the Moral Challenges of Aesthetic Narration," appropriates Leela Prasad's evocative account of aesthetics and morality to query how comic narratives present stereotypes and style as moral provocations. Here I want to explore how stereotypical depictions of others through line, font, color, and graphic calligraphy offer modes of ethical engagement and deflection. Comic styles yield moral claims to foundations—a sense of moral certainty and order—as well as ethical modes of instability and flow. The very lines on a page can even expose negotiations between order and flow, opening an inviting hybridity and boundary crossing. One can see this in Will Eisner's *A Contract with God* (1978) and his appeal to moral order (through Hebrew calligraphy) even as he points beyond moral certitude to divine capriciousness (through strategic use of lightning bolts and the absence of comic frames). This doubleness returns in Craig Thompson's *Habibi* (2011) but in ways that channel Eisner's tragic world into a fantastical orientalist image of exotic others. This static other, as a mere projection of the orientalist frame, undermines Thompson's ethical desire for religious reconciliation. Yet both Eisner and Thompson employ stereotypes to represent moral positions within their ethical frames, thereby erasing a stylistic flow that could lead to a broader, more imaginative ethics of representation. By including the Vakil brothers' *40 Sufi Comics* (2011) and J. T. Waldman's *Megillat Esther* (2005) in this discussion of aesthetic moral representation, we see how style evokes certain modes of ethical reflection and containment.

The second chapter analyzes comic translations of sacred literature and uncovers the moral force of scriptural works for graphic narratives. In "The Ethics of Scriptural Play: Gender, Race, and Moral Sources," I ask how comics open scripture to ethical play and possibility and how they sensationalize, racialize, and sexualize those texts in new visual modes of representation. There are a number of recent comics that turn to sacred texts as compelling testimonies and resources for visual representation, and I will focus on three of them: Robert Crumb's *The Book of Genesis Illustrated* (2009), Mike Allred's *The Golden Plates* (2004), and Steve Ross's *Marked* (2005). Literary scholars such as Robert Alter tend to find these visual renditions far too constricting, especially when they are compared to the openness of the written word. Alter's critique of Crumb articulates this view quite well: for biblical texts, "these ancient Hebrew stories use the resonance and the reticence of well-chosen words to proliferate possibilities of meaning," whereas graphic representations too easily pin down and reify those meanings.[35] Certainly images can work in the ways Alter criticizes here, but they can also function like "well-chosen words" and so open the text to imaginative, ethical reflection. I want to trace how graphic translations of sacred texts work in both registers, with a special eye to the racial and gendered depictions of religious selves.

Comic artists often depict those religious selves as superheroes. Indeed, students of graphic narratives such as Greg Garrett visualize superheroes, erroneously in my view, as modern-day representatives of religious figures.[36] But the popular appeal of comics and their superheroes, and perhaps the equally moving portrait of religious figures as superheroes in their own right, still do ethical work for our sense of justice—and in this regard I think Garrett's work is quite compelling. The third chapter of this book, "Imagining (Superhero) Identity," looks at non-Western superheroes and the ethical representation of model selves. I delve into two revelatory texts—A. David Lewis's *Lone and Level Sands* and the *Ms. Marvel* series—to better assess how artists frame the West, the others that surround the superhero, and the American superhero tradition. These comics offer alternative visions of the superhero but tend to work within a politics that limits identification to those who look much like their superheroes. In presenting the ethnic body as superhero, these comics move readers to consider what superheroes *should* look like and how visual performance enacts moral goods. Here too I wish to engage how these non-Western texts lean heavily on classical superhero motifs; still, they construct alternative models of religious selves—persons who challenge familiar narratives of the heroic, revealing unfamiliar stories about the superhuman.

These are new stories: narratives about skin color and ethnic stereotypes, loneliness and the inner self. What kind of moral work do religious stories enable? The fourth chapter, "The Nativist Imagination in Religious Comic Stories," looks at Craig Thompson's *Blankets* (2003) and Joann Sfar's *The Rabbi's Cat* (2005)—two comics about religious maturity, the native self, and the religious other. Moral philosophers have already mined and still return to the narrative genre for ethical value but in comics readers see that moral imagination in visual play. And that play is a serious one for religious selves yearning to move beyond the confining structures of home to less secure but more open, hybrid, and creative expressions of religious practice. I begin this chapter with Kirin Narayan's sensitive account of the native anthropologist and her pursuit of more hybrid, complicated identities for informants and ethnographers.[37] Both Thompson and Sfar traffic in these narrative appeals to the native, but the one grows out of a rigid, evangelical Christianity to expose more troubled, scarred accounts of identity (Thompson), while the other travels within a safe and ultimately insular pluralism, inevitably returning to a more comfortable, nativist framework (Sfar). Together, these comics expose the limits of religious seekers. Their more chastened visions of religious freedom, as I read these texts, reveal the limits and possibilities of the moral imagination and a more nuanced account of nativist identity, one that informs and continues to haunt their moral worlds.

Comics are haunted by more than a nativist logic; they have participated in a representational history of violence. The fifth and final chapter, "Graphic Violence and the Religious Self," scrutinizes the role of spiritual violence in forming religious selves. The comic tradition has a long, rather tortuous history with graphic violence, at one point even creating a comics code of self-censorship to prevent American government interference in the 1950s. I draw from Cynthia Baker's thoughtful account of the term *Jew* to explore how religious violence works to define the religious other, to establish mythical narratives of perpetual violence, and to embody violence as constitutive of the religious self. There are numerous comics that do this kind of work, but I focus my attention on the *Jack Chick* cartoon series of the past thirty years, Douglas Rushkoff's *Testament: Akedah* (2006), and Grant Morrison's "The Coyote Gospel" (1989). All three of these comics depict violence as critical features of religious expression, but they do so in distinct ways that bear on the moral imagination. *Jack Chick* tracts define the non-Christian other (or really, the nonevangelical Christian other) as essentially violent, and so they categorically distinguish those saved through faith from those damned to eternal violence in hell. *Chick*'s separation of those faithful who live in peace from the violent evil that inhabits religious others functions much like Jan Assmann's "Mosaic Distinction," in which no translation is possible between competing cultural frames. As Assmann astutely notes, "False gods cannot be translated."[38] For Rushkoff and his modern adaptation of the biblical sacrifice of Isaac by his father, Abraham, we are all unknowingly entrapped in a religious battle for authenticity. In *Akedah*, Rushkoff seeks to liberate us from this ever-recurring violence, but the battle for freedom never recedes, and neither does the savagery. This is true as well for Morrison's "The Coyote Gospel" within his *Animal Man* series, although Morrison harbors little hope that we can free ourselves from divine and human violence. But Crafty, the Christlike and tragic coyote in this comic, glimpses a world outside these cyclical horrors, and it is this vision beyond vision—an imaginative sight beyond imagination—that opens our moral worlds to new, yet-to-be-seen lives beyond horrific violence. This is the comic challenge to the moral imagination.

I conclude *Drawing on Religion* with a meditation on what it means to imagine beyond imagination, and I do so through a review of Jonathan Lear's moving portrayal of Plenty Coups.[39] In significant ways, reading the religious in comics is akin to the radical hope that Lear traces in Plenty Coups's attempt to maintain his tribal culture. For like Plenty Coups, graphic narratives can expose worlds beyond our imaginative capacities, but they can also call into question our own framed cultures and so move us to reimagine and thus resituate moral boundaries, sometimes even pushing us to explore beyond the frame. But the ethical stakes before Plenty Coups are vitally different in at least one respect: very few readers encounter the cataclysmic challenges that this tribal leader did. He faced the extinction of his people and their way of life. Unlike Plenty Coups, readers of graphic novels have the luxury to endure in critical and reflective postures and to slowly absorb the moral quandaries before them. In this more welcoming temporality, graphic narratives portray worlds that engage the imagination in pleasurable and painful modes of reflective, pedagogical encounter. They are graphic reminders that the violence perpetrated by those who attacked *Charlie Hebdo* cannot silence our imaginative play with words and images. Comics show us those playful worlds in image, text, and image-text; the pedagogical challenge is to linger in that space and see those worlds well, both with ethical sensitivity and moral imagination.

CHAPTER 1

Stereotypes and the Moral Challenges of Aesthetic Narration

Telling stories is a moral act of bodily gestures, pitch, tone, and expression, all requiring a sense of timing and purpose. It is a stylistic encounter with listeners, viewers, and readers who are often challenged by the strong claims of ethical narration. Here is but one example of such an encounter. Robert Orsi introduces his edited volume, *Gods of the City* (1999), with a none-too-subtle distinction between the common fantasy of the urban holy and the more realistic, gritty, and far more complex notion of urban religion. For those who wish to absorb the city as "alien desire," as a source for redemption among the poor and the unkempt, the urban holy marks a charged space of personal salvation in which pleasure seekers and spiritualists "could bring order out of chaos, unity out of diversity, whiteness out of color." But such absorption and even consumption of the city "obliterates the lived reality of the other." That reality Orsi describes in much different terms: "Immigrants recrafted inherited traditions, invented new ritual practices, and reconfigured the meanings of cities with improvisatory religious practices of stone and space. They recreated particular spaces in the cities to better serve their religious needs." Reading "through and across the fantasy of the city"—a fantasy that attempts to organize and survey by means of structured cartographies and sculptured landscapes—reveals instead a city bustling with recrafting, invention, reconfiguration, and improvisation. Where the one closes down creative play, the other lives by it; if one yearns for simplicity of purpose and encounter, the other erupts with vitality and the unknown.[1] These descriptive narratives are also normative ones, for they each portray the city as a charged, ethical space of moral contest. They divide those seeking recognizable structure from those who thrive within creative forces. We can imagine Orsi verbally repeating this story with movements and stylistic tones that mimic the sometimes staid and sometimes lively urban religious experience. The ethical posture of storytelling can reveal how to listen to the well-ordered structures and vibrant energies that inform the lives of others.

But even Orsi would admit that this story is too clean, almost too generic, and simply too either/or. For Orsi recognizes as well that city dwellers absorb modes of bodily comportment as they mimic their elders and appropriate cultural norms. Hardly ever is it a mode of creativity rather than of order, for even the most fluid of urban citizens appeal to religious maps to navigate through the city.[2] In another context, Orsi recognizes this kind of negotiation as a critical feature of religious relationships: "Rarely is it a simple matter of either resistance or submission, but rather of negotiating compromises that are often tragic in their inevitability."[3] Moral narratives are not lived as wholly one or the other, as either bustling complexity or rooted simplicity. Instead, ethical stories often rely on notions of propriety—what is fitting and acceptable as a moral, narrative choice, even if that choice leads to inevitable conflicts. Some moral decisions are simply tragic ones, but others capture something profoundly human, sensitive as they are to the ethical moment.

Leela Prasad, in her magnificent *Poetics of Conduct* (2007), writes about "dramatic propriety" as a positionality that bridges "connections between aesthetics and persuasiveness." Here, Prasad helpfully repositions ethical inquiry to accept how "moral narration is intimately tied to the aesthetics of narrativization." She presents a number of compelling stories to textually draw out this claim, none more fascinating and moving than this one about Dodda Murthy: "He asked me if I knew the tragic manner in which the resident's father had passed away many years ago. When I said no, he started to recount the incident, but then stopped in midsentence, noticing that I had brought a cup of boiled milk for him. 'Let me finish this first,' he said. 'It isn't right to drink milk after narrating such a story.'" Prasad summarizes Murthy's ethical sensitivity in this way: "To have drunk the milk after narrating such an episode would have been an inappropriate and callous mixing of 'tragedy' with 'satisfaction.'"[4] Murthy has absorbed cultural notions of propriety, and Prasad recognizes how proper style marks an ethical stance. This is not the fantasy of cultivating order out of complex heterogeneity, as Orsi has described the fantasy of the urban holy. This is, by contrast, a more subtle form of ethical reflection. It is one in which moral style requires an attuned sensibility to the tragic dimensions of human lives, to bodily needs and the compassionate embrace of others, to dramatic presentation within the context of empathy and vulnerability.

Graphic narratives embody these ethical accounts of sensibility, style, and warmth, and being attuned to their scripted narratives helps to cultivate a more expansive ethical imagination. But comics also undermine these subtler forms of ethical reflection, often appealing to common stereotypes that reify mixed representations of character and moral complexity. In these ways, graphic narratives mirror what Orsi tells us about the complexity of lived religion and the impoverished fantasies of ordered lives: sometimes they simplify, organize, and flatten, even as they also burst through their confining frames to reveal sensitive moral textures.

In this chapter I want to explore how comic style both reifies and expands the moral imagination through representations of religious traditions and experiences. Comic readers can usually scan a shelf and immediately find their favorites, for many artists have mastered a style that continues throughout their publications. But I am less concerned with this kind of attributive style than I am with the thickness of lines, the contours of panels, the textures of drawings, and the aesthetic dimensions of religious practice as they provoke and conceal moral claims to foundations, hybridity, and open encounters. We want to look at *how* comics present religion through images and texts and to notice how these image-text representations suggest ethical postures. Movements in lines and closed borders, much like bodily movements when telling a story, can open up or attenuate empathetic encounters with others. The argument here is that we want to become the kind of comic readers who recognize these swerves of recognition and refusal.

To facilitate this encounter, I will explore four extraordinarily different comics: Will Eisner's *A Contract with God* (1978), the Vakil brothers' *40 Sufi Comics* (2011), J. T. Waldman's *Megillat Esther* (2005), and Craig Thompson's *Habibi* (2011). Eisner's *Contract* is a master work of gritty Jewish tenement life in which Frimme Hersh confronts God's contractual obligations to Jewish believers. Famous for drawing comics without borders, Eisner uses shades, line formations, and distinct panel borders to open a dialogue about commitment, power, and moral order. It is a complex and ambiguous work, for even as *Contract* recognizes human tragedy and mystery, it also appeals to moral foundations and deploys stereotypical depictions of Jews, Protestant bankers, and the attractive shiksa who brings shame on the more upright Jewish man. In my reading, *A Contract with God* establishes recurrent narratives of moral complexity and hurtful representation—themes we will encounter in the other comics discussed in this chapter.

40 Sufi Comics, a minimalist ethical treatise on upright living, offers compelling stories as Muslim pearls of wisdom. Grouped under such topics as "Ethics" and "Existence of God," the moral import is clear, direct, and designed to instruct. The stark lines, strong borders, and lengthy quotes from the Qur'an leave little to the imagination; readers are not meant to explore the political dimensions of moral reasoning but instead are positioned to ingest the wisdom of the ancients. This is less an opening or closing of moral thought than a confining of it within reflective freedom: the imagination resides within the self, bounded by mystical reflection. A very different kind of evasiveness can be gleaned from Waldman's *Megillat Esther*. As is well known, the name of God never appears in that biblical book, even though the rabbis read God into it as the guiding force that breaks Haman's rule through Esther's and Mordecai's clever reversals. Indeed, the constant swirls in text and image, and Waldman's own clever physical reversal of the comic itself (one must turn it upside down to finish the story), invite the reader to share in Waldman's imaginative account of religious politics. Through a playful script about power and caprice, *Megillat Esther* explores the limits of the moral imagination. Craig Thompson's *Habibi* meets these limits head-on but with familiar ambivalence. Even as his magisterial drawings weave Arabic letters into the very bodies of his characters, suggesting inscription but also the possibility of reinscription, he still represents those bodies as sexualized objects of play and power. We see in *Habibi* what an imaginative ethics looks like in both its expansive and closed forms. Together, these four texts reveal how style motivates ethical postures that enable but also hinder our moral imaginations. Representing religion in these comics is a stylized ethics of scripted and imagined encounter.

A Contract with God (1978)

Will Eisner (1917–2005) is perhaps the most successful storyteller and artist in the comic book industry, and he has influenced how Americans see comics as a serious art form. His earliest works included the 1940s comic *The Spirit*, and he later published a number of important works in "sequential art," including *Fagin the Jew* (2003) and what many consider his masterwork, *The Contract with God* trilogy: *A Contract with God* (1978), *A Life Force* (1988), and *Dropsie Avenue* (1995).[5] He taught the art of cartooning in New York City and published pioneering books on the trade. According to Jeremy Dauber's insightful essay on Eisner's life and work, he "is known in the field of comics for two fairly distinct achievements: his creation of the Spirit, a groundbreaking adventure hero (but an adventure hero nonetheless), and his invention of the graphic novel."[6] Eisner's invention is in full view in *A Contract with God*, a story about the immigrant Frimme Hersh who, as a young boy in czarist Russia, authored a contract with God to ensure that God would justly respond to Frimme's good deeds in America. The contract with God is an ethical pact between a just God and a good man. But after Hersh's adopted daughter dies, "plucked, as it were, from his arms by an unseen hand—the hand of God," Hersh rebels against God for abandoning their contract: "If God requires that men honor their agreements . . . then is not **God Also**, so Obligated??" Because he only accepts a God who recognizes and keeps contractual promises, Hersh commissions three rabbis to draw up a new contract, a "genuine" contract that requires God's consent. As Hersh tells God, "**This time, you will not violate our contract!** This time, I have three witnesses!"[7] But just as those words leave Hersh's lips, he grabs his chest in pain and then falls to the floor, with the contract beside his limp hand. As Eisner artfully explains in his *Comics and Sequential Art*, readers do not really see this movement or sequence; instead, we imagine it happening in the empty gutters between and among the panels.[8] But Eisner leaves nothing to the imagination in his depiction of the bolt of lightning as an "angry" response to Hersh's contractual demand. It is not only that, as Laurence Roth nicely phrases it, these contracts are "distinctly unglamorous and unfulfilled agreements"[9] but also that this God is unmoved by human demands for justice. Eisner contrasts this natural and divine volatility with the human demand for a just God to consistently act justly, generation after generation, as his "Epilogue" to *A Contract with God* makes clear; after discovering Hersh's stone contract, the young boy Shloime Khreks "signed his name below that of Frimme Hersh . . . thereby entering into a contract with God."[10]

The moral cry for justice, from Frimme as much as from Shloime Khreks, is certainly Eisner's working out of the tragedy of his daughter's death some eight years before he wrote *A Contract with God*. And as I will argue later, we can see this moral dilemma play out in the very style of Eisner's comic drawings. But we also see it in Eisner's heavy use of stereotypical character portrayals. As I argued in the introduction to this book, although stereotypes are a staple feature of comics, this trademark only expands our responsibility as readers to uncover their pernicious effects. Even Eisner was keenly aware of this, as he makes clear in the foreword to his *Fagin the Jew* (2003). Here, Eisner finally comes to terms with his character Ebony in *The Spirit*, who "spoke with the classic 'Negro' dialect and delivered a gentle humor that gave warmth to balance the coldness of crime stories." An older and wiser Eisner now understands how he "was nonetheless feeding a racial prejudice with this stereotype image." Yet with honest and clear intentions, Eisner harbors little guilt over his character.[11] Although stereotypes can generate reflective critical awareness—as they do, for example, in Spiegelman's *Maus*—they work in *A Contract with God* to stabilize prejudicial depictions of the other. When readers encounter the white banker, the female alcoholic shiksa, and the tenement-owning Jew, their moral imaginations are truncated and abused by a comic shorthand that projects a moral simplicity representing characters "suspended in time."[12] Eisner's use of stereotype closes down the reader's moral imagination, I argue, even as his stylistic use of font, lines, and panels expands our ethical worlds.

Eisner's two-page spread (*Contract with God*, 32–33) of Hersh's encounter with the white banker contrasts dark, foreboding spaces with an airy brightness touched with the high power of money, as Hersh wins the banker's acceptance. Frimme has just completed his mourning for his departed daughter and shaved his beard as a sign of his lost faith in a just God, and now he marches down to the bank—and it is a literal movement down on the page—to buy the very building on Dropsie Avenue in which moments before he prayed to his God. The banker, sitting behind a clean and elegant glass desk, is a picture of straight lines, perfectly combed hair, and tasteful cufflinks with a thin, pressed tie. Here we encounter an image of cleanliness, establishment, sophistication, control, reason, and power. We see the elite, the Protestant work ethic in action, the air of whiteness before a far more disheveled Hersh, who is bent over, while the banker's back is gracefully angled. Frimme's jacket and pants are rumpled and ill-suited to his lumbering physique, and he grabs his hat in nervous anticipation before the staid, controlled banker. While Eisner hides the banker's eyes behind blank glasses—preventing us from gleaning his intentions—we can see Frimme's cagey look and recognize his need to implore before power. Indeed, we even *hear* this sense of groveling from below in the intonation captured in Eisner's speech bubbles. As the banker opens their conversation with the slow deliberation of one who is being pursued ("Well, now . . . it's an expensive piece of property"), Frimme's pleading answer reflects the Yiddishized English of the greenhorn immigrant: "What e-x-p-e-n-s-i-v-e? Please, Mr. Johnson."[13] Where Frimme speaks in the colloquial dialect of the streets and dresses the part, Mr. Johnson responds with the high finance talk of "financial worth" and "ample equity." On the second page, the one that concludes the transaction with a handshake, we witness the disparity between the powerful white banker and the one who beseeches from below. Frimme looks up to the banker with reverence and gratitude, his hunched back drawn in contrast to the straightened but elegant beholder of money (or, in this case, financial bonds). All Frimme grasps is his wrinkled hat; the bonds in the banker's left hand, positioned above the hat and the handshake, are straight and catalogued to match the banker's pressed suit (see figs. 1 and 2).

These visual and linguistic details reveal how Eisner works with stereotypes to depict class, status, and power. He deploys stereotypes to deliver bits of information in very quick succession. The banker is lean, dominant, and

FIG. 1 Frimme negotiating with white banker. From *A Contract with God and Other Tenement Stories: A Graphic Novel* by Will Eisner. Copyright © 1978, 1985, 1989, 1995, 1996 by Will Eisner. Copyright © 2006 by Will Eisner Studios, Inc. Used by permission of W. W. Norton & Company, Inc.

FIG. 2 Frimme concluding transaction with white banker. From *A Contract with God and Other Tenement Stories: A Graphic Novel* by Will Eisner. Copyright © 1978, 1985, 1989, 1995, 1996 by Will Eisner. Copyright © 2006 by Will Eisner Studios, Inc. Used by permission of W. W. Norton & Company, Inc.

disciplined: an authoritative figure who represents the white Protestant elite establishment of high finance. Frimme's suit can barely contain his protruding anxiety: he is the shifty Jew who can turn a less-than-honest deal into a financial treasure (those bonds were not his but belong to the synagogue). Yet this is not the last we see of the banker; four pages later we recognize that same elegant figure now working for Frimme—who replaces Mr. Johnson, literally, by sitting behind the same clean desk, this time with a more fitting suit to match the sparse interior design. The Protestant establishment now relies on the scheming Jewish financier, a role reversal that plays on the stereotypical depiction of Jewish immigrants taking over American finance. None of this, I submit, challenges the common representations of Protestant establishment or Jewish immigrant culture. Eisner instead trades off these stereotypes to move the sequential narrative forward at a brisk pace.

Compare this conventional narrative, one in which the reader's moral imagination never requires activation or refinement, with Spiegelman's explicit depiction of stereotypical behavior. Artie and Françoise visit Vladek in the Catskills, and while driving home they come across a hitchhiker in need of a ride. But that is not what Vladek sees: "A hitch-hiker? And—**oy**—it's a colored guy, a **Shvartser! Push quick on the gas!**" Appalled, Françoise retorts, "That's **outrageous**! How can you, of all people, be such a racist! You talk about Blacks the way the Nazis talked about the Jews!"[14] This scene works to discomfort readers in two quite different moral registers. In one, we see racism as hypocrisy ("how can you, of all people"). Vladek worries that the hitchhiker will steal his groceries in the back seat, displaying in body and language how stereotypical prejudices undermine human concern and empathy. But the other register traces back to Artie's own anxiety of representing his father as the "racist caricature of the miserly old Jew."[15] One senses an ambivalent overcoming of the father, in both word and deed.

In both registers, however, Spiegelman presents the stereotype as problematic representation. As Marianne Hirsch artfully phrases it, "Spiegelman lays bare the levels of mediation that underlie *all* visual representational forms."[16] But we do not see these levels of sophistication in Eisner's *A Contract with God*. Whereas Spiegelman breaks the narrative flow to highlight the ethics of representation, Eisner runs past the moral problem to efficiently move the narrative forward. Comic artists should deploy stereotypes, according to Eisner, because their use "speeds the reader into the plot and helps the storyteller gain the reader's acceptance for the action of his characters." As a plot device, the stereotype hurries up the reading by appealing to an "ingrained set of accepted stereotypes" to quickly deliver information.[17] The artist positions the reader as a passive receiver to cultural norms. Eisner expects his reader to instantly recognize character rather than to creatively interrogate accepted practices. His use of stereotypes appeals to an unreflective moral imagination that accepts visual depictions of others as harmless plot devices rather than as vicious accounts of the self.

Spiegelman's depiction of Vladek shows us that comic stereotypes need not work like this; they can enliven imaginative readers to confront ethical complexity. But Eisner closes this down, offering a quick unreflective encounter. We see this clearly in Eisner's depiction of the non-Jewish female alcoholic shiksa—Frimme's girlfriend who announces his status in high society (see fig. 3). Although Frimme harbors some guilt for raising the rent and providing fewer services to his former neighbors on Dropsie Avenue, his shiksa from Scranton, Pennsylvania, suggests that a good, strong drink can cure his "black hole inside o' you." With blond hair, makeup to cover all facial lines, an expensive dress with fur coat, and an elegant figure, she chides Frimme for his cheapness: "We never go nowhere, Frim! What kind of life is this?" She even proposes converting to Judaism to help cure Frimme's blackness.[18] But Frimme rebuffs her brightness, peeling her inviting hand away as he hunches by the window, displaying the black hole that no longer resides within. He believed that taking a mistress, one "more appropriate to his new station" (38), would whiten that blackness. But this shiksa remains permanently other to his immigrant Jewish sensibility. This is not Anzia Yezierska's world, in which the passionate immigrant Jewess encounters the rational Protestant American male.[19] Instead, Eisner presents the shiksa with the same stereotypes that Jews typically had of white America: sexy, fashionable, full of forbidden pleasures, but intellectually light, and lacking in substance. Even as it entices, America is the gentile other to Frimme's Jewish burdens. My point is that these two worlds never engage; they never cross over or break the frame of Eisner's plot. The focus here is not on challenging these representations but on using them to quicken the narrative arc. Turn the page, see what happens next, but do not ponder the ethics of representation.

Eisner's stereotypes prevent more expansive accounts of moral complexity, but his use of font, lines, and style represent religion in ethically complex ways and works to undermine the limiting effects of stereotypes. This is, to my mind, why *A Contract with God* is such an important text for recovering the ethics of representation in graphic novels. Here we see the crosscurrents of ethical choices: the very same text both closes down and opens up the moral imagination and does so in its depiction of religious practice and belief. The splash page brings these competing frames to the fore (see fig. 4). Eisner draws the word *God*, chiseled in stone above the dispirited Hersh, in a font evocative of Hebrew script. The stone drips with pouring rain, drenching Hersh below even as it physically wears away the hewed contract. Behind the stone, looming quite large in the background, is 55 Dropsie Avenue— the source of Hersh's pain (the death of his daughter) and wealth (as the eventual owner of the building). Eisner directly links this image with the

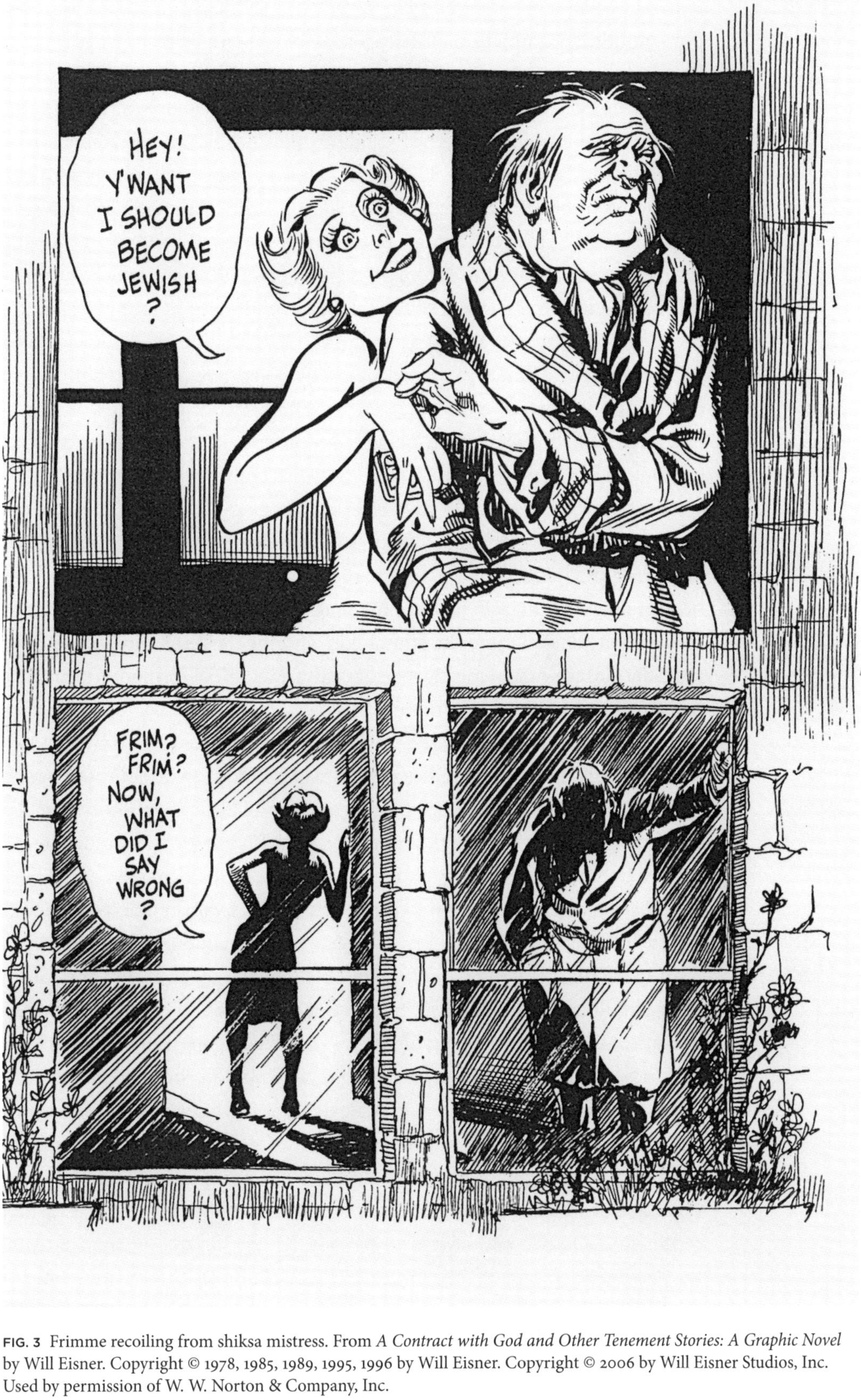
HEY! Y'WANT I SHOULD BECOME JEWISH ?
FRIM? FRIM? NOW, WHAT DID I SAY WRONG ?

FIG. 3 Frimme recoiling from shiksa mistress. From *A Contract with God and Other Tenement Stories: A Graphic Novel* by Will Eisner. Copyright © 1978, 1985, 1989, 1995, 1996 by Will Eisner. Copyright © 2006 by Will Eisner Studios, Inc. Used by permission of W. W. Norton & Company, Inc.

biblical Ten Commandments—a contract also etched in stone—in his *Comics and Sequential Art*: "A stone is employed—rather than parchment or paper, for example, to imply permanence and evoke the universal recognition of Moses's Ten Commandments on a stone tablet. Even the mix of lettering style—Hebraic vs. a condensed Roman letter—is designed to buttress this feeling."[20] Eisner quite effectively undermines that permanence, of course, with a torrential downpour. It is as though the flood from Noah's time had returned to erode the transcendent power of the Hebrew God at Sinai. The stone seems to force Hersh into a bowed position, not because he is showing respect but because of the arduous weight of biblical commitments. With so much rain cascading down, Hersh himself turns into a puddle of wetness, and the fire hydrant arrives almost as the comic other, an unnecessary object in a sea of water. But a darker, far more menacing object overshadows both Hersh and the stone contract. The tenement building is both menacing backdrop and mountain, both Sinai and curse. It does not weather like God's contract, and it does not bow to the harsh conditions. Eisner draws raindrops as thick, wide streams of water; they are relatively enormous drops that pound on Hersh's back. The rain behind and around 55 Dropsie Avenue is even, vertical, and ordered. One gets the sense that the contract with God does not belong here. It hovers in midair without foundation as a kind of imposition to the steady, ever-present rain. The contract, in short, gets in the way.

In at least one respect, this splash page functions like Eisner's stereotypes: he conveys all kinds of information in a very constricted space. But the data here is equivocal, and if readers hover over this image as the contract does over Frimme, their moral and religious imaginations can be activated. A stereotype of Judaism, for example, might portray an assertive authority etched in stone. But Eisner textures that authority with a hovering ambivalence; framed by the lived lives at 55 Dropsie Avenue, beaten down by a pelting rain, and hovering in midair, the contract's weight still retains force over a bending Hersh. It is both weighty commitment and beleaguered obligation, both traditional authority over and foreign object to the more earthy and messy tenement life. Although the contract is out of place and even overshadowed by a gritty Dropsie Avenue, it still retains the authority of tradition. Together, font, style, and lines present competing representations of religion as storm: it has a presence, perhaps even as a plague, but it will eventually pass away. Yet that eventuality might outlast those it devastates in its wake. Hersh would like to write a new contract with a new God who recognizes just measures. But a contract of this type, especially one that hovers over as biblical presence, cannot be discarded and rewritten so easily. It takes decades, if not centuries, for water to erode stone. This image of religious authority raises the specter of temporal dislocation: Hersh moves forward, but the contract seems to follow him wherever he goes. A contract with God hovers as atemporal presence.

FIG. 4 *A Contract with God* splash page. From *A Contract with God and Other Tenement Stories: A Graphic Novel* by Will Eisner. Copyright © 1978, 1985, 1989, 1995, 1996 by Will Eisner. Copyright © 2006 by Will Eisner Studios, Inc. Used by permission of W. W. Norton & Company, Inc.

Here we see how the ethics of representation and the graphic medium align to activate the moral imagination. Comics render time in space; sequential art squeezes the past, present, and future into a single frame and so organizes time as a spatial category. Scott McCloud captures this sensibility in "Time Frames," the title of one of his chapters in *Understanding Comics*, and notes how a comic "tangles up time beyond all recognition!"[21] In positioning the contract with God as above but in time, Eisner deploys the comic medium to situate religious time in city-space. That contract does not belong there visually, hovering as it does above Hersh before the towering tenement dwelling. But comics enable the collapse of time into space, and we see this visually in Eisner's splash page depiction of the biblical contract with God. It both belongs and does not belong here, and this collapse of temporal worlds stakes a claim to moral presence. The ethical issue here, as I see it, is how to account for a presence that ought not to be there, that remains out of place in its place. The law of gravity, and even the law of erosion, suggest that the contract with God should not be there or will soon melt away. But the comic medium, in its singular ability to render time spatially, does not frame the contract in this way. The splash page, after all, is not framed; it "bleeds" over to the right side following Hersh's movements. Even as the contract hovers in place, it will follow Hersh down the street. What we have here is less a moment in time than a moment that collapses time altogether. Religious time is not merely weighty but also inescapable. If readers hover over this image, then they too mimic the collapse of time in space, recognizing a presence out of place. And that is how comic style reveals moral perplexity: How can we be obligated to commitments out of but in time, out of but in place? How can we linger there with the displaced presence of religious commandment?

Eisner depicts religious obligations as an inescapable presence out of place, utilizing the comic medium to collapse time into a frameless page. The design of whole pages without borders is a style often attributed to Eisner but is nonetheless not unique to him. Craig Thompson, for one, appropriates Eisner's frameless pages to great effect, as we will see later in his *Habibi*. But this sense of a religious presence suspended in time and out of place is what makes *A Contract with God* particularly challenging for the moral imagination. The problem is not that Frimme must abide by a contract that forever pursues him. The challenge is how to recognize his unceasing duties to a God who remains an out-of-place presence. But even more, this God does not hold reciprocal commitments. For just as the weight of those commandments lingers over Frimme, unceasingly, as he slogs down Dropsie Avenue, so too does God's own response to Frimme's demand for justice come out of the whirlwind as divine caprice. This reference to Job's cry for justice and to God's capricious response has been nicely argued by Leonard Kaplan in his essay on Eisner and the Book of Job. Kaplan believes *A Contract with God* offers, both in its account of suffering and in its depiction of God, an extended rabbinic midrash on Job.[22] Eisner invokes this biblical God in his frameless drawing of God's angry response to Frimme's demand for a new contract. In this image, God delivers an angry bolt of lightning out of the blue, as it were, without "a drop of rain." Delivered in retaliation for Frimme's apparent return to Jewish life and commitment, the lightning bolts rent the page as if they arrive from outside the text altogether yet are also directed singularly at 55 Dropsie Avenue. Eisner deploys lightning at other moments in this comic to suggest God's angry response to Frimme's moral concerns. This divine rupture fractures both the page and the timeless contract etched in stone. By presenting religious experience as both contractual presence out of place and as divine capriciousness beyond the ethical, Eisner challenges the moral imagination to hold together two competing visions of religious commitment: the demands of moral obligations framed within a world without divine sanction for them. *A Contract with God* reveals how moral perplexity and ethical commitment remain forever suspended, if not engraved, in human endeavors to act justly. There is no moral certitude under a contract with God.

Like God's response to Job, Eisner offers little consolation for Frimme's moral outrage. Neither a bedrock certitude nor an ethical foundation nor an objective sense of meaning and order can be found in these pages. The contractual obligations still remain in place, even if they are out of place in the tenement streets of Dropsie Avenue. I read Eisner here as social psychologist: we yearn for a moral certitude that is denied us by a capricious God. But that neither means we are now released from ethical duties nor suggests that we live in a disenchanted world. We do maintain and can defend moral claims and acts, but we cannot do so by appeal to objective standards or revelatory truths. Those commitments hover over us, like the stone on the splash page, as aspirational duties to one another. The aesthetic style of *A Contract with God* makes this very point: the bleeding pages and the frameless drawings open the narrative to boundless possibilities without the certainty of closure. What we lose in foundations we gain in the freedom to explore beyond the frame. It is this aesthetic move that motivates the moral imagination in the very act of reading. This hermeneutical encounter, in which reading invokes moral judgment and imagination, can productively unwind the debilitating closures of Eisner's stereotypes.

A Contract with God is really a fractured text, at once limiting our moral resources through stereotypical depictions and opening our ethical imaginations to live in a world committed but uncertain, dedicated without assurance that our faithful love will be returned in kind. A generous aesthetic like this one does indeed make aspirational claims on us. Eisner asks us to stand up tall where Frimme bends low before the weight of those claims.

40 Sufi Comics (2011)

There are few graphic narratives as compellingly different from Eisner's work as Mohammed Ali Vakil's and Mohammed Arif Vakil's *40 Sufi Comics* (2011). The contrast has less to do with religious tradition than with aesthetic force. Whereas Eisner draws with shades of grey, in both color and moral temperament, the Vakil brothers offer stark, carefully crafted spiritual truths from the mystical Islamic tradition. I do not mean to suggest that Jewish teachings are morally ambiguous while Islamic lore is clear, level-headed, and authoritative. Both Jewish and Muslim traditions are far too historically and theologically complex for any one text, much less graphic narrative, to fully explain. But Ali Vakil and Arif Vakil present the Islamic Sufi tradition—a remarkably diverse mode of religious practices and ideals that traces its origins to the early medieval period—as a foundational source of wisdom for life's increasingly robust challenges to personal integrity and religious faith. Minimalist in aesthetic design but maximalist in religious certitude, *40 Sufi Comics* follows a clear stylistic pattern: each comic page (and they are *all* one-page comics) tells a story as moral lesson. The ethical teaching on the left (verso) side of the open page precedes two sections on the right (recto) side that contain a related quotation from the Qur'an and additional sayings from the Islamic interpretive and narrative traditions. At times, Ali Vakil will add his own commentary and stories to supplement both the visual and written material. This continuous pattern structures all forty comics. One turns the page not with expectation or curiosity; rather, one reads to learn wisdom in a structured, visual environment. Only the black-and-white ink on the page suggests any form of continuity with Eisner's *A Contract with God*. Whereas Eisner's aesthetic cultivated openness and moral perplexity, the Vakil brothers draw most of their pages with heavy, straight, and impenetrable frames to offer moral guidance in a complex world. But there are significant openings in the written narratives that appeal to the moral imagination, and one powerful comic page deviates from the structured norm to present a model of Sufi imaginative yearnings. Here, too, style presents moral claims and suggests a world of ethical certitude in which imagination has its place. Yet that place resides within the contemplative lives of the mystic. If Eisner both limited and expanded a reader's ethical imagination, the Vakil brothers locate it within a philosophical world of inner freedom. In *40 Sufi Comics*, the moral imagination never appears to break the frame.

The very first comic, within the section called "Ethics," establishes the fundamental aesthetic patterns echoed throughout *40 Sufi Comics*. The title for this comic moral, "Justifying Wrong Actions," straightforwardly directs attention to a reader who often does this very thing (see fig. 5). This is a tale for those of us who often justify actions we know to be wrong. Many of the comic

FIG. 5 "Justifying Wrong Actions." From *40 Sufi Comics* by Mohammed Ali Vakil and Mohammed Arif Vakil. CC BY-ND 3.0.

narratives in this volume include a man (and the actors in these forty comics are almost all males) who attempts to outwit or ridicule the Sufi mystic. So it is in this comic narrative: a man steals bread and fruit from a shop but offers them to the poor. The thief proclaims that he earns more good deeds by giving away the food than by stealing it, and thus he mocks the imam's sense of justice. But the Sufi sage will have none of this. Quoting the Qur'an and employing a different logic, he argues that the man accrues "eight sins but not a single good deed." The insincere thief has no response to this holy logic, and textual silence implies his (and our) acceptance of the Sufi's argument.

The moral is clear, as is the aesthetic dimension of the comic page. The Qur'an arrives to challenge our "raving poetry" with its "measured tone." Too often we abuse logic in order to accrue merit; the Qur'an subverts those petty desires. And the very aesthetic features make this moral point as well. The lines are strong, straight, and thick, with a kind of minimalist design that highlights text over image. The point is not to be dazzled or to be impressed by beauty; *reading* lies at the heart of this comic. Indeed, the bold title ("Justifying Wrong Actions") together with the abundance of words on the page cohere to locate the visual dynamic within the process of reading. This is also how Ali Vakil understands the Qur'an in his "Artist's Notes" to this comic page: "The verses of the Quran cannot be understood if the reader approaches them by imposing his ideas on them. Rather, they should be approached with an open & sincere heart to understand their outer and inner meanings. The Quran can have an empowering effect on the reader. It is a book that challenges, debates, criticizes, and inspires the reader. At times, one may feel that they are not reading the Quran, but rather that the Quran is reading them."[23] Reading is at the center, whether I am the object or subject of that process. The strong frames break up the comic page to suggest quick, tidy, and clear visual sections that mimic quotations on the page—we follow the words, not the visual design. If the Qur'an reads us in order to subvert our misguided logic, then it does so through the sheer force of textual meaning. Our moral imaginations must be driven out to make room for revelatory truths. To open the heart to meaning, as Ali Vakil suggests we do, is really a process of suppression. To be read means not to read imaginatively; indeed, for many comic readers, it means not to read at all.

40 Sufi Comics asks us to open our hearts to a new Qur'anic perspective that overwhelms predominant modes of rational and scientific discourse. Although most of the comics make this point textually, highlighting the ethical point through language, the Vakil brothers present this morality tale through an evocative aesthetic design. We see this in one of my favorite comic pages, where the modern, scientific doctor once again tries to embarrass the Sufi master (see fig. 6). A wealthy merchant invites both a doctor and a Sufi mystic for dinner and beseeches the mystic to pray for his ill daughter. The doctor, as the devoted student of scientific progress, rejects this mumbo jumbo yet becomes angry when the Sufi calls him a donkey for misunderstanding the power of prayer. In the end, the Sufi mystic has the last laugh: if the word *donkey* could dilate his blood vessels and increase his heartbeat, then "the name of our creator can have a healing effect" also (*40 Sufi Comics*, 47). Once again, Qur'anic logic trumps modern sensibilities as the Sufi master turns the tables on narrow, provincial reasoning. Arif Vakil masterfully portrays this turn of events through his depiction of the two protagonists. The structural frames remain rigid, strong, and deterministic, much as they did in the "Justifying Wrong Actions" page. But here we see a calm, focused, and plain Sufi mystic as opposed to the angry, agitated, and elitist doctor. The scientist, with his necktie and distinguished jacket, is the modern counterpart to the more traditional sensibility of the mystic, with his plain robe and traditional head covering. With his well-kept beard, the mystic appears somber, grounded, and religious, but the doctor almost breaks the frame, leaning forward in anger with his modern glasses and long, fashionable hairstyle. This aggressive gesture has moral force since "The Power of Prayers," as the Vakil brothers label this comic, suggests an ease with this and other worlds, with a healing that connects and binds rather than progresses according to science. This is the Sufi's point, and Arif Vakil draws it to perfection. We *see* the power of prayer in the Sufi mystic, just as we recognize how scientific progress is a false god. The aesthetic matches the ethic: modern progress must bend to the rational and mystical simplicity of prayerful acceptance. Only God's revelatory healing can break the frame from the outside.

With stark, straight lines and a Qur'anic moral order, it would seem that the Vakil brothers leave little to the moral imagination in reading or being read by *40 Sufi Comics*. If the "Follow Principles" comic is any indication, modern spiritual seekers should "not follow personalities [but] follow principles" (21). Our goal, Ali Vakil tells us, "should be to follow divine principles" so that we can "see the world without prejudices."[24] Moral decisions, in this model, reside in understanding what God wishes to tell us through the Qur'an. Where, then, might the moral imagination reside, or even play a role, in this divine ethic? So far as I can tell, the imagination appears only once in *40 Sufi Comics*, but it does so in a fascinating and important account of mystic inner worlds (see fig. 7). Although Arif Vakil maintains a strong frame, *inside* the frame we see the blind astronomer, who conjures up "the greatest universe" within his own body. The suns, moons, and stars of his world all reside within the self as the past, future, thoughts, imagination, intellect, desires, emotions, mind, and soul. Here the imagination is part of a vast universe of worlds that swirl in an ordered pattern around the soul. As the text on the opposite page makes clear, "your consciousness is within you, though you do not know."[25] Yet just as it remains within the self, it also undermines the controlling logic of the strong,

FIG. 6 "The Power of Prayers." From *40 Sufi Comics* by Mohammed Ali Vakil and Mohammed Arif Vakil. CC BY-ND 3.0.

rectangular frame, even if it never breaks with it. The astronomer's imaginative universe appears ready to burst beyond the page, but his grounded, seated body indicates that he is going nowhere. At the very moment when the Vakil brothers suggest a more expansive, perhaps even more critical, role for the moral imagination, they confine it within the ordered world of the comic frame. Imagination allows us to access inner worlds, but these worlds remain universes bounded by Qur'anic structure. As the blind astronomer tells us, he "watches" this grand universe, but he does not act on it.

Reading for the Vakil brothers is a form of acceptance, but it is not the active work of the moral imagination. The comic page continually frames the

FIG. 7 "The Blind Astronomer." From *40 Sufi Comics* by Mohammed Ali Vakil and Mohammed Arif Vakil. CC BY-ND 3.0.

meditative practices of seeing and reading, for the astronomer gazes within the self but does not yearn for worlds outside. Although our inner lives are rich with emotions, desires, and imaginative possibilities, they are still trapped within the self. One must practice a form of denial that opens the self to Sufi logic and morality. Freedom has constraints, as it were, and throughout *40 Sufi Comics*, Arif Vakil presents a consistent aesthetic page that reveals those constraining borders. There is something here like Roland Barthes's notion of the photographic "flat death," in which the image remains forever static, fixed, and already dying.[26] There are no imaginative leaps beyond the flat page; as readers being read, we absorb that flatness and that moral aesthetic. In this sense, the strong bordered lines of *40 Sufi Comics* structure the self much like the Qur'an does in reading our souls. *40 Sufi Comics* does more than constrain the moral imagination; the comic page flattens the self within an ordered world of Qur'anic truth.

Megillat Esther (2005)

The bordered frames in *40 Sufi Comics* reflect the revelatory logic of the Qur'an that arrives from the outside to constrain moral lives on the inside. The repetitive structure drives that point home, as do the long, straight lines that frame each comic page. So it is altogether jarring to move from the minimalist but consistent formalism of the Vakil brothers to the aesthetic anarchy of J. T. Waldman's *Megillat Esther*. His is a book of subversions, one that mirrors the plot twists and disruptions of the biblical text as well. Whereas the Sufi mystic arrives as master of Islamic ethics, we discover in Waldman's comic something else entirely in the story of Mordecai and Esther: political intrigue, ethnic pride, role reversals, and ambiguous moral codes. It is a masterful retelling of the book of Esther that fuses biblical Hebrew, English translation, rabbinic midrash, and thoughtfully creative black-and-white images. Waldman has achieved broad acclaim, and deservedly so.[27] It was clearly a labor of love, exhibiting painstaking detail and subversive development. But in the introduction to this work, Moshe Silberschein tends to sidestep the twisting plots within the comic in order to underscore the basic storyline. He notes that the book of Esther, while never mentioning God, is "merely one chapter in the ongoing battle between the forces of evil and the forces of good in a frightening world where the presence of God is hidden."[28] How then does Waldman, who elsewhere has described himself as "a third-generation secular American Jew exploring his roots,"[29] actually depict, in word and image, a moral imagination bereft of divine certainty? Silberschein may still believe in God's hidden presence, but I can find few signs of that faith in Waldman's comic narrative. Indeed, God's absence opens space for Waldman's brilliant creativity: the moral imagination is his, as creator, and ours, as readers of that creativity. The objective here is not to challenge or expand the imaginative impulse; it is instead to illustrate it and in so doing offer a creative example for exploratory readers. *Megillat Esther*, with its overflowing and disruptive aesthetic narrative, is itself an imaginative performance, and Waldman calls on his readers to creatively inhabit his visionary world.

As Waldman depicts Esther's entry into the king's palace and the eventual overthrow of Haman, he interweaves various interludes as creative modes of midrashic interplay within the text. In the first of these interventions, Waldman conjures up the game show "Mashiach for the Day," pitting against each other two familial lines that end with either the son of David or the son of Joseph as the Messiah (Esther and Mordecai belong to this latter family tree). But the second interlude, following the end of the second chapter in the book of Esther, directly concerns the effacement of God (see fig. 8). In this image, Waldman quotes Deuteronomy 31:18: "I will surely hide my face on that day because of the evil people have done." He notes how interpreters often relate this text to Esther herself, for the Hebrew name *Esther* contains the root of the word that means "to hide."[30] The biblical context for this reference, however, is quite different. In Deuteronomy 31:14, God informs Moses of his impending death and calls for Joshua to join Moses in the Tent of Meeting so that God can inform both of what will soon pass: the Israelites will break the covenant, but they will quickly blame their infidelity on God's absence, even as the fault lies in their turning to other deities. To Moses and Joshua, God wants to be clear: "I will surely hide my face on that day because of the evil people have done." But note Waldman's image in the midst of this Deuteronomy text; this is not the face of God but the face of King Achashverosh. Here is but one obvious example of God's effacement, but there are other, more subtle forms of displacement in Waldman's narrative. Hegai, the "keeper of woman," arises out of a bottle, genie-like, to help Esther emerge as the best of maidens for the king. Waldman depicts the imagined East as a magical palace, a Persia full of fanciful clothes, incense, and enchantment. Even Stephen Tabachnick, in his reading of Waldman's *Megillat Esther*, buys into this fantastical occultism: "All characters are rendered—correctly—as ancient Persians, with a different standard of beauty than Western standards."[31] But this standard is not one in which God works in the background to move events along. It is Hegai, not God, who advises Esther to remain silent about her family origins and who earlier strategizes about how best to position her as the king's chosen one. Even in Waldman's depiction of the showdown between Haman and Mordecai—in which Mordecai refuses to bow and worship before the king's servant—we see a world of lordship and servants but no God. In this battle of good against evil, God is nowhere to be found.

FIG. 8 Deuteronomy 31:18. From *Megillat Esther* by J. T. Waldman. Copyright © 2005 by J. T. Waldman.

To be sure, as Silberschein makes clear in the introduction to Waldman's work, "Esther is the only narrative portion of the entire Bible that omits the name of God, and actually goes out of its way to avoid mentioning 'it.'"[32] But Waldman does not have to go out of his way; he instead chooses to do so. He clearly takes imaginative license with his Mashiach game show episode, and he creatively interweaves midrashic discourse into the Esther narrative.

Why, then, has he decided to efface God as the guiding power from behind the magical scenes?[33]

Perhaps Waldman is less concerned with divine presence than he is with the Jewish moral imagination. Let's take a closer look at Waldman's aesthetic depiction of Deuteronomy 31:18. Like all other pages in the comic, this one contains both Hebrew and English translations. A reader can view the Hebrew or English as stylized image or can read either language as text (in many of these comic pages Hebrew works as calligraphic script, as both text and image). Here, Waldman scripts the English chapter title on the top left and the Hebrew chapter on the top right. This follows convention, because since we read Hebrew right to left we expect the Hebrew to begin on the right side of the page. But the verses do not follow this expectation; instead, the Hebrew begins in the middle of the page, between the chapter headings in both scripts, and the English begins to the right of that initial Hebrew word. Both texts then work around the image of King Achashverosh, with the English traveling along the right side (opposite its chapter heading), and the Hebrew following along the left side (also opposite its chapter heading). To read both languages, the reader must rotate the page—counterclockwise for the English and clockwise for the Hebrew. Almost all of this, I want to suggest, subverts expectations for how one *should* read English and Hebrew.

This motif of subversion is certainly within the overall theme of the biblical text and the comic. But Waldman's visual depiction forces a reader to make some unlikely choices. Recall how Eisner justified the use of stereotypes, claiming that comic authors need to deliver information in a short span of visual time, and stereotypes are the most effective means of doing so. We can see here in *Megillat Esther* how Waldman subverts that ideological reading practice as well. As I scan this page, I am initially perplexed about how to read it. Where should I begin? And even if I figure that out, it might not be clear where I should end (hint: at the beginning). I must take physical hold of the comic text and turn it, turn it, as the midrashic saying goes, until I force meaning out of the text. In this physical interactive space in which the aesthetic dimensions motivate reader response, Waldman's imaginative leaps yield to the reader's. As the reader, the text now becomes my own, as my hands grab and turn the text, as I make readerly choices to follow the Hebrew or English, and as Achashverosh's finger continually points at me, even as I rotate the book. So it is not really a question about hiding God's face, or even the king's face. The question is now directed squarely at me as reader. The problem is not God's absence but my own absence from this narrative tradition.

Waldman's direct appeal to the reader, as I read the aesthetic language on this page, is a call to the moral imagination. It asks the reader to leap into that tear duct, that hole in the mirror, or whatever that oval shape might conjure up for a reader of this interlude. Achashverosh's finger points at me to jump in and imaginatively see myself as part of this story, as part of this comic text, as a character wrapped by Hebrew and English, and in ways that might quickly subvert my religious expectations. At the very tip of the king's head Waldman has stylized a diamond-shaped figure that marks the beginning and end of the English sentence—it marks the boundary between the *I* to its right and the *Done* to its left. But it also allows the Hebrew word for *I* to bleed into the English *I* (which looks more like an *H* until you begin to rotate the page correctly). This hemorrhaging within the page—the turning, wrapping, and undoing—offers neither border frames to constrict and control nor a sense of the insider who can secure a geographical border to ward away the foreign speaker. English and Hebrew intermix, subvert, and penetrate *as* image-text. If this page calls for presence, as I claim it does, then the moral question is this: Whose presence? Who is allowed inside? Who is allowed to tell this story, and who is allowed to read it? Perhaps this image as teardrop suggests that hidden faces—those not allowed to appear, those not allowed to stand as presence—stand for the evil done.

There is, of course, another kind of evil invoked in this text: the death of thousands at the hands of the Jews. This role reversal, in which the Jew as victim becomes Jew as heroic warrior, is an ambivalent legacy. The modern carnivalesque Purim, with its masquerades and gift-giving treats, valiantly attempts to mask this foundational violence. This too is a form of erasure. But Waldman presents the brutal killings as a kind of holocaust, a method of wiping out and erasing heritage. In the image depicting verse 9:16 (*Megillat Esther*, 139), the Judeans kill off "those that hated them," some seventy-five thousand people (see fig. 9). We see countless individual battles at the very top of the page, including young fighting young, women slaying children, and warriors stabbing, beheading, and strangling. As the Judeans celebrate in the lower left corner of the page, we see the dead being dragged to a mass grave in the lower right corner. That pile of dead bodies we have seen before, at Babi Yar or, if not there, in Art Spiegelman's famous drawing of dead mice on the floor of his *Maus* studio.[34] Waldman hints at this tragic violence when he portrays one character lying down, with hand to head in disbelief, gazing at that pile from just above the raucous celebration. "What did we do?" he asks (139). Saved from destruction, the Jews have become the destroyers. Waldman depicts celebration right up against mass genocide: we see ecstatic dancing at the very edges of dead bodies. This convergence of borderless revelry and mass grave site, where bodies move liberally and lie inert, is but one aesthetic dimension of moral presence. Those outside the story lie dead within it, murdered by those who tell the story. Waldman moves us to ask not only whose story we tell but what kind of story we wish to tell, to ourselves and to those we have abandoned.

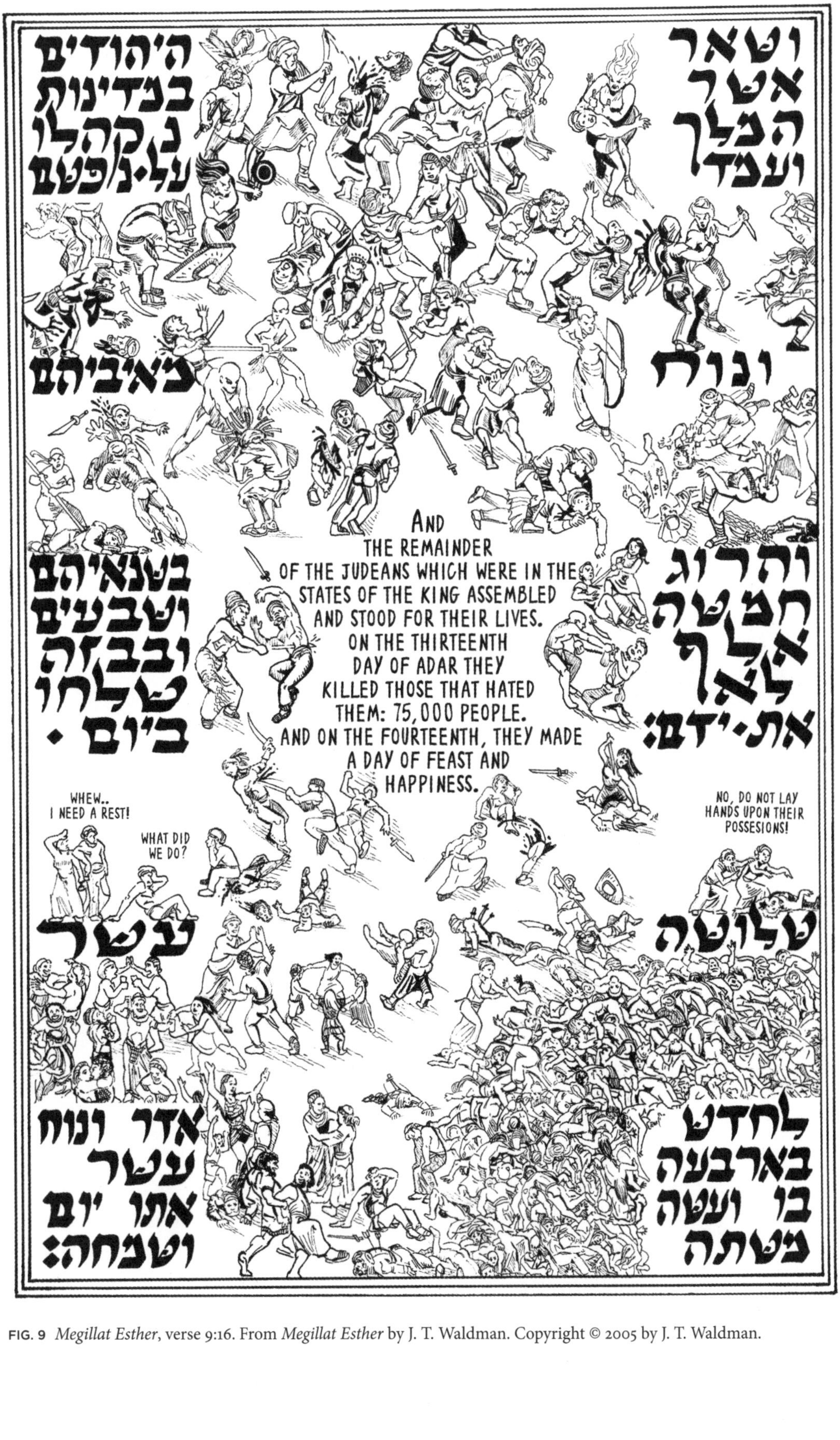
ושאר
אשר
המלך
ועמדו
היהודים
במדינות
נקהלו
על-נפשם
ונוח
מאיביהם
AND
THE REMAINDER
OF THE JUDEANS WHICH WERE IN THE
STATES OF THE KING ASSEMBLED
AND STOOD FOR THEIR LIVES.
ON THE THIRTEENTH
DAY OF ADAR THEY
KILLED THOSE THAT HATED
THEM: 75,000 PEOPLE.
AND ON THE FOURTEENTH, THEY MADE
A DAY OF FEAST AND
HAPPINESS.
והרוג
חמשה
אלף
לא
את-ידם:
בשנאיהם
ושבעים
ובבזה
שלחו
ביום ·
NO, DO NOT LAY
HANDS UPON THEIR
POSSESIONS!
WHEW..
I NEED A REST!
WHAT DID
WE DO?
שלושה
עשר
לחדש
בארבעה
בו ועשה
משתה
אדר ונוח
עשר
אתו יום
ושמחה:

FIG. 9 *Megillat Esther*, verse 9:16. From *Megillat Esther* by J. T. Waldman. Copyright © 2005 by J. T. Waldman.

In calling us to leap imaginatively into his text, Waldman also asks us to recognize those left behind or out of that text. This is, in part, why I read *Megillat Esther* as critical response to Eisner's use of stereotypes and as alternative comic to the Vakil brothers' moral Qur'anic certainty. In exploring his roots, Waldman uncovers moral perplexity, if not downright ugliness. If an appeal to the moral imagination is ever an exercise in identity formation, it can also work to expose shame, violence, and regret, as it clearly does in the pages of *Megillat Esther*. Waldman's imaginative aesthetic, much like our own, reveals the pleasures of fanciful reversals of fortune and unexpected narrative turns. But it also recovers the underbelly of those diversions, suggesting that engaging the moral imagination can be a painful exercise in self-exposure and reckoning.

Habibi (2011)

In *Habibi* (2011), a monumental work of the graphic narrative imagination, Craig Thompson suppresses any sense of agonizing self-reflection to construct a pleasing and problematic caricature of the Orient. He appeals to this oriental sacred through Arabic calligraphy, weaving sacredness into the visual and textual narrative of the imagined, exotic other. The exotic and even erotic forms of calligraphy stylize an openness to the moral imagination, even as they severely constrict ethical boundaries through stereotypes and repressive gendered norms. I want to call this double movement—the way that Thompson both appeals to and undermines the moral imagination—the oriental gaze of calligraphic form. This image-text aesthetic weaves an oriental tapestry that subverts and widens critical ethical reflection. We can see this in Thompson's landscape drawings, in his mythic and salvific animals, in his appeal to Islamic textual traditions within the Hadiths and Qur'an, and in the material body of Dodola, who captures the young Zam's erotic fantasies. Thompson deploys calligraphy to open Islamic and Arabic culture to the moral imagination in ways both problematic and inviting.[35]

Habibi is the love story of Zam and Dodola, who meet when a young Dodola saves baby Zam as they escape together from a slave market. The two live in seclusion on an abandoned ship in the desert as brother and sister until Zam witnesses Dodola's rape—a recurring bodily violence that she endures as she negotiates for food from desert travelers. Haunted by his own latent sexual desires for Dodola and the shame of visual witness, Zam searches for food and water to spare Dodola from a more physical, abusive shame. But the two are separated—Dodola is sold into slavery once again, becoming the prized catch within the sultan's harem, while Zam escapes to the city, cuts off his sexual organ to remove his erotic shame, and then gains employment as a eunuch at the sultan's palace. When Zam recognizes Dodola and saves her from execution by drowning, they escape the palace, adopt a baby girl, and leave the city as parental lovers.

To be sure, this story of budding romantic love, erotic inhibition, physical abuse, and the exotic East are fantastical tales within the imagined Orient of Richard Burton's *1,001 Arabian Nights*.[36] Indeed, Craig Thompson modeled a good deal of his graphic narrative on that text, and he self-consciously appropriated its orientalist project. He locates his oriental gaze in Wanatolia, a city of his own creation that over the course of the story transforms from slave market into desert wasteland and from the sultan's harem into the heart of a bustling, commercial city. Like Will Eisner, Thompson appropriates stereotypical depictions to set the scene for this coming-of-age story. But this is a dubious appropriation: he sexualizes Dodola and the entire notion of Arabia even as he also grounds constructive and uplifting power in Dodola's gendered, inscripted body.

Within this gendered space and gaze, Arabic calligraphy takes on the aesthetic force of the moral imagination. Thompson deploys calligraphy as an image-text to naturalize the orientalist discourse in material space. Dodola tells stories from the Qur'an, weaving them within the meandering lines of Arabic calligraphy learned from her first husband. Zam literally sees the calligraphic forms as letters, animals, mountains, and bodies. He encounters calligraphy as that material script within nature: a writing of and in the world as the naturalized sacred. In this sense, the comic form is not image alongside text, or even the interplay of these two mediums, but a bridging, or bricolage, of textual and visual forms. In *Habibi*, calligraphy is the sacred text as comic image-text, braiding together the play of sacred inscription and oriental gaze. This is the force of the moral imagination: we see the orientalist visions of Arabia *through* calligraphy, as we do through Dodola's sexualized body. But we also envision the power of material inscription to write anew, to reinscribe power and authority. In calligraphic form, Thompson presents debilitating stereotypical accounts of sexualized others *and* offers a vision to empower readers to overcome that oriental gaze. The calligraphic image-text reveals both a world of exotica and the empowering possibilities of moral persuasion.

There is by now a vast literature deeply critical of Thompson's oriental framework. Note, for example, Nadim Damluji's blanket condemnation of Thompson's oriental writing, gestured in the very title of the essay, "Can the Subaltern Draw: The Spectre of Orientalism in Craig Thompson's *Habibi*." For Damluji, *Habibi* "is a tragically familiar Orientalist tale" that "fails to escape many classic Orientalist trappings."[37] One finds a similar critique from a number of online blogging communities, interviews with Thompson, and book reviews. Even the *New York Times* panned *Habibi* with the pithy title, "The Graphic Novel as Orientalist Mash-Up."[38] Yet even as these readers condemn the oriental frame, they consistently praise the stylized calligraphy as largely outside that discourse. Damluji's tribute is quite typical: "First let's discuss what *Habibi* gets right. The good is found foremost in the calligraphy and geometric patterns Thompson employs throughout *Habibi*."[39] My claim here is that calligraphic geometry is a critical feature of Thompson's oriental gaze *and* his presentation of the moral imagination. It is problematic script as it reveals both closed and more unbounded forms of moral inquiry. We see this double movement in the comic's animals (the snake, among others), exotic landscapes (Wanatolia and the desert wasteland), and bodies—especially in Dodola's sexualized, penetrated form. Calligraphy is a critical, problematic feature of Thompson's moral vision, flowing through the scenic forms as a mode of visual, ethical encounter.

Dodola's body and a large, dark snake visually and thematically frame Zam's fantasies (see fig. 10). Zam watches in amazement as the snake repeatedly takes the form of various Arabic letters, spelling out the corners of the *buduh*—an amulet from Dodola to protect Zam in the wilderness (*Habibi*, 138). Note too how the *buduh*, with nine frames, mirrors the very design of the page. The *buduh* as comic page sacralizes and legitimates the comic book as sacred text and, by extension, the space of imaginative gestures. It is never clear whether Zam is truly seeing or only imagining the snake and its calligraphic form. This subversion of sight, or the confluence of vision and imagination, becomes a marker of the comic page and the *buduh*. The moral play here, as I see it, opens sacred script to imaginative insights. By sliding within and around fantasy and transforming into various natural shapes and calligraphic lettering, the snake marks imaginative vision as mysterious, subversive, exotic, and enticing. As the serpent transfigures into written script, calligraphy becomes the very shape and form of the oriental gaze.

In *Habibi*, Thompson visually distinguishes Arabic stories with elaborate frames. These darker markings tend to separate Zam's fantasies from reality, but his desert wanderings blur the line between fantasy and reality as the two bleed together into the oriental frame. Thompson constructs this fantastical weaving through the calligraphic form. The beguiling snake transforms into Zam's linguistic guide through the barren desert, leading him to a pure and abundant water source. Zam believes the serpent is a magical being in its transformative capacity to become script. Calligraphy *moves* Zam between fantasy and reality: we see it in Zam's magical amulet, written into the landscape and inscribed into animal flesh. This is not a kind of tattooing that inscribes the flesh from without;[40] this is a tattooing from within, as it were, from the very core of the natural world. Reflecting back Zam's facial expression, the river water dissolves into flowing Arabic script as Zam dips his finger into the watery substance (141) (see fig. 11). Calligraphy grows and dominates the page spread, capturing Zam's and the reader's imaginations. Thompson

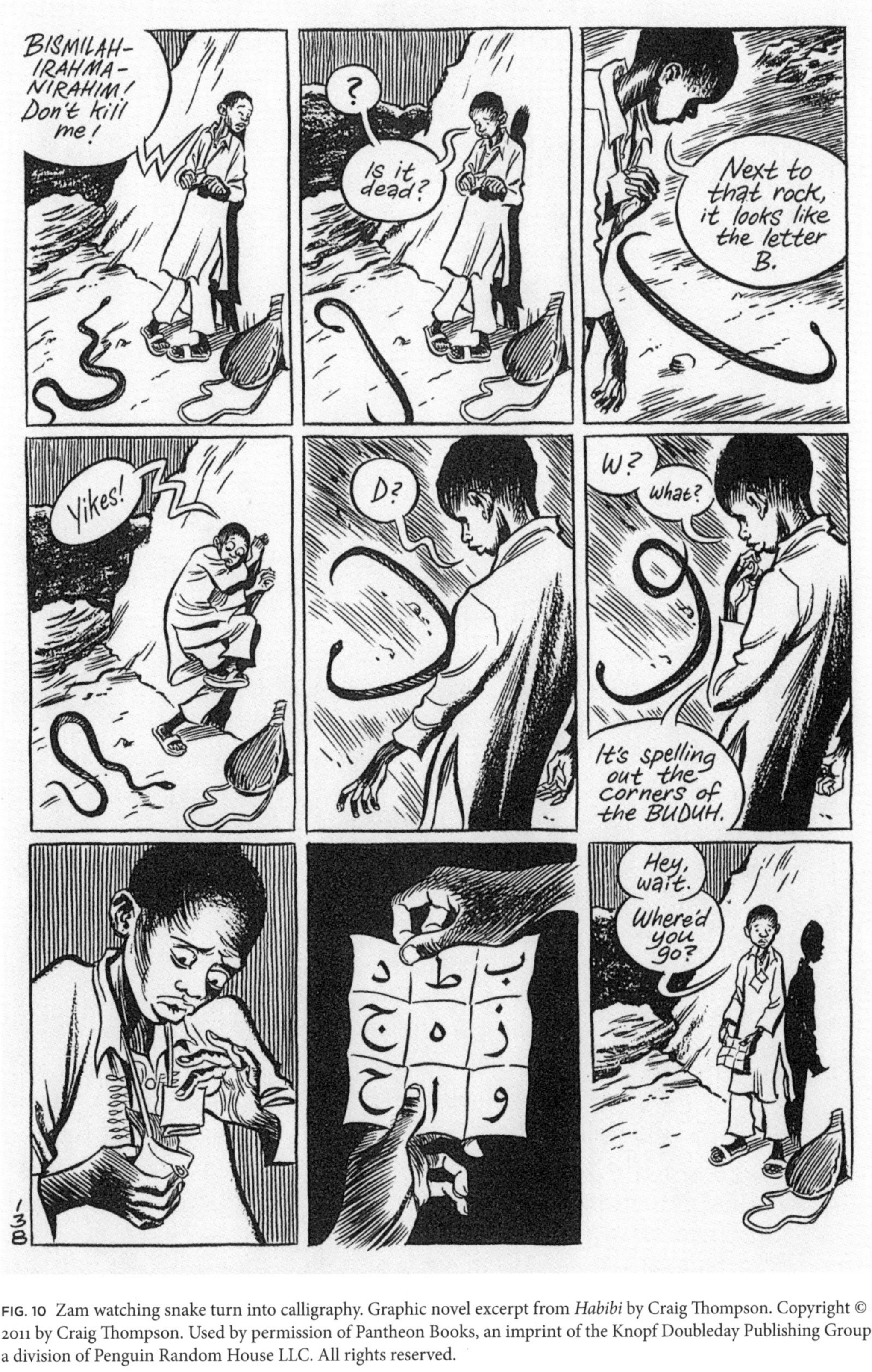
BISMILAH-IRAHMA-NIRAHIM! Don't kill me!
?
Is it dead?
Next to that rock, it looks like the letter B.
Yikes!
D?
W?
What?
It's spelling out the corners of the BUDUH.
138
ب ط د
ز ه ج
و ا ح
Hey, wait.
Where'd you go?

FIG. 10 Zam watching snake turn into calligraphy. Graphic novel excerpt from *Habibi* by Craig Thompson.

FIG. 11 Zam gazing at river with calligraphy. Graphic novel excerpt from *Habibi* by Craig Thompson. Copyright © 2011 by Craig Thompson. Used by permission of Pantheon Books, an imprint of the Knopf Doubleday Publishing Group, a division of Penguin Random House LLC. All rights reserved.

uses calligraphy and Islamic sacred stories to construct this world, one both mysterious and seductive. As Zam gazes into script, so too does the reader: his point of view becomes ours as well, and we see the world as material script. We are all lost in the magical realism of calligraphic forms and fantastical, natural shapes. This scripted gaze, I want to suggest, is not just orientalist in perspective but also imaginative in moral force. It moves us to see the world differently, to see it as inhabiting sacred language. Calligraphy as comic aesthetic challenges us to constitute the world anew as sacred story.

Thompson writes calligraphy into the landscape, infusing it with the magical dimensions of Islam and rooting it in the neverland mysticism of *1,001 Arabian Nights*. He presents the sacred not only as exotic and material script but also as a form of writing that disarms and deceives the reader's visual imagination. Each page of *Habibi* is painstakingly illuminated, and Thompson warmly embraces the artistic possibilities of an ancient and venerable Arabic tradition of calligraphy. At times he uses calligraphy to approach Islam with reverential respect, illustrating stories and commentaries from the Qur'an—for example, Muhammad's ascension to heaven—with thoughtful attention to detail. Yet alongside this deference Thompson also sexualizes Dodola's body through calligraphy. Her sexual encounters, which are often violent or unwanted, travel within the orbit of magical stories about talismanic squares and occult numerology—all inscribed by Arabic calligraphy. Thompson frames Dodola's rape within calligraphic forms, drawing her body as fluid water. Like the pure water Zam discovers at Wanatolia's dam, Dodola's body is sacred as calligraphic script. With Dodola's body inscribed with calligraphic ink, we see her body not merely as embodied script but also as a landscape delimited and defined by it. Thompson positions his reader to gaze at and thus penetrate into Dodola's liquid body. To push this metaphor a bit further, we could say we swim in it, and so in part we remake the curvature of her embodied frame. This is imaginative vision as possession, and it suggests a violent moral penetration. Dodola's body is the passive receiver to the readers' invasive gaze as they rewrite her body with calligraphic script. Rather than being challenged by the other's material presence, readers visually acquire the other's body for consumption. This is the oriental gaze in *Habibi*, and this is the debilitating, closed space of the moral imagination.

Readers engage the moral imagination through Dodola's calligraphic body. She engenders moral knowledge in *Habibi*; she reads and writes sacred stories and weaves both religious and cultural fantasies. Dodola is a permeable figure, and her naked body is persistently violated by Zam, desert travelers, and spiritual forces. As sacred, visual body, she both controls and is subjected to the power of calligraphy. Dodola's only recourse, her one great source of power, is the subversive capacity of calligraphy to wind its way between fantasy and reality—bending time and space to create a transcendent sacred order.

In her desperate attempt to escape the sultan's gross sexual needs, Dodola takes shelter in the palace stables among horses and exotic birds. Deep in an opium stupor, the sultan envisions Dodola as the *buraq*—a mythical creature in the hadith literature that's part horse, part woman, and part bird (282). Although impaired, the sultan's gaze becomes the reader's own, transforming Dodola's sexualized body into a mythic object. Here we see how Thompson writes Dodola into Islamic lore, but this imaginative world remains a sexual and masculine space of domination. The sultan is only aroused by this mythic site and must possess her sexually. This hypersexuality continues in other frames as well, and Thompson links the riding of horses to the sultan's own grotesque riding of Dodola. And whereas the sultan's desires (and even Zam's snake) reflect male potency and ownership of space, Dodola's frame remains a weak, impotent, penetrated vessel. She retains little agency or ownership over her own body when de-scripted from sacred calligraphy. Without that holy script to frame her body, she becomes a mere receptacle for male aggressive fantasies. And the comic works to implicate readers in this male imaginative vision as we project Dodola's sacred sexuality onto an illusive mythic potency. As her body transfixes and beguiles the sultan, so too does she capture the reader's imaginative leaps. The sudden and almost effortless shift between Dodola as sacred *buraq* and Dodola as naked, violated body—violated by the reader's vision as much as by the sultan's penetration—highlights the acquiring, desensitized readings of her sexualized body.

Dodola is embodied as calligraphy, an inscribed physicality reinforced by Zam's and the reader's visual penetration of her written surface. It is a kind of tattooing that goes all the way down, penetrating to a depth that reads from the inside out. There is no room here for the moral imagination, no space for ethical play or for imagining different configurations of human flourishing. Indeed, Thompson inhibits these moral flights; he restricts them to an oriental gaze that penetrates the calligraphic surface to find only an objectified, sexualized body. This vision is paramount in Zam's frantic attempt to see Dodola once more in the palace. As Zam climbs atop the roof, peering through the lattice into the sultan's garden, Thompson draws a series of vertical panels of Dodola's face and then leads the reader's gaze to the full panel on the opposite page with Dodola in silhouette (405) (see fig. 12). Created with Islamic calligraphy—some of it recognizable, some of it mere doodles—Dodola's body is the passive receiver of sacred script. She no longer tells the stories with language; that language now works on and through her. This bodily inscription winds through and creates her frame, accentuating and objectifying her sexualized figure as sacred text. As Zam's gaze becomes the reader's own, we do not imagine a sacred body so much as penetrate it. Calligraphy transforms the material body into a gendered, erotic, and sacred

FIG. 12 Dodola's body as calligraphy. Graphic novel excerpt from *Habibi* by Craig Thompson. Copyright © 2011 by Craig Thompson. Used by permission of Pantheon Books, an imprint of the Knopf Doubleday Publishing Group, a division of Penguin Random House LLC. All rights reserved.

FIG. 13 Dodola ingesting sacred writings. Graphic novel excerpt from *Habibi* by Craig Thompson. Copyright © 2011 by Craig Thompson. Used by permission of Pantheon Books, an imprint of the Knopf Doubleday Publishing Group, a division of Penguin Random House LLC. All rights reserved.

text. We visually consume Dodola's body through calligraphy, and we see the word—the sacred script—become flesh.

Dodola embodies sacred calligraphy through the male gaze, but she also literally consumes calligraphy as a prophylactic against the filth and disease of the modern city. Zam and Dodola escape from the palace by means of a water system that funnels pure, clean water from the desert oasis to the palace but spews waste to the rest of the city. Doused in this toxic sewage and approaching death, Dodola limply drapes over Zam's arms as he carries her to safety, far from the deathly waters. Thompson illustrates the septic waters in grotesque detail, as the waters take on the comic form and style of feces. Dodola's condition is so severe after drinking the noxious refuse that even Zam cannot nurse her back to health, and so he must seek out (with the fisherman Noah's help) a medical healer. The shrouded, enchanted doctor arrives with magical implements for healing that work a material encounter with calligraphy as prophylactic. Cloaked in mystery and occult knowledge, the doctor mixes ink with water to create a magic bowl of healing. After dissolving the sacred calligraphy, the doctor hands the curative liquid to Dodola as protective, palliative script. By ingesting the letters into her material body, Dodola gives witness to the material power of sacred writing as prophylactic, magical cure (see fig. 13). The alchemy works to revive Dodola, who now embodies not only the form but also the magical substance of oriental script (472–75).

Magical bowls and squares existed throughout the pre-Islamic period.[41] Even as some forms of Islam rejected magical readings of the Qur'an, the practice continued as a material and protective encounter with the sacred. Writing boards were a magico-religious tradition that transferred the sacred power of Arabic calligraphy to material and consumable form. Travis Zadeh cites Islamic scholars from the fourteenth century who argued that "the act of writing verses of the Qur'an in ink, immersing the paper in water, and then drinking the water, was also a tradition accepted by many in the early community."[42] The "charismatic and medicinal qualities of the Qur'an," including those invoked by writing on a bowl, were more than isolated incidents in medieval Islam. Magic bowls and writing boards served functional rather than aesthetic purposes, and in *Habibi* we see that the calligraphy inscribed by the healer is less ornate than the flowing script Thompson usually employs. The calligraphy used for prophylactic purposes is a "symbolic act of soliciting the spiritual assistance of God using a message that is destined not for human eyes but for those of God."[43]

Yet as Dodola imbibes the sacred script it takes on aesthetic significance and moves from the purview of God to the reader's gaze. Dodola's body becomes a sexual vessel for calligraphy that serves orientalized, aesthetic ends. Her body projects and is projected onto sacred writing that controls her. And this sense of Dodola as a passive receptacle also deadens the moral imagination. To be written is to be subsumed into someone else's narrative. It is to be controlled, subjected, and violated. This sense of full exposure recalls Roland Barthes's distinction between pornography and eroticism, in which the former reveals all and thus leaves little room for imaginative play.[44] So it is here too, as Thompson does not raise the oriental, sexualized gaze as problematic moral vision. Images of Dodola's body are pornographic but not erotic. Calligraphy is less sacred script than inscribed sexuality written onto Dodola's body. And so it is crucial that Dodola does not ingest the prophylactic writing on her own; she requires Zam's powerful male hand to do this for her (475). Male bodies control access to the feminine other. And that gendered figure becomes a sexualized body when Thompson positions Zam's gaze as the reader's own. Thompson effectively colonizes Dodola's body through calligraphy, establishing her sexualized form as the material object for a pornographic gaze. There is nothing to imagine here.

Paradoxically, Dodola can regain her bodily integrity only through a male gaze that scripts her body with calligraphic form. Like the desert landscape, calligraphy remaps Dodola's body, and we read sacrality through her. But as iconic and sacred image-text, calligraphy both objectifies and empowers Dodola. She comes to own and to command her body through calligraphy, allowing her to embody a sacralized and protective script. Dodola can read against the male-inscribed penetration, and this reappropriation of bodily integrity opens space for reimagining her scripted stories. Here, the moral imagination, both hers and the reader's, works to unravel the sexualized consumption of her body. Although Dodola is at the mercy of the sultan, she never fully submits to him, and she practices her independence through fantasy, sacred stories, and the study of the occult. By presenting her body as sacred script, Dodola challenges a gaze that merely appropriates her as a passive vessel. She can own her sexuality by becoming erotic rather than pornographic, by reimagining her body as *producing* rather than being consumed by sacred writing. In this sense, calligraphy transforms into a kind of tattooing that reveals the self—it arrives from the inside out, as it were, rather than from a violent penetration from the outside in. Dodola can actively script what has been inscribed on her body by the male gaze. And this taking back of the self opens room for a moral revisioning of embodiment, in which our bodies, however inscribed and narrativized, become our own sacred stories. We can reimagine embodiment as a sacred writing of self-exposure. Dodola's moral imagination—her taking hold of script as her own material form—works as a counternarrative to the consumptive gaze. *Habibi* challenges readers to embody that moral sensitivity.

The locale of the moral imagination lies in reenvisioning Dodola's written body. Thompson positions the reader to see through Zam's gaze and thereby provokes a visionary choice: to reimagine the body as material writer of stories or to consume that body as male possession and appropriation. In this latter mode, gazing at Dodola is a form of oriental consumption, one mediated and produced by the sacred script of Arabic calligraphy. But a reader need not see through Zam; she can reposition her gaze to see as Dodola might see, to look from within and behind her, and not, like Zam, at her. A moral imagination that looks *at* functions as an idolized gaze at an object and so objectifies the embodied other.[45] But to see as Dodola might see is to refocus that moral sight; it is to shift one's embodied perspective to another's body. The moral challenge, then, is not whose body I see, but from which body do I see it? In *Habibi*, Thompson presents us with a double vision, one that looks *at* and *is seen by* material, embodied script.

Conclusion

Comics do more than tell stories; they create alternative visions of the good. Those visions are both substantive and aesthetic, and much of their moral force weaves style and content together to produce robust accounts of the moral imagination. In many ways, to distinguish the aesthetic features of comics from their narrative arc is really to undermine the allure of the image-text. One cannot escape from Thompson's oriental story, for example, in order to isolate the aesthetic dimensions of calligraphy. Indeed, calligraphy works as both text and image, as both material encounter with the other and problematic visual aesthetic.

I have attempted to bleed image and text together in the very title of this chapter. Aesthetic narration is a kind of visual story in which we see through image to the text, even as the text informs how we see, work, and re-vision image. But this kind of visual narrative demands readers who linger in moral complexity and who thereby deny the pace and simplicity of comic stereotypes. But in both stereotypical and more imaginative depictions, the comic aesthetic has moral force. Eisner's borderless pages conjure up time in space, creating temporal dislocation and presence out of place. Here, ethical questions about traditional obligations and religious commitments torment moral certainty and stereotypical expectations. That moral perplexity, I have argued, is altogether muted in *40 Sufi Comics*, a work that projects strong boundaries to confine the moral imagination within the self. *Megillat Esther* works hard to burst that self-confinement to present, through material frames and aesthetic reversals, a challenging world of moral presence and absence. The moral force of all this is ambiguous and disturbing, as it is in Thompson's oriental gaze through calligraphy. But clarity should not be the goal of a robust, critical, moral imagination. The graphic narratives discussed in this chapter expose how style materially inscribes others as visual spectacles. How we see those others—with a compassionate embrace of vulnerability or with the stereotypical violence of objectification—is the challenge, and the peculiar responsibility, of the moral imagination.

CHAPTER 2

The Ethics of Scriptural Play

Gender, Race, and Moral Sources

Aesthetic narration makes claims on the moral imagination, and as I argued in the previous chapter, those claims both enable and hinder an imaginative ethic. This was certainly clear in Craig Thompson's *Habibi*, in which he objectifies female bodies as the passive receptors to male sexual fantasies but also inscribes those bodies with empowering script to reimagine the sacred gaze. Thompson's exotic appropriation of orientalism is more than aesthetic gesture, however. It also seeps into how he reads sacred texts. One subtle but noticeable undercurrent in *Habibi* is Thompson's reading of the sacrificial chosen son as Ishmael in the Muslim tradition or Isaac in the Jewish and Christian texts. Although the allusions to Jesus remain clear throughout, Thompson reads this foundational story to help rebuild relations between Jews, Christians, and Muslims in a post-9/11 world. He believes these communities share a common story about familial obligations and community that mitigates more violent desires for sacrifice.

My interest in this chapter lies in how someone like Thompson reads sacred texts through visual image. In one stark and powerful drawing, Thompson portrays both Ishmael and Isaac climbing up a mountain, preparing for their sacrifice by their father, Abraham. Both boys appear as young teenagers, one with dark hair (Ishmael) and the other with light-blond locks (Isaac). Thompson glosses his image on the page by noting that Ishmael was a "willing participant" but Isaac "was tricked," and he quotes surah 37 from the Qur'an and Genesis 22:7 as prooftexts for those claims. Now, for both traditions, this story of sacrifice is far more nuanced and uncertain than Thompson allows for in his comic drawing. All three traditions continually reread these texts, in part because they remain so unsettling. One such detail involves the ages of Ishmael and Isaac. The texts tell us nothing in this regard, and religious scholars have struggled with this issue for centuries. And their age makes a difference if we want to fully understand what it means to be a willing or tricked participant in sacrificial slaughter. Thompson has truncated an enormous body of conflicting biblical readings into a bifurcating account of religious foundations: either willing or tricked, obedient or horrified, Eastern exotic or Western blond. This is less an imagined leap into an ethics of toleration in a post-9/11 world than it is a form of visual trickery in which complex religious traditions become simplified exemplars of moral instruction.

Imagining comics such as this one as problematic visual midrash, in which textual gaps allow for rewritings of the biblical story, enables us to see how graphic narratives translate biblical texts into moral sources. David Burke and Lydia Lebrón-Rivera argue that midrashic practice "has helpful implications for the work of adapting Scripture from print text to formats involving text and image,"[1] and I want to follow their lead in understanding the dynamics of midrash as a visual practice. I use the term *midrash* here as a heuristic device of the imagination, in the same way that David Stern locates the "spirit" of rabbinic exegesis. Rather than being interested in midrash as an activity or mode of study in the first five centuries of the common era, or even as a particular literary form,[2] I am interested in what midrash does within a visual medium. Stern nicely examines how rabbinic midrash functioned as a *heard* text; in this chapter, I want to creatively appropriate the term *midrash* as a visual mode of inquiry that is similar to the mode in which Ben Schachter uses the term *visual midrash*.[3] For Schachter and me, *midrash*, in both its aural and visual capacities, fills in visual and silent gaps in the text. Thompson can depict Ishmael and Isaac as teenagers because the textual silence allows his imaginative leap. Still, creative play such as this can assert more truncated, even harmful representations of the other; Thompson shows this here in his exotic depiction of the Arabian Ishmael and the light-skinned blond Isaac. Visual midrashic reading does more than fill in the gaps; it is more than background story. Visual midrash transforms textual silence into a morality tale and thus enacts the ethical imagination. By appealing to an imaginative ethics in which readers envision biblical characters and stories, graphic narratives offer subtle but powerful accounts of identity that both diminish and enlarge our ethical frontiers. Thompson's account of the sacrificial son, for example, exploits male bodies to ground a more ecumenical, inclusive community. This serves only to restrict a more expansive, fluid view of racial and gendered inclusion. But other graphic depictions of sacred texts do enable this imaginative negotiation, and we want to become sensitive to how comics both enable and frustrate these ethical visions.

Visual midrash functions to expose what Erich Auerbach once famously described as background to the biblical story. In the first chapter of *Mimesis*, "Odysseus' Scar," Auerbach compared Homer's *Odyssey* to the story in Genesis 22 of the binding of Isaac. The Greek text, Auerbach argued, was simply "foreground" in representing all meaning to the reader, but the Hebrew text revealed only the slightest hints of its inner depths and left much room for a reader to interpret what was left in the "background."[4] Visual midrash, as we will see in this chapter, exposes that background as graphic design, repositioning it before the reader as fully perceptible. For a literary critic such as Robert Alter, this foregrounding of biblical interiority wrongly solidifies the multivocal significations of textual utterances: "My own preference as a reader is to relish the shimmer of murky possibilities, including the more lurid ones, even if I am left without a concrete or confident picture of what actually happened. Pictorial representation forces you to decide one way—which, however appealing or plausible that way may be, imposes a limit on the story told in words." For Alter, "the image concretizes, and thereby constrains, our imagination."[5] This is not always the case, as I hope this chapter makes clear, for comics can expand our interpretive horizons just as it can close them down. But Alter's point still helpfully reveals how visual midrash functions to impose a "concrete" view of sacred texts. And illustrators cannot help but do this—they must decide how to depict Isaac and Ishmael in physical bodies as these kinds of children. As Alter suggests, they must impose a vision, and these choices foreground what the text leaves in the imaginative background. This chapter focuses on how graphic adaptations of biblical stories accomplish this work of foregrounding, especially in their exposure of racial and gendered bodies.

There is a growing list of graphic narratives that translate sacred literature into the comic medium, but the comics I focus on in this chapter all engage the ethical imagination in expansive and debilitating ways. I want to explore how these comics translate biblical scenes into the comic imaginary and what these translations do to the visual scope of scriptural texts. Comics as visual midrash are the scriptural play of the moral imagination, in which ethical horizons recede and extend through a medium that both integrates and subverts the image-text divide.

I want to pay careful attention to exposures of race, gender, and sexuality in three graphic narratives that reread sacred texts: Robert Crumb's *The*

Book of Genesis Illustrated (2009), Michael Allred's *The Golden Plates* (2004), and Steve Ross's *Marked* (2005). Crumb's work has received much praise and blame, mirroring a good part of his illustrious career. Although Crumb is infamous for his sexist and even admittedly pornographic depictions of women, his *Genesis Illustrated* is a masterful aesthetic experience in reading and visualizing sacred texts. Crumb argues that his work is only a "straight illustration job," deviating little from the written word by remaining true to the text. But this cannot be the case if he illustrates the text and so makes visual choices about gender, race, and sexuality. We can see this within three particular biblical scenes: the creation stories of Genesis 1–3, the account of Lot and his daughters, and the binding-of-Isaac narrative. Gender and sexuality play important roles in the first two of these accounts, and in Isaac's binding we engage the ethical dilemmas in picturing foundational stories for Jewish and Christian traditions.

Allred's *The Golden Plates* engages the racial and ethnic politics of biblical interpretation. *The Golden Plates* is a masterful pictorial translation of the first fourteen books of Nephi, the first book in the Book of Mormon. But we see how dark and light coloring suggests moral worth, as do the shades of skin color attached to Nephi, his brothers, and the savages they meet in the new land of America. Women embody seductive attractions who can either lure men from their sacred duties or enable them to become appointed leaders. The biblical text itself is relatively silent on these matters; Allred enlivens this background through his graphic midrash on the Book of Mormon.

Ross's *Marked* is certainly one of the most creative adoptions of the Gospel story of Mark in the New Testament. This is a self-conscious reimagining of the Gospel account, and it neither pretends to be a straight illustration job nor worries about poetic flights or even grotesque fantasy. I find this creative study refreshing, but I want to look closely at Ross's portrayal of the androgynous Jesus and the women whom he meets, heals, and loves, together with how race subtends much of his retelling. In all three comics—Crumb's *The Book of Genesis Illustrated*, Allred's *The Golden Plates*, and Ross's *Marked*—readers should recognize the illustrated choices to depict bodies as sacred, graphic bodies. These imagined renderings of sacred texts may be scriptural play, but they are visually alluring as problematic exposures of selves. Encoding racial and gendered images in visual midrash gives voice to the silent undercurrents of ethical representation in religious traditions.

The Book of Genesis Illustrated (2009)

Robert Crumb (b. 1943) is well known from the underground comix movement of the 1960s and 1970s, and some of his best-known illustrations (*Fritz the Cat* and *Keep on Truckin'*) have become legendary and mainstream. He is the subject of films and a fine documentary, because his work has inspired a generation of comic illustrators even as it has offended many others.[6] The front cover of the expulsion from Eden in *Genesis Illustrated* is classic Crumb (see fig. 14). For those accustomed to his comic drawings, Eve will look familiar: strong, sexually alluring, and tougher, perhaps even more subversive, than the meek Adam. The visual jokes are here too, despite Crumb's dismissal of them in his introduction. The cover of the book promises complete exposure ("Nothing Left Out!") and suggests—with adult supervision recommended for minors—a lurid side to "the Bible, graphically depicted." That lurid side is more than enticing promise: like God's finger directing Eve and Adam away from the garden and into the desert, this cover points to how Crumb embodies biblical characters in gendered, racial, and sexual bodies. The meek Adam uses one hand to work the harsh land with a tiller, but he uses the other to hold Eve's hand firmly. Eve, although emotional with flowing tears, still gazes back to God with defiance and sexual allure. God is the stern father in this imaginative reading of Genesis—a ghostly whiteness that highlights the tanned-but-still-light-skinned figures of his creation. This is not, then, just Crumb's illustrated Genesis: it is a concrete vision, to appropriate Alter's phrase, of what sacred bodies look like.

From the front to the back cover, Crumb portrays God as a stern taskmaster who is by turns caring, demanding, cruel, and forgiving. Yet Crumb rarely considers his illustrations as anything but fair portrayals of biblical characters and scenes. In a somewhat apologetic tone, Crumb defends his illustrated Bible as an evenhanded, literal translation, claiming that "if my visual, literal interpretation of the Book of Genesis offends or outrages some readers, which seems inevitable considering that the text is revered by many people, all I can say in my defense is that I approached this as a straight illustration job, with no intention to ridicule or make visual jokes. That said, I know that you can't please everybody."[7] But what does a straight illustration job look like to Crumb? How does one portray the God in Genesis, or Adam and Eve, in a literal way? At times, Crumb tends to think of a literal reading as deferential rather than as satirical. In a 2009 interview with Neal Conan of National Public Radio, Crumb explains that he "decided just to do a straight illustration job, because the stories themselves are so strange that it doesn't need satirizing. It doesn't need, you know, making fun of or taking off on or anything. It just stands up on its own as a lurid, you know, comic book." *The Book of Genesis Illustrated*, then, is precisely that: a straight illustration of the original comic book of Genesis. As Crumb puts it, his work is "just exposing the text with illustrations."[8] So a nonsatirical comic book is less interpretation than immediate revelation: a considered, visual exposure of words rather than an imaginative visual reading. We witnessed this denial of imagination in the

FIG. 14 Front cover of *The Book of Genesis Illustrated*. From *The Book of Genesis Illustrated* by Robert Crumb. Copyright © 2009 by Robert Crumb. Used by permission of W. W. Norton & Company, Inc. Artwork © Robert Crumb. Published by arrangement with Random House Children's Publishers UK, a division of The Random House Group Limited.

Vakil brothers' *40 Sufi Comics*. There, readers did not interpret the Qur'an so much as the Qur'an interpreted them. For both the Vakils and Crumb, the text requires little interpretation; it only needs visual exposure. Some of Crumb's critics, amazingly, maintain that he did not fully deliver on his claim of a straight illustration job. As Peter Sattler sees it, "The problem with *Genesis* is not that Crumb is too literal. The problem is that he is very often *not literal enough*."[9] But Rubén Dupertuis, in his essay "Translating the Bible into Pictures," notes how comic book illustrators often claim objective status for their images, as if they faithfully picture the text without embellishment. Dupertuis argues, to the contrary, that comic images create biblical meaning and do not just cleanly translate it.[10] Crumb's illustrations are interpretive pieces—as Robert Alter and Gary Anderson have suggested in their book reviews[11]—that encourage a far more embodied depiction of biblical scenes than a straight illustration job would suggest. A literal reading, in this sense, is always imaginative, creative, and productive. It is also very often, as we have seen on the cover image, raced and gendered. The point is not *that* Crumb genders God, Adam, and Eve, although this is in itself a rather contentious issue. My query concerns the choices he makes—it is *how* he genders them.

So what of this bleached male God with the long, flowing white beard, pointing harshly at the way out of the Garden, encased in a halo of light? Crumb's imaginary derives from Cecil B. DeMille's classic and engaging epic "The Ten Commandments" (1956), and he often pictures God, not just Moses, as the Charlton Heston type. It was hard depicting God, Crumb admits, because he "ended up with the old stereotypical Charlton Heston kind of God, long beard, very masculine."[12] (This, I should add, despite Heston's role as Moses in the film.) In his interview with Conan on *Talk of the Nation*, Crumb speaks of a dream sequence back in the year 2000 in which he "saw God for a brief instant, . . . and it was very powerful. . . . He was very severe, kind of like Mel Gibson when he's angry, you know? Like that."[13] Appeals to Mel Gibson and Charlton Heston suggest the influence of popular culture on Crumb's imaginary, and Don Jolly notes how Crumb's God "is a caricature of the pop cultural images that have come to be associated with the figure of God and the Bible in general."[14] We have already seen in Eisner's *A Contract with God* how stereotypes move readers quickly along a narrative arc but at the great cost of reifying complex images and securing problematic social and cultural biases. For Crumb, Gibson and Heston track common visual tropes for God and Moses, illustrating Hollywood's immense cultural power to naturalize a particular form of male whiteness. Rather than challenging these truncated views, Crumb leans on them heavily, authorizing them as revelatory dream visions. Even more, as I will discuss later, Crumb's God draws on a disturbing image of the Old Testament God as a stern, patriarchal father. But clearly it is simply not true, as Stephen Tabachnick argues, that Crumb's drawings "give a sense of realism rather than hyped-up beauty and are, therefore, very believable." Crumb's illustrations do not offer "credibility and persuasiveness to the biblical story"[15] but instead reproduce common gendered and racial depictions of the biblical God.

Crumb's stern God on the cover of *Genesis Illustrated* recurs throughout his telling of the Genesis narrative, but he also portrays God as a caring and protective father. After the death of one of their sons by the other, Adam and Eve bear a third child (Seth). Crumb depicts the older couple with some compassion and concern and symbolically relates Adam's doting image to God's protection of a much younger Adam and Eve. In this transition from chapter 4 to chapter 5 in Genesis, Crumb draws a shining sun behind both the first couple and God and pictures Adam as only a slightly younger God—with the same flowing beard and hair, just not quite as long (see fig. 15). In the last frame on this page (bottom right), Adam is old and dying, but he still resembles his younger self, which to my eye is indistinguishable from God himself. Crumb's God is decidedly human in appearance and even dress, emanating a tenderness matched only by Adam and Eve's love for their child.

But note Crumb's English version of the initial verses for chapter 5. In the introduction to his work, Crumb appeals to trustworthy translations, claiming that he has "faithfully reproduced every word of the original text, which I derived from several sources, including the King James Version, but mostly from Robert Alter's recent translation, *The Five Books of Moses* (2004)."[16] Crumb's use of biblical translations is much more complicated than he admits here. At times he appropriates Alter's version and then turns to the King James Bible, but he also appears to use the Jewish Publication Society translation as well. This is classic graphic mash-up, but it has important consequences for seeing gender in Genesis. Here is Crumb's version of Genesis 5:1–2: "This is the record of the lineage of Adam: On the day that God created the man, in the image of God He created him. Male and Female He created them. He created them, and He blessed them and called their name man on the day they were created." But this is how the King James Bible and Alter's translation present the same Genesis text:

This is the book of the generations of Adam. In the day that God created man, in the likeness of God made he him; Male and female created he them; and blessed them, and called their name Adam, in the day when they were created.[17] (King James Version)

This is the book of the lineage of Adam: On the day God created the human, in the image of God He created him. Male and female He created them, and He blessed them and called their name humankind on the day they were created.[18] (Alter, *Five Books of Moses*)

AND ADAM AGAIN *KNEW* HIS WIFE, AND SHE BORE A SON AND CALLED HIS NAME SETH, WHICH MEANS, "GOD HAS GRANTED ME ANOTHER SEED IN PLACE OF ABEL, FOR CAIN HAS KILLED HIM."

AND TO SETH, TO HIM ALSO A SON WAS BORN, AND HE CALLED HIS NAME ENOSH. IT WAS THEN THAT MEN BEGAN TO CALL UPON THE NAME OF THE LORD.

Chapter 5

THIS IS THE RECORD OF THE LINEAGE OF ADAM: ON THE DAY THAT GOD CREATED THE MAN, IN THE IMAGE OF GOD HE CREATED HIM. MALE AND FEMALE HE CREATED THEM. HE CREATED THEM, AND HE BLESSED THEM AND CALLED THEIR NAME MAN ON THE DAY THEY WERE CREATED.

AND ADAM LIVED 130 YEARS AND HE BEGOT IN HIS LIKENESS BY HIS IMAGE AND CALLED HIS NAME SETH, AND THE DAYS OF ADAM AFTER HE BEGOT SETH WERE 800 YEARS, AND HE BEGOT SONS AND DAUGHTERS. AND ALL THE DAYS ADAM LIVED WERE 930 YEARS. AND HE DIED.

FIG. 15 God and Adam in Genesis. From *The Book of Genesis Illustrated* by Robert Crumb. Copyright © 2009 by Robert Crumb. Used by permission of W. W. Norton & Company, Inc. Artwork © Robert Crumb. Published by arrangement with Random House Children's Publishers UK, a division of The Random House Group Limited. From *Genesis: Translation and Commentary*, translated by Robert Alter. Copyright © 1996 by Robert Alter. Used by permission of W. W. Norton & Company, Inc.

The interpretive difficulty lies with the word *Adam*, a term often rendered as man. All three translations deal with this term somewhat differently, but Alter helpfully explains both the dilemma of Genesis 5:1 and his solution to it: "*Adam*. The lack of a definite article would seem to indicate that the term is being used as a proper name. But the two subsequent occurrences of '*adam*,' here and in the next verse [Genesis 5:2] equally lack the definite article and yet clearly refer to 'the human creature' or 'humankind.' God's calling 'them' by the name '*adam*' (verse 2) is also an explicit indication that the term is not exclusively masculine, and so it is misleading to render it as 'man.'"[19] I think Alter's is the more faithful translation, but even if Crumb has it right he has still produced an image in strong contrast to the biblical text. For in Crumb's image, God stands over and blesses not just Adam but Eve too; yet Crumb's translation refers only to the man Adam ("He blessed them and called their name man"). Note, too, a similar ambivalence in Crumb's illustration of Genesis 1:26–27, in which God creates Adam as "man" in one panel but then creates "male and female" as Adam and Eve in the next, as though they were two different creations. Why would Crumb struggle with such image-text dissonance in a straight illustration job? Perhaps Crumb only *sees* the strong, white masculine type—read Heston and Gibson—when he imagines God blessing His creation (and Crumb seems to be following the Jewish Publication Society translation in chapter 5 but still diverges from it).[20] In Crumb's rendition, it is Adam, not Eve, who appears godlike in his compassionate embrace of son and spouse (Genesis 4:25). God created the man, and not Eve, in His image. When Crumb envisions Adam and Eve in God's image, he sees popular models of Hollywood leading men. As Alter suggests, there are strong grammatical reasons not to see or imagine in these ways. But race and gender work in Crumb's drawings as stereotypical mimings of pop culture so that viewers see their icons naturalized in sacred bodies. The Genesis text is just a Hollywood screening and thus never demands a viewing beyond the film-market economy.

This charged framing of Adam and Eve runs throughout Crumb's depiction of Eden, especially in his depiction of Eve's creation at the end of chapter 2. After creating all the animals for Adam to name but still finding no fitting mate for him, God creates Eve, according to Crumb, from one of Adam's ribs; Crumb even shows God's hand holding that rib. God introduces her to Adam, who then names her woman. This all arrives as justification for social norms: a man leaves his parents and clings to his woman/wife, and without shame they become one flesh in their nakedness (this despite the fact that Adam has no human mother or father). Crumb's drawing of this scene is, I would think, a clear example of what he claims to be a straight illustration job. He literally shows Adam and Eve joyfully clinging to one another in their nakedness. In some strong sense, he brings two naked bodies together without shame. But the pictorial movement from Adam's naming of Eve to him clinging to her nonetheless reveals gender and sexual hierarchies grounded in Crumb's moral imagination and not rooted in the textual narrative. In the framing of Adam's recognition of Eve, Crumb depicts Adam and Eve as equal partners within a halo of light. Although Adam is taller than Eve, he stands upright as a mirror image to Eve's strong gaze. In hair and physique, both Adam and Eve do seem flesh of each other's flesh. But when Crumb imagines this Adam clinging to woman, both of them with naked and carefree bodies, he projects sexual domination into the picture. In this stylized image, the halo of light in the background still frames Adam and Eve, but now Adam lustfully takes hold of Eve from above, and she energetically accepts his powerful advance (see fig. 16). It seems that Adam has tackled her to the ground, and now in his clutches, she becomes the pursued to his pursuer. Regardless of whether this is all fun and games or a welcome sexual advance, Adam and Eve are literally no longer on the same plane. He controls from above; she acquiesces from below. Crumb has twisted his straight illustration job to project sexual and gender norms onto a text that is at best ambiguous or even silent about them. Clearly, images do things to texts, and this kind of visual exposure illustrates how Crumb encodes his sexual imagination in sacred texts.

FIG. 16 Adam and Eve. From *The Book of Genesis Illustrated* by Robert Crumb. Copyright © 2009 by Robert Crumb. Used by permission of W. W. Norton & Company, Inc. Artwork © Robert Crumb. Published by arrangement with Random House Children's Publishers UK, a division of The Random House Group Limited. From *Genesis: Translation and Commentary*, translated by Robert Alter. Copyright © 1996 by Robert Alter. Used by permission of W. W. Norton & Company, Inc.

To be fair, sexuality is not foreign to the Genesis text, but it is rarely "straight." As Alter suggests, biblical texts usually "proliferate possibilities of meaning" rather than close or pin them down. One such explicit sexual scene in Genesis arrives in chapter 19, when Lot's daughters fear they will be childless and so move their father to drink in order to secure his sexual complicity (see fig. 17). Crumb's depiction of this scene is masterful as he depicts a woozy Lot and two sisters who have quite different experiences with their father. The rabbinic tradition has tended to blame the older sister for this socially aberrant sexual tryst. She is the one, after all, who convinces her younger sister of the plan, even though the rationale for it—that "there is no man on earth to come to bed with us"—seems odd and perhaps downright implausible. Crumb follows this Jewish tradition by depicting the older daughter as the one who gleefully offers her father wine, while the younger lies to the side watching, her expression hidden from us. And yet the frame immediately below suggests a far more fearful look from the younger daughter than from the older. While the older daughter cooks dinner, the younger clutches her body with both hands in a state of uneasy expectation as the older boldly suggests it is now her turn to lie with their father. The two frames to the right of these scenes explore the two sexual liaisons. Lot is equally intoxicated and clueless, but the older lies beneath him with a pleasurable countenance, while the younger dominates from above yet still looks away with disgust and shame. There are many ways to read this text and these pictorial images, and I think Crumb has brilliantly offered a number of possible readings. This gives the lie to Alter's preference for linguistic richness: Crumb shows how images too can proliferate "possibilities of meaning." And yet nothing in the Genesis text warrants Crumb's depiction of it—not the older sister's enjoyment, not the younger sister's ambivalence, and certainly not the entanglement of bodies from below and above. This is visual midrash as creative imagination. Readers of Genesis, and not just the Jewish rabbis, have struggled for centuries with how to read this text. Crumb shows us that we also struggle to visually imagine this scene in the act of reading. According to W. J. T. Mitchell, we imaginatively "create much of our world out of the dialogue between verbal and pictorial representations."[21] We enact texts visually, Mitchell suggests here, and Crumb illustrates a form of this visual reading as sexed fantasy.

I am not arguing that it could be otherwise, that somehow Crumb could imagine this biblical scene beyond sex. But he could have made other pictorial decisions, to be sure. To queer a text like this, for example, might open up new imaginative possibilities of meaning. But what responsibility does Crumb hold to do so? Should we demand a more expansive, explorative, even creative pictorial imagination? When we consider the ethics of representation, these questions rise to the fore, in part because images really do things to texts, as they do here, and sometimes these things harm our intuition for empathy and

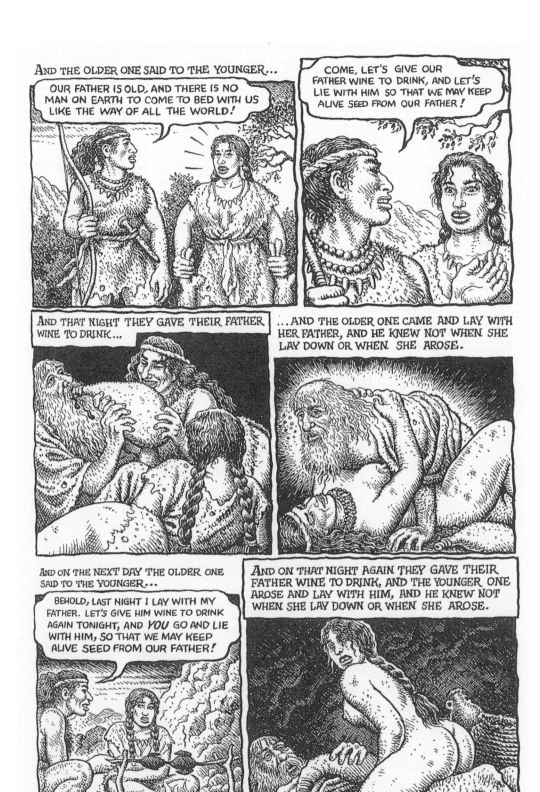

FIG. 17 Lot and his daughters. From *The Book of Genesis Illustrated* by Robert Crumb. Copyright © 2009 by Robert Crumb. Used by permission of W. W. Norton & Company, Inc. Artwork © Robert Crumb. Published by arrangement with Random House Children's Publishers UK, a division of The Random House Group Limited. From *Genesis: Translation and Commentary*, translated by Robert Alter. Copyright © 1996 by Robert Alter. Used by permission of W. W. Norton & Company, Inc.

compassion. Crumb dismisses this kind of criticism by appealing to his illustrations as "straight," that is, as images that merely "expose" the text. Alter is
right to argue that this is not what images do; images interpret texts, and those
interpretations move viewers to *see* and solidify those texts in particular ways.
But are there more compassionate, engaging, and opening ways of doing this?
One cannot hide behind the text, as Crumb would like to do, and claim a form
of interpretive innocence. When the older sister looks fervidly into her father's
eyes from below, even as the younger appears frightened from above, this is no
longer an innocent exposure. Representing texts visually is an ethical act, for
Crumb and for viewers of Crumb's comic works. To see is to imagine a world
of possibilities or of closures, of moral compassion or sexual domination, and
perhaps of a clinging to others that is more than controlling desire.

Picturing foundational religious stories, in Eden or in a father's bed, runs
straight into the ethical imagination. One cannot remain neutral here, either
as artist or as viewer. Graphic narratives can help train us to explore ambiguous meanings and textual nuances, or they can pretend to simply expose a
ready-made text through straight illustration. Responsible seeing, I believe,
means cultivating a capacity to recognize Crumb's artistic decisions as creative
interpretations of the moral imagination. This does not mean that we must
recognize moral compassion where there is none, but it does mean that we
must raise these ethical questions to the fore and take some responsibility
for them. We should become reflective viewers of biblical scenes, even when
artists deny responsibility for their imaginative license.

This kind of moral vision helps us to critically appraise Crumb's account
of Genesis 22, in which God commands Abraham to sacrifice Isaac (see fig.
18). Erich Auerbach discussed this chapter as fraught with background, one
in which a story remains unclear and silent on what appears to matter most
to both actors and readers. This foundational religious scene opens with God's
call to Abraham and his steadfast reply of "Here I am!" The insertion of the
exclamation mark (biblical Hebrew has no inscribed punctuation) suggests
that Abraham is willing and prepared for God's command. There are good
reasons to read this preparedness here, but Crumb misses an opportunity to
draw the textual parallel to Abraham's equally steadfast reply to his son in
Genesis 22:7. Still, Abraham looks above to God's voice only; Crumb decides
to hide God's body from view. This is not always the case—in chapter 12, when
Abraham first hears from God, Crumb depicts God's face within the halo. But
in Genesis 22:1, Abraham and readers see only that bright halo and a voice
emanating from above. With only aural but no visual certainty, Abraham
faithfully responds to God's test and prepares his young boy for the slaughter
(see fig. 19). But when Abraham is told to relinquish his desire for sacrifice
(and in this scene he appears as a wild, crazed father), a compassionate figure
appears to him, one reminiscent of another popular image: that of an angelic

Jesus calling out from the heavens. What accounts for only the heavenly voice in one verse and the voice plus the material presence of God (or God's son) in the other?

I do not know how Crumb understands the binding-of-Isaac narrative, but his illustrations suggest one reading made prominent by the eighteenth-century philosopher Immanuel Kant: Abraham misheard God's voice, for a just and moral God could not have commanded Abraham to sacrifice his son. The problem with voice, according to Kant, is that we "could still never *know* that it was God speaking. . . . But in some cases man can be sure that the voice he hears is *not* God's; for if the voice commands him to do something contrary to the moral law, then . . . he must consider it an illusion." As Kant argues in the footnote to this text, Genesis 22 provides the most illustrative example of this fantasy.[22] In Crumb's *Genesis*, God's voice calls out from heaven to test Abraham's resolve, but God (or God's son) appears to prevent the slaughter. The one, according to Kant, reveals an immoral god, whereas the other conforms to our sense of the moral law. If Crumb harbors similar misgivings about a God who commands human sacrifice, and if his illustrations depict that unease—perhaps this is why Abraham appears crazed and unhinged—then Crumb's God, like Kant's, cannot be the one who commanded Abraham to sacrifice his son. For Crumb, God appears only as the ethical voice of a compassionate, if sometimes angry, father/son.

But the appearance of the Jesus figure in Genesis 22:12 suggests a far more disturbing view of the biblical God, because Crumb appropriates the stereotypical distinction between the stern Old Testament God and the compassionate, loving one of the New Testament. The Jewish tradition generally depicts this dynamic as the God of justice and the God of mercy, and perhaps Crumb also plays with God's dual nature in Genesis. But too often, Christian readers depict a stern God of the Hebrew Bible to transfigure that text into an Old Testament that points to, and at times even requires, the compassionate God of the New Testament. Consider this exchange between Crumb and Neal Conan of National Public Radio:

Conan: How did you decide—was there a debate in your mind about how to picture God?

Mr. Crumb: Well, drawing God was hard. That was the hardest part. But I had this dream in the year 2000 that I saw God for a brief instant in my dream, and it was very powerful. It was a lucid dream, and he talked to me, but I couldn't bear to look at him longer than a split second. And he looked even more severe and more pained than the God that I drew. He was very severe, kind of like Mel Gibson when he's angry, you know? Like that.

(*sound bite of laughter*)

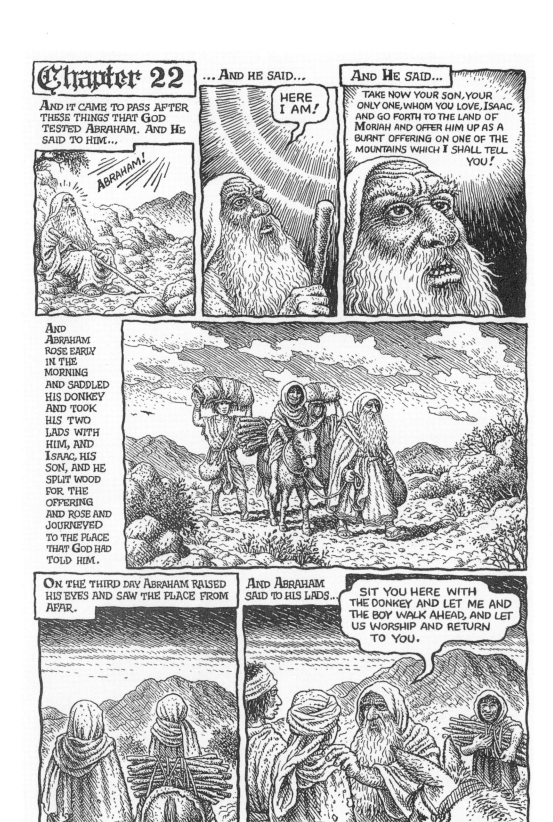

FIG. 18 God calls to Abraham in Genesis 22. From *The Book of Genesis Illustrated* by Robert Crumb. Copyright © 2009 by Robert Crumb. Used by permission of W. W. Norton & Company, Inc. Artwork © Robert Crumb. Published by arrangement with Random House Children's Publishers UK, a division of The Random House Group Limited. From *Genesis: Translation and Commentary*, translated by Robert Alter. Copyright © 1996 by Robert Alter. Used by permission of W. W. Norton & Company, Inc.

FIG. 19 The Binding of Isaac in Genesis 22. From *The Book of Genesis Illustrated* by Robert Crumb. Copyright © 2009 by Robert Crumb. Used by permission of W. W. Norton & Company, Inc. Artwork © Robert Crumb. Published by arrangement with Random House Children's Publishers UK, a division of The Random House Group Limited. From *Genesis: Translation and Commentary*, translated by Robert Alter. Copyright © 1996 by Robert Alter. Used by permission of W. W. Norton & Company, Inc.

Mr. Crumb: He kind of looked like that, but you know, at the same
time, he had the long, flowing white hair and beard like
Michelangelo's God in the Sistine Chapel. You know, this is
the patriarchal God of Western civilization, you know, the big
father in the sky that we all fear so deeply.

(*sound bite of laughter*)

Conan: You should excuse the expression the Old Testament God.

Mr. Crumb: Yeah.

Conan: Literally.

Mr. Crumb: Which, you know, Jesus is the good cop. You know, he
comes, and he's, you know, he's the nice side of God, the compassionate, the victim side of God, you know?[23]

Crumb's repetitive utterance, "you know," suggests a cultural familiarity with
these figures. We all know—literally, according to Conan—the patriarchal,
fearful God of the Old Testament and the "good cop" of the new one. This
disturbing interview comes off as insider talk, in which Crumb appeals to
anti-Jewish stereotypes—but winks at his viewers to "excuse the expression"—
and Conan plays along with common, sometimes even vulgar stereotypical
images. Picturing biblical sacrifice, heavenly voices, moral dilemmas, biblical
promises, and obligations of fathers to sons all seems like a fun sound bite, a
material script for light and airy banter, but not the stuff for reflective moral
vision. There are serious ethical issues here, and if Conan and Crumb will
not see them, then readers of *The Book of Genesis Illustrated* should do that
visionary work in their stead.

What do readers see when they read Genesis 22? One scene that Crumb
envisions, and I imagine many other readers do also, is Isaac walking down
the mountain with Abraham after the ordeal. But the text never mentions
Isaac; it says only that "Abraham returned to his lads" (Genesis 22:19). Some
commentators suggest that this omission highlights Abraham as the main
protagonist and so fits well with the very first call to sacrifice his beloved
son. Although Jews of medieval Europe often turned to Isaac as the principal
character of this story as they too went to slaughter by the crusaders, the test
here is Abraham's, and he is the one who is rewarded for his commitment
to God. Still other interpreters, however, see traces of a very different story,
in which Abraham actually did sacrifice his son, and so only Abraham came
down from the mountain (and in some accounts, Isaac was later brought back
to life, a clear precursor to God's only son, Jesus).[24] However we imagine this
scene, Genesis 22:19 functions like a textual gutter: we have to envision an
event left out of the script. And this means we must see with a moral vision
because it matters *ethically* whether Isaac is with his father at the end of this
chapter. Crumb *assumes* Isaac is there, but careful readers of Genesis should

see differently and so enact a more reflective kind of moral and visual imagination. To imagine Isaac with his father, here and throughout this story—"and the two of them went together" (Genesis 22:8)—is to tell one kind of ethical narrative. To perceive a different ending, though, one focused on Abraham alone, is to recount another kind of moral drama. Cultivating an active moral imagination, one that recognizes how texts *and* images "proliferate possibilities of meaning," queers Crumb's straight illustrations into more elastic, open, and transformational encounters with sacred texts.

The Golden Plates (2004)

Michael Allred calls his graphic narrative "an adaptation" of the Book of Mormon, "one [of] the greatest books on the face of the earth." Presenting himself as an inspired insider, Allred carefully situates his comic as his own testimony "to the absolute proof that Jesus The Christ is in all fact the son of God, the Savior of the world." *The Golden Plates* is both personal witness and pictorial depiction of God's revelation: "Many wonderful and terrible things have transpired in my life—All bringing me to this commitment—the inspiration that led me toward attempting this project. My true intent is to do this work justice—to provide an easily accessible visual thread through all the events in *The Book Of Mormon*."[25] Allred has never fulfilled the promise to illustrate the entire *Book*, but he has given us a wonderfully rich account of the first fourteen chapters in 1 Nephi, together with two additional volumes: *The Liahona and the Promised Land* (volume two) and *The Lord of the Vineyard and Discovering Zarahemla* (volume three). This appeal to accessibility was never Crumb's concern: he sought to simply translate the biblical story into the comic medium. According to him, that translation was possible because Genesis presented itself as a kind of comic. "If you actually read the Old Testament," Crumb asserted, "[God is] just an old, cranky Jewish patriarch. It's a lot of fun doing Genesis, actually. It's very visual. It's lurid."[26] Allred maintains a very different sensibility toward his sacred text. The Book of Mormon is for Allred an inspired work that commands visual inspiration from the comic artist. It's important that many wonderful and terrible things have happened in Allred's life, because that life simultaneously testifies to the power of the Book of Mormon and authorizes the artistic adaptation of it.

As an insider witness to the tradition he portrays to outsiders, Allred struggles with the status of his graphic narrative. Because it is an adaptation, the comic need not be considered a faithful translation, although Allred does adhere almost verbatim to the original wording. As we will see later, however, Allred deviates from the original text in crucial scenes, and these discrepancies are ethically productive. What troubles Allred is the necessity of his work; if the Book of Mormon "is a true and inspired record," then why the need for its graphic adaptation? Here is how Allred justifies his labor: "Most importantly, let me make clear that this is in no way a substitute for *The Book Of Mormon* itself, which is a sacred book. This project is a primer at best. It is a visual guide, flaws and all, that will hopefully make the events of the actual scriptures come alive and more easily understood when they are read in full as they should be. The Gospel in it's [*sic*] fullness will be found in the sacred scriptures—not here. But hopefully the spirit will be present in these pages as you, dear reader, turn them."[27] Allred worries that his graphic narrative might be taken as a replacement for or, even worse, a better adaptation of the original story. But as a "visual guide," the danger is even greater, for in visualizing the scriptural text, Allred might envision a very different kind of story than a reader might when reading it. W. J. T. Mitchell's work in visual studies has maintained a consistent focus on the ways we *see* texts, and most recognize this reading strategy when they encounter the movie adaptation of an engrossing book. Rarely does the movie conform to one's visual imagination of the written word. As Alter pointed out, visual images can all too easily codify meanings in a far more ambiguous textual tradition. So as a visual guide, Allred's *The Golden Plates* might do more than translate a mysterious work into a well-understood one; it might instead *transform* that text as a very particular kind of sacred writing and seeing.

As a visual primer, Allred's graphic narrative genders and racializes the Book of Mormon in ways that appeal to problematic stereotypes of female and black bodies. Now, this is certainly not Allred's intent, as he makes clear on the inside jacket covers. He implores his readers to "seek out *The Book Of Mormon*." But if a reader comes to that text by means of this comic one, the Book of Mormon will appear with dark bodies and enlightened, white angels. It will show the female body as sexual, dangerous, and transgressive. This is not about understanding sacred texts "as they should be"; this is about the ethics of representation.

The first books of Nephi read as heritage production—an engrossing tale of Lehi's family roots in ancient Israel, narrated by his son Nephi. It begins in the reign of King Zedekiah, which Allred claims is around 600 BC, at a time when prophets arose in Jerusalem seeking repentance for their people. Lehi is overcome by the Lord's spirit and is blessed with visions and prophecy. As he begins to minister to his people, the Book of Mormon relates this telling scene:

> And it came to pass that the Jews did mock him because of the things which he testified of them; for he truly testified of their wickedness and their abominations; and he testified that the things which he saw and heard, and also the things which he read in the book, manifested

plainly of the coming of a Messiah, and also the redemption of the world. And when the Jews heard these things they were angry with him; yea, even as with the prophets of old, whom they had cast out, and stoned, and slain; and they also sought his life, that they might take it away. (1 Nephi 19–20)

Let us leave aside the issue about the status of the Jews in 600 BC; what is crucial here is how Allred narrates, in text and image, the following scene in his comic adaptation: "He truly testified of their wickedness and abominations; and also the things which he read in the book, and manifested plainly of the coming of a Messiah, and the redemption of the world. And they were angry with him. Just like they were with prophets of old, who they had cast out, and stoned, and slain. And now they wanted to take away my father's life as well" (see fig. 20).[28] Allred has erased all mention of "the Jews" in his text, and he leaves out altogether how they mocked Lehi's testimony. Indeed, when reading this comic in light of Crumb's, the Israelite mob doesn't even look Jewish! Crumb depicts his Israelites as having light-skinned, toned bodies, and as they age, like Abraham, they tend to look like "old, cranky" Jews. But Allred's Lehi is of noticeably lighter complexion than those who gather to hear and ultimately to cast stones upon him. They are dressed in long gowns and headdresses associated with popular scenes from the Levant, especially Egypt. These are not Crumb's cranky old Jews but are the much darker Israelites of Allred's imagination.

This erasure of Jewish presence is all the more noticeable for Allred's fairly consistent word-for-word translation of the Book of Mormon. There are very few instances such as this one in which Allred deviates from the sacred text. But the silence here reveals Allred's missionary zeal. The Book of Mormon portrays Jews much like other Christian sources that focus on their scorn for prophecy, their denial of honest testimony, and their failure to recognize revelatory truth. If Allred wishes his comic to be a guide to the Book of Mormon, he would do well to leave out suggestions of Jewish pride and ridicule. But Allred fills in that silence with murky colors; he and Laura Allred, who authors the coloring, consistently portray the mob in darker hues throughout the comic. Note how the Allreds portray Lehi, Nephi (who relates this tale), and Nephi's two older brothers, Laman and Lemuel. The older ones resist Lehi's and later Nephi's prophetic command, and they, like the Israelite mob, murmur and complain about their father and younger brother. Only Nephi and Lehi radiate light skin; the "bad" sons and brothers are much darker, with far more sinister expressions. This darkening also applies to Lehi's wife, who remains unnamed. In chapter 5, she too mocks her husband for his prophetic zeal, saying, "You have led us from our land and home, and my sons are no more, they have perished in the wilderness. We will perish as well. And for what? Visionary man!" These last two sentences are Allred's—he adds this mocking tone to her complaint, and he portrays her with teary eyes as she stares resolutely back at her disgraced husband. Lehi defends himself as an inspired prophet, and she acquiesces to his authority as he comforts her in a tender embrace. This rendering of gender hierarchy, so pronounced with male authority and female betrayal, is raced and colored; complaining women show a darker complexion, whereas the two other women mentioned in this comic—Ishmael's daughter (and Nephi's love interest and future wife) and Mary, the mother of Jesus—are noticeably light skinned. Skin color marks the belief and betrayal of these ancient Israelites.

Perhaps the most disturbing racialized scene in *The Golden Plates* appears in chapter 12, when God's angel grants Nephi a vision of the future. He beholds a vision of Jesus as the lamb of God, descending from the heavens all in white: his skin, his robe, and even the brightness that engulfs him are white.

FIG. 20 Lehi ministers. From *The Golden Plates* by Michael Allred. Copyright © 2004 by Michael Allred.

FIG. 21 A dark, loathsome, and filthy people. From *The Golden Plates* by Michael Allred. Copyright © 2004 by Michael Allred.

Yet soon after Jesus blesses the twelve apostles, and the Holy Ghost descends upon them, things quickly take a turn for the worse. As the generations pass, so too does righteousness, and Nephi beholds his progeny fighting against his kin: "And because of the pride of my seed, and the temptations of the devil, I beheld that the seed of my brethren did overpower the people of my seed" (1 Nephi 12:19). These internecine wars continue to ravage Nephi's descendants, and as a sign of disbelief they become a darkened people: "And it came to pass that I beheld, after they had dwindled in unbelief they became a dark, loathsome, and filthy people, full of idleness and all manner of abominations." Allred's text is almost a direct translation from 1 Nephi 12:23 (the biblical text reads "a dark, and loathsome, and a filthy people"). If mention of "the Jews" had bothered Allred in the opening scene of *The Golden Plates*, visions of dark, unbelieving bodies fail to register here as ethically problematic (see fig. 21). The strong contrast in light and dark colors delivers the message in full—whereas the angel stands in bright white robes and almost bleached-white skin and Nephi kneels as a tanned, strong man unable to look at such filth, only the blackened bodies bend over in disgrace.

This message has deep, historical, and painful roots in the Mormon church. Not until 1978 were male bodies considered dark in complexion allowed to stand for ordination to the priesthood or be married within the temple.[29] The church has offered conflicting theological and cultural accounts to justify this distinction. Joseph Smith was somewhat ambivalent in his position toward African American males, but Brigham Young was not, for he both supported "servitude" in Utah and instituted the priesthood ban for black-skinned males in 1852.[30] The Mormon church has recently condemned Young's view but argues that his position merely "echoed the widespread ideas about racial inferiority" in Utah of his time.[31] Some of those views included the curse of Cain and Ham, which Mormon theologians (as well as others) believed to be a curse on black-skinned people as Cain and Ham's progeny. One can read these theological views in such pamphlets as *Mormonism and the Negro*, a work published in 1960 by Professor John Stewart, then professor of journalism at Utah State University.[32] Americans have inherited this racial history, but the Mormon church has been somewhat deaf to its cultural impact. There is a noticeable absence of "black people and black traditions in church-sanctioned art, literature, music, and temple rituals."[33] Although the Mormon church has labored to be more inclusive, some still feel left out, and the church's cultural relations with Native Americans might be even worse. The Allreds work within this religious history and discourse, and readers might expect a *visual* sensitivity to this racial injustice, even if the sacred text lacks it.

But if *The Golden Plates* reads as primer to the Book of Mormon, it does so by showing *how* skin tone reveals faith. In the second volume, *The Liahona and the Promised Land*, the Allreds make this all too clear in their depiction of Eve and the devil. Eve is the innocent white female who is undone by the black devil—a clear indication of the ways gender and race conspire to articulate hierarchies of value (see fig. 22). For those cognizant of American racial history, this scene recalls the racial narrative made famous in the film *Birth of a Nation* (1915), in which southern whites were called on to protect their fair women from black aggression. Reading this racist, gendered imaginary back to Eden reveals how the Allreds see race and gender in sacred texts. But this only continues what the Allreds depict in this first volume of "a dark, loathsome, and filthy people." Yet what should truly shock a viewer here is the cannibalism of the black bodies. As they savagely eat the intestines and arms of other darkened bodies, we too wish to look away, like Nephi, and reject that darkness for lighter hues. The Book of Mormon tells us of their darkness; *The Golden Plates* shows us what this darkness *means*. As viewers, we can look at that black grotesque or look away and seek protection from the light. Allred makes this *our* choice by visually enacting blackness as lurid animality. *The Golden Plates* is not a primer for the Book of Mormon; it is instead a racialized, gendered fantasy of it, one that draws from a Mormon cultural and theological legacy on blackness.

Throughout *The Golden Plates*, depictions of whiteness highlight this visual dichotomy between faith and disbelief. One of the more vivid scenes in the Book of Mormon is Lehi's vision of a man "dressed in a white robe" who reveals to him a tree "whose fruit was desirable to make one happy" (see fig. 23). Like Eve before him, Lehi takes of this fruit, but it is more than just good to eat: "The fruit was white, above all the whiteness that I had ever seen." Lehi calls to his family to eat of this white fruit also, only to be rebuffed by his two wicked sons, Laman and Lemuel. Lehi then envisions a multitude

FIG. 22 Eve and the Devil. From *The Golden Plates* by Michael Allred. Copyright © 2004 by Michael Allred.

who must choose between this white tree of life and "the great and spacious building" across the river that shelters those who mock the ones blessed by the white fruit. Whiteness saves the elect from the abyss, and Allred translates this textual vision into a colored dichotomy: the saved hold the white fruit close at hand as if to ward off the evil emanating from across the river (see fig. 24). There, the Allreds portray the lost souls as modern selves dressed in "very fine" clothing as they scorn the more simple, innocent, religious types who cling to white things. When Nephi requests visions like his father's, the very same "Spirit of the Lord" in white robes shows him, in Allred's graphic narrative, an even larger tree with equally grand white fruit that "did exceed the whiteness of the driven snow." And on the following page, when Nephi sees the coming of the Christ, the color white dominates the two-page spread. Quite simply, it's good to be white in the Book of Mormon, and even more so in *The Golden Plates*.

Allred's text is not a primer or a neutral visual guide to the Book of Mormon, despite his pleading intentions listed on the inside cover. He could

FIG. 23 The white fruit. From *The Golden Plates* by Michael Allred. Copyright © 2004 by Michael Allred.

FIG. 24 The lost souls. From *The Golden Plates* by Michael Allred. Copyright © 2004 by Michael Allred.

have chosen to mute those bleached tones, as he certainly did when the sacred text mentions the Jews of old. In his second volume, *The Liahona and the Promised Land*, Allred does include a number of textual referents to Jews, but here the appeal retains a far more inclusive and encompassing tone, as a petition to the restoration either of the Jews in the latter days or of "all the nations of the gentiles and also the Jews." They have not disappeared, although before those latter days and like the gentiles, the Jews too will be drunk "with iniquity" (2 Nephi 27:1). Still, in the latter days the Jews will be grafted back onto the tree of life, even if, as Allred's third and last volume in this trilogy makes clear, the children of Lehi are the true inheritors of God's original covenant.[34] Here and elsewhere in *The Golden Plates*, the images tell us *how* to read the text, how to envision and represent it as a story about restoring a lost heritage, a moral fable about saving whiteness, or even a tale of the inevitability of succumbing to darkened error. We see this clearly, for example, in the way Allred portrays a white Jesus who heralds the Jewish return to God, when the biblical Book of Mormon mentions only God's, and not Jesus's, call to the Jews (see fig. 25). My point here is that Allred's images do not reflect the text so much as color it with his Christocentric reading. This reading has deep roots in Mormon racial history, but coloring in comics informs the ethics of vision, for it can move readers to see bright dichotomies when more subtle variations might be in order. In one crucial scene that I will explore later, Allred brilliantly challenges the ethic of whiteness in Nephi's narrative. He understands how coloring and shading reveal ethical nuance and ambiguity. So when the Allreds image blackness as ugly, animalistic, and morally corrupt, they are not merely adapting a sacred text into comic form. They undermine a more textured account of the moral imagination and the ethics of representation.

This closure of moral ambiguity appears in gendered accounts as well. When God's angel reveals the future to Nephi, he foresees the virgin Mary, who is "exceedingly fair and white." Her purity, imagined here in skin color, is also connected with her femininity. Allred shows her drawing water from a well, and with baby Jesus in hand on the very next page, she is imaged as the domestic provider and mother. But she is not the only female who embodies purity of heart and domestic bliss. When Ishmael and his family journey with Lehi, one of Ishmael's daughters defends Nephi before his jealous older brothers. The Book of Mormon offers only a general account of this scene, as follows: "One of the daughters of Ishmael, yea, and also her mother, and one of the sons of Ishmael, did plead with my brethren" (1 Nephi 7:19). The Allreds take great liberty here, both in image and text, by imagining Laman ready to strike out against Ishmael's daughter as she pleads, "Stop this! We know our father leads us to safety and we mean to follow." As Laman, fist raised, yells "Out of my way, girl," one of Ishmael's sons intercedes to protect her, saying,

FIG. 25 The coming of Christ. From *The Golden Plates* by Michael Allred. Copyright © 2004 by Michael Allred.

"Don't you dare touch her." At the same time, Sariah, Lehi's wife, reprimands her older boys. None of this can be found in the Book of Mormon, but this scene certainly guides readers on how to read gender and race in that text. White women here require male protection, in part because they represent virtue and righteous order. They defend their men but also reprimand those who stray from the sacred path. They enable righteousness, yet neither produce nor enact it. But even as they keep their men on the straight and narrow, they can also seduce them away from their chosen journey. After Lehi laments the loss of his Laman and Lemuel because they did not partake of the white fruit, the Allreds depict Ishmael's daughter as temptress, not only to the older brothers but to the righteous Nephi as well. She is embodied white seduction, and by looking back over her shoulder at the tempted Nephi, she understands her role and how to play it well. If, indeed, *The Golden Plates* works as primer to the Book of Mormon, then it also functions to gender and race that text in ways that sacralize women as dangerous bodies who, with a push of their hands or a look over their shoulders, can deceive and empower with equal measure.

In *The Golden Plates*, white women move men to righteousness or dishonor; they seduce, complain, seek comfort, provide, and protect. These are well-worn cultural norms for women as enablers, both for good and ill. These stereotypical images harm our capacity to imagine other modes of envisioning gender and race and thus impede the expansion of our ethical imaginations. But *The Golden Plates* also facilitates this more expansive imagination in a troubling scene in which Nephi is asked to kill Laban, a man of great power who holds the historical records of Lehi's family history (see fig. 26). Laman had failed to secure those records, and as the older brothers again rebel against Nephi, the spirit of the Lord descends to command Nephi to return to Jerusalem, for "the Lord will deliver Laban into your hands." Nephi discovers Laban drunk outside his own house, immediately takes hold of Laban's sword, and "was constrained by the Spirit that I should kill Laban" (1 Nephi 4:10). But Nephi resists this command, and the Mormon text narrates an internal dialogue between the Lord's spirit and Nephi. Finally persuaded that he must kill Laban for the greater good, Nephi "did obey the voice of the spirit." Both the Book of Mormon and *The Golden Plates* are clearly uncomfortable with a God who demands murder from a faithful servant. And both texts suggest that Nephi never willingly accedes to this request: he is both constrained by and obedient to the Spirit's voice, but he does not actively choose to kill Laban.

Allred displays this inner turmoil in ways that both heighten the moral complexity of this scene and undermine the simple bond between the good and whiteness. The passive tense suggests to Allred that Nephi's will is bound and constrained, and he reluctantly obeys the order to kill the drunken Laban. He visually portrays this internal struggle by situating the Spirit's presence within Nephi's eyes, thereby commanding Nephi's vision and, by extension, his moral will. Note the top right panel, in which the white background bleeds into the figure of the Lord's spirit, who appears at Nephi's side as the two of them gaze together at the drunken Laban. The middle panels on this page all brighten Nephi's eyes with that whiteness, suggesting how the Spirit occupies Nephi's soul. But to reveal Nephi's resistance to that white possession, Allred shows Nephi's eyes flushed with tears, as if he wishes to defy and struggle against the Lord's command. Those tears, in the final panel on the lower right of this page, turn to resolve as Nephi "smote off his head with his own sword." The moral sensibilities here are ambiguous, as are Nephi's intentions. As Nephi labors to convince himself of the necessity of this deed, he is either ashamed at his loss of innocence or rebellious against a God who demands murder. Whereas the color white signified pure goodness in other scenes in *The Golden Plates*, here it announces spiritual possession and a kind of moral consequentialism, in which "it is better that one man should perish than that a nation should dwindle and perish in unbelief" (1 Nephi 4:13). But Allred complicates this moral thinking by enhancing Nephi's passive acceptance and active resistance. This internal negotiation, in which the eyes shine bright with tears, advances a far more ambivalent, textured account of the sacred book and the ethical dilemmas it presents. There is no resolution here, no quick and easy dichotomy between white beauty and darkened animality. The hero, to be sure, becomes the strong, controlling man on the very next page, but Allred has uncovered his moral vulnerability. In this complicated scene of ethical valor and intention, *The Golden Plates* works as primer and guide by revealing a sacred text as an ambiguous moral source.

Allred never intended his comic to display moral ambivalence. As he argued in the inside front cover of the first volume, the Book of Mormon "is a true and inspired record" of Jesus as the Christ.[35] He thinks of his graphic narrative as a transparent window into the sacred text: "And so I just happen to draw comic books. For this project the classier 'Graphic Novel' moniker seems more appropriate to describe what Laura (my gorgeous, patient wife and colorist) and I are doing. We simply want to share what we know to be true through our favorite artistic medium."[36] But when they share the sacred truth through their most beloved comic, they envision a text that is both racialized and gendered in ways that are anything but "true and inspired." They visualize, in other words, a certain kind of sacred text, and not one discovered, as they claim, by Joseph Smith in 1830. It is not only that the words in their graphic novel are not always the same as those in the Book of Mormon. The comic images transform those words into visual metaphors and do so in ways that highlight how reading is, among other things, a visual exercise of the imagination. A sacred text becomes so through the visual, moral imagination, and this making sacred also informs visual claims to race and gender. Allred's

FIG. 26 Spirit moving Nephi to kill Laban. From *The Golden Plates* by Michael Allred. Copyright © 2004 by Michael Allred

anxiety that his comic may in some way substitute for the Book of Mormon is a very real one. Readers may indeed read that sacred text "through" his favorite artistic medium. The challenge for these comic viewers is to envision sacred writing through the ambiguity of ethical reflection rather than through the bifurcated gendered and racial dynamic so pronounced in Allred's moral imagination.

Marked (2005)

Crumb intended his *Book of Genesis Illustrated* as a "straight illustration job," and Allred understood his work as an accessible "visual primer." But we have come to recognize how images texture sacred literature such that appeals to straight jobs or visual accessibility undermine critical visual reflection. Those images project contentious moral representations of gender and race. With Steve Ross's *Marked*, we encounter a more expansive form of biblical commentary. Both Crumb and Allred remained close to the biblical text, imagining their comics more as clear illustrations of a biblical story. This is only partly so in *Marked*. Knowledgeable readers of the biblical Gospel of Mark, as Elizabeth Coody nicely argues, can follow Ross's *Marked* as it works through the Gospel's plot. But for those new to this biblical story, "*Marked* can be a confusing read."[37] Ross sets his Gospel story in the urban present, where greed, economic disparity, and those "marked" as outsiders become the background and locale for Jesus's good news. Like in the biblical Gospel, we encounter a Jesus who drives out evil spirits, who portends his tragic end in Jerusalem even when those around him fail to see the signs, and who constantly interprets his parables to his unenlightened disciples. But Ross desires a different kind of Jesus than "the long-haired white middle-class guys who have co-opted Christianity." These tyrannical images of the biblical Jesus have suffused American culture, so Ross believes, and he wants us to see the Gospel and its message in a new light: "I just wanted to see if I could receive the Gospel of Mark with a lover's heart and then recount it with a troublemaker's eye. . . . Like Picasso stripping away layer after layer of preconceptions until he finally arrived at a new way of seeing."[38] In many ways, both Crumb and Allred believe their graphic narratives reflect the biblical one; for Ross, his all black-and-white comic seeks to "mark" the Gospel with a new vision of engagement. We move from desired transparency to troublemaker's challenge and so leave Crumb's straight illustration job and Allred's devoted witnessing to see how Ross imagines sacred texts.

One of Jesus's many confrontations with Jewish scribes offers a clear example of Ross's creative repurposing of the Gospel. In Mark 12:18–27, the Gospel recounts how the Sadducees confront Jesus about Jewish law with the hope of revealing his failings. The issue concerns sibling obligations to a brother who dies but leaves his wife childless. The law requires the male next of kin to marry his brother's wife and to raise the resulting children as if they were his deceased brother's progeny. In this fantasy tale in Mark, each of the seven brothers ends up marrying his brother's wife because each brother dies in turn without producing children. The Sadducees, who according to this text do not even believe in resurrection, then ask Jesus, "In the resurrection whose wife will she be? For the seven had her as wife."[39] Jesus's response is either cryptic or evasive, but Ross turns this entire scene into comedic, television-drama farce. Ross substitutes a television game show host for the biblical Sadducees, and his Jesus seems perplexed by the celebrity and purpose of the televised game ("What's the Law?"). The television host repeats the biblical conundrum with sarcastic flair, saying, "But guess what? The brother slips in the bathtub, suffers a severe concussion and, you guessed it, he also dies! So the third brother steps up to the plate and marries her uh oh. . . . He chokes to death on a hazelnut." Ross portrays the absurdity of the problem as well as the "gotcha" quality of the text. Jesus won't play, however, and as the young woman turns off the show in disgust with a quick click of the television remote, she offers Ross's assessment of the whole thing: "I hate it when they ask trick questions."[40] Jesus works on a different plane and in a different medium than do the Sadducees of the Gospel or the game show host in Ross's comic. He does not arrive to answer to the law but to challenge and reimagine it.

But that reimagining still traces the problematic representations of gendered and racial images at the heart of this chapter. In *Marked*, Jesus arrives as an androgynous being who, while projecting beyond gender and racial boundaries, still grounds male whiteness as normative. Ross introduces Jesus as a carpenter with long black hair (and bandanna to keep it back from his eyes) and a somewhat unkempt goatee. He looks enough like "the long-haired white middle-class" Jesus for readers to recognize him immediately. Upon hearing John the Baptist's liberatory and revolutionary message, he trots down to the lake to be baptized and then returns home dazed and confused. Staring into the bathroom mirror, he cuts off all his hair, along with his goatee, and he rejects his carpenter clothes for a long white robe. Ross is at his most clever here, as Jesus's mother knows something is up ("Did something happen at work?" she asks), but she cannot fathom the depth of her son's transformation. This the reader learns only on the next page, when a Hollywood-type mogul, arriving in a limousine, plays the role of God as movie producer: "Simply perfect. Not too white, not too ethnic. Young. Strong. Male though slightly androgynous. Working class yet intellectual. Young man, I always trust my instincts and my instincts tell me you are the find of the epoch. Come with me now. I'll drop all my other clients. You'll be my only purpose in life. Exclusively" (see fig. 27).[41] Ross indicates that this

FIG. 27 Male, though slightly androgynous. From *Marked*. Copyright © 2005 Church Publishing Inc. All rights reserved. Used by permission of Church Publishing Incorporated, New York, NY.

"slightly androgynous" being can appeal to all types. He transcends gender and ethnicity, class differences, and racial hierarchies. He bridges divides ("working class yet intellectual") by asserting a strong sense of self. But note the dichotomies throughout this Hollywood trip: white is still normative as the baseline for identity, and so too is maleness. Jesus is white and male, just

FIG. 28 Black mammy figure. From *Marked*. Copyright © 2005 Church Publishing Inc. All rights reserved. Used by permission of Church Publishing Incorporated, New York, NY.

FIG. 29 Adoring black mammy figure. From *Marked*. Copyright © 2005 Church Publishing Inc. All rights reserved. Used by permission of Church Publishing Incorporated, New York, NY.

not enough to be out of touch with other ethnic and gender groups. Jesus can pass as unmarked, even when Ross clearly marks him as just-enough white and male. His androgynous appearance allows him to slip through boundaries, which he does only because he never upends the normativity of male and white bodies.

Another figure who has tyrannized the American psyche is the black mammy figure, and she also appears in *Marked*. As Donald Bogle explains this stereotype, the black mammy is always female and is "usually big, fat, and cantankerous."[42] This racialized figure appeared in minstrel shows as Aunt Jemima in the early twentieth century, as cartoon and comic book characters, and in Hollywood movie productions. She makes her appearance in *Marked* as one overcome by an evil spirit. Jesus saves her from a deathly fever, and she recovers almost immediately as the mammy she apparently has always been: "You kids today! You think you can tear around, saving the world, without a proper breakfast. Sit." Humbled, Jesus can only reply, "Yes, M'am" (see fig. 28). With big lips and sagging breasts, she is sexed in a way that the androgynous Jesus is not. Her body provides food and commands respect, but it does not reveal sexual desire. She is not marked in that way. Instead, this black mammy exists as dominant servant, as the mother whom white boys listen to from within a bemused status reversal. But she knows the light shines on him, because the following page reveals her gazing adoration at her shining star (see fig. 29). The black mammy is protector and admirer in Ross's *Marked*, for she saves Jesus from the evil spirit (and so repays him for his divine help), provides a hearty meal to rejuvenate his powers, and looks to him with longing affection. This is indeed a troublesome image, for it draws on the white fantasy of willful black enslavement. Blacks admire whites even in their own servitude; this is what they were meant to do and feel. I am not suggesting that Ross believes or even intends this moral representation. But the juxtaposition of the servile black maid with the adoring one is steeped in stereotypes of vicious, gendered, and racial images. If this is an American scene, and not just one in the Gospel of Mark, then it revives a hurtful and damaging stereotype to reimagine sacred literature.

This is not the whole Gospel, however, and it is not solely representative in *Marked*. Ross embraces contrasting images of black Americans that go a long way in undermining these more damaging ones. In Ross's depiction of this modern dystopia, in which governments and the elite control food, resources, and the market, children arrive to remind adults of their better selves. This is Ross's version of Jesus's call that children will more easily enter the kingdom of God. To confront the truth of this claim, Ross depicts a young black girl who refuses to follow her mother's advice to keep her lunch to herself because, as the mother says, one does not "get ahead by sharing." But this young child recognizes injustice, for "everybody around [her] looks so hungry, and scared." It takes that kind of innocence to know that "Mom is wrong," and she offers her sandwich to the nearest white adult, who munches on it greedily. Somewhat abashedly, as he realizes his own self-absorption, he offers the young girl a bite to eat of her own sandwich, and like the fish from the Galilee, the sandwich appears to multiply and then feeds the entire community. In some ways we can see how the young girl acts very much like the adult mammy: they both feed adult white boys, and these men listen and respond well. But in rooting this scene in child innocence and relating that innocence to blackness, Ross works against the white fantasies and fears of black aggressiveness. Whereas Allred imaged black as evil and subhuman, here Ross marks that skin color as morally sympathetic, thoughtful, and steadfast. But he also identifies those traits as feminine, and so again we see how gender and race work together in ethical representations. Black innocence is also female innocence, a conflation only enhanced by the child's feeding of adult white men. What would this scene portray if that young child were a black boy, or even an androgynous or queer one? Did Ross fear that his readers would be less inclined to associate innocence with a male or queer body? Perhaps this too explains Jesus's androgynous features: he is just enough to the other side of the male body to appear innocent and naïve—Jesus can be marked in any way readers wish to see him. Ross opens space to imagine race and color in ways that move beyond the mammy stereotype, but he appears to limit gendered readings that might truly open the moral imagination to new configurations of identity formation. Although children may indeed enter the kingdom of heaven, they do so here in *Marked* as gendered and racial selves.

In the scene immediately following the young girl's virtuous sharing of her lunch, Ross imagines two elder black men looking upon this impressive mass feeding "from a single sack lunch." Ross draws them to appear like Frederick Douglass and a young Louis Armstrong, perhaps the two African American heroes most recognizable to white Americans. As they quickly disappear from Jesus's sight, he follows the musical notes, which Ross deploys effectively to draw out the musical resonance of the textual referent, "those with ears . . . let them hear."[43] As Jesus climbs to the top of a distant mountain, he trustingly walks off the cliff only to be suspended in midair with Douglass and Armstrong by his side (see fig. 30). In the Gospel of Mark, this scene of transfiguration (Mark 9:2–8) reveals how Elijah and Moses appear with Jesus. Ross's makeover is brilliant: Armstrong heralds the metamorphosis by blowing out butterflies from his trumpet, while Douglass plays the role of Moses as he and Jesus look together at a bound book. As Coody suggests, it helps to know the Gospel of Mark in order to pick up on Ross's imaginative reading. Douglass is the wise man, but as Moses, he is also bookish and so leans on the coupling of Moses with law and text. Yet unlike the mammy scene in which she stares adoringly up at the young white Jesus, here Jesus plays the student to the wiser, older, black man. And here too, we should see how race and gender commingle in distinctive and somewhat troubling ways. These are black male heroes who have wisdom and artistry to impart on the young Jesus. Arriving just after the young black girl's noble gesture, these heroes suggest the kind of adult models to which she may very well aspire. But wisdom here attaches to male bodies, while Ross ties her young feminine virtue to innocence. All this, to be sure, unwinds the white imaginary of black bodies, but it does not conceive new gender constructions and virtues. The moral worth of black bodies, it appears, still attaches to naturalized constructions of gender.

Readers encounter another black adult male body at the very end of *Marked*, but this one appears as a forlorn, somewhat overweight clown (see fig. 31). According to the Gospel, Mary Magdalene; Jesus's mother, Mary; and Salome arrive at Jesus's tomb and discover "a young man sitting on the right side, dressed in a white robe" (Mark 16:5). Most scholars believe that verse 16:8 marks the end of the Gospel (the "shorter" ending), whereas verses 9–20 were added somewhat later (the "longer" ending).[44] The shorter ending is somewhat cryptic, for the three women were so astonished and afraid that "they said nothing to any one." The "longer" ending seeks a more uplifting note as the good news spreads to Jesus's disciples. Ross appropriates this mystery to great effect in his comic, and the clown face works to widen the Gospel's puzzling ending, whether long or short. I do not know what Ross intends here or what or whom the clown might signify. But the grand impression of the full-page spread in which readers first see the clown is clear: this black man/clown is not the expectant Jesus. As Jesus's stand-in, he is neither androgynous nor white, young, strong, or working class, and he is practically anti-intellectual. Blackness here is far less regal and enchanting and so too is the flabby male

FIG. 30 Jesus, Frederick Douglass, and Louis Armstrong. From *Marked*. Copyright © 2005 Church Publishing Inc. All rights reserved. Used by permission of Church Publishing Incorporated, New York, NY.

FIG. 31 The forlorn clown. From *Marked*. Copyright © 2005 Church Publishing Inc. All rights reserved. Used by permission of Church Publishing Incorporated, New York, NY.

body hiding not-so-well behind the clown face. This is neither the dignified blackness of Douglass nor the whimsical artistry of Armstrong; instead we encounter a kind of gloominess, a sense of loss and belatedness, and perhaps even a blackness covered over by the lightness of clown face. This clown is worn down.

I do not believe we can read clear meanings here, and the Gospel of Mark suggests we should not, in any case. But we do not have to see those signified meanings clearly to recognize how gender and race work to project moral representations of self. Black male bodies and young female bodies produce images of gender and race in Ross's *Marked*, and they do so in complicated, creative, and sometimes harmful ways. When Ross creates an androgynous Jesus, a body "simply perfect," he still marks that body as white, male, and young. It may not be too white or too male, but it is male and white enough. And that is how gender and race work in graphic narratives such as *Marked*: race is not just about color, and gender is not just about bodies. The title of Ross's comic is a nice pun on the Gospel story, but it also offers a reflective claim about the moral imagination. We see bodies and colors as *marked* things, as objects with certain values and traits. There is no neutral, perfect, androgynous, unmarked being. Jesus, after all, is never discovered at the tomb. Instead we encounter a dispirited clown, one so beaten down by life's tragedies that he can only deadpan to Jesus's mother the trajectory of her son's life, saying, "It's simple. Your son died. He was buried. And now he's alive."[45] The clown does not "read" this narrative; he offers no consolation or meaning to lighten Mary's suffering. It is just what happened. It is, we might say, unmarked. But Ross does not conclude his Gospel here. He too adds to this shorter ending an image that demystifies the text: he draws a wilting flower that buds to life out of the carcass of dead bones. The flower's whiteness looms large over the black vulture who has apparently picked the white bones dry. This final black-and-white image renders the sacred text too as black and white—a divide that nonetheless "marks" gender and race as co-constructed categories of the visual, moral imagination.

Conclusion

The markings of gender and race are rarely intended, but they still animate the moral imagination in the three comics discussed in this chapter. Authorial intent is difficult to discern, but the practice of reading comics rarely leads back to those intentions. Comic studies often refer to the gutter as a comic device used to establish readers as co-creators in the production of graphic narratives.[46] Generating those imaginative scenes remains part of the joy and thrill of reading comics. So when comic authors such as Crumb, Allred, and

Ross map gendered and raced images onto biblical scenes as if they were natural modes of *seeing* gender and race, we need to step back from that process of co-creation in order to recognize the ethical and visual dilemmas these scenes present to comic readers. This kind of second-order reflection, in which we do not simply move from panel to panel but instead tarry within a panel to observe its representative claims, means that we should slow down as comic enthusiasts rather than take the gutter's bait. Recall how Will Eisner defended the use of comic stereotypes: authors need to move the plot along, and the stereotype presents large amounts of information in a very short space of time. But the cost of this quickening is the short-circuiting of moral reflection; the active pleasures of reading comics through the gutter might indeed be enhanced, but we will undermine reflective accounts of being human in the world.

We will also undermine the capacity of sacred texts to challenge what appears as normative and natural. When Crumb describes his work as a straight illustration job, or Allred positions his comic as a window into the Book of Mormon, they naturalize gendered and racial constructions as sacred. Even Ross draws from contemporary depictions of gender and race to reimagine the Gospel of Mark, although his is far from a straight reading of that sacred text. Yet we have also seen how comics work to challenge some of these gendered and racial assumptions about human identity. *The Book of Genesis Illustrated*, *The Golden Plates*, and *Marked* are composite, multivocal texts that visualize human identity in sometimes promiscuous ways. To queer these straight texts in this way means to recognize the eclectic, multiple claims to gendered and racial identities in comics *and*, just as importantly, in sacred texts as well. Comic readers should take Alter's critique seriously that images constrict the open-endedness of literary meaning. Comic images can indeed work in this way. But that is not how we should read or see them. The ethical obligation of comic readers is to recognize gendered and racial stereotypes as a visual challenge and to respond to that challenge by conceiving new images of being human in comic and sacred forms.

CHAPTER 3

Imagining (Superhero) Identity

What do superheroes look like? When I ask that question in this way, I obscure by erasure the tension explored in this chapter: What do superheroes look like in comics, and what do superheroes look like *to me*? There is, of course, a significant dynamic at work here, for superheroes may appear to me precisely as they do on the comic page. But this has not always been the case, Carolyn Cocca explains, because readers publicly hold their artists to account for gendered, racial, and sexualized depictions of their heroes. This form of talking back, in which readers present their concerns about destructive stereotypes such as "the brokeback" pose (an unnatural and even superhuman arching of the spine so as to expose the female curves, both front and back), suggests a determined coming-of-age for responsible visual depictions of our better selves. And those selves are diverse and multifaceted, so the white, heterosexual, middle-class, normative, gender-conforming hero speaks less and less to a readership demanding representation.[1]

This is a very different dreamscape than the one inaugurated by Jerry Siegel and Joe Shuster in June 1938 with their Superman comic. Superman represented everything the two Jewish kids from Cleveland were not and wished to be. Siegel recalls his own frustrations and desires as a high-school youth in this way: "Those attractive schoolgirls in the classes and corridors didn't care that I existed. But!! If I were to wear a colorful, skintight costume! If I could run faster than a train, lift great weights easily, and leap over skyscrapers in a single bound! Then they would notice me!"[2] Even more, as Danny Fingeroth argues, Siegel may have had deep personal reasons to create a superhero who could transcend familial tragedies.[3] But these boyhood fantasies have given way to something very different; instead of superheroes who fulfill heterosexual desires and the need for parental authority, many readers want superheroes who look like them and who struggle and mess up just as they do. Superheroes are super because they are us. This is what it means to imagine the superhero as the authentic self.

We all know the classic superhero type, one that generally follows B. J. Oropeza's seven-part schematic: (1) most superheroes have super powers (Batman is perhaps the most famous exception to this one); (2) they receive their powers by accident; (3) they wear costumes (usually spandex); (4) parental guidance is, shall we say, wanting; (5) superheroes tend to experience a great tragedy or challenge; (6) most have ambivalent relations with law and authority (perhaps Superman is the great exception here); and (7) many superhero myths are rooted in religious accounts.[4] But when readers wish to see themselves in their superheroes, only categories four, five, and six reflect everyday situations. Scholars tend to pinpoint this shift from the superhero as pure mythic type to one far darker, more complicated, and more terrestrial to two landmark works published in 1986 by DC Comics: Alan Moore's *Watchmen* and Frank Miller's *Batman: The Dark Knight Returns*.[5] In these comics, superheroes break out of Oropeza's confining schema to offer more complicated, ambivalent selves who resonate with an equally disenchanted readership. Yet even as Moore and Miller redefined the superhero genre, it remained a white man's world (and Dr. Manhattan's otherworldly blue complexion only reaffirmed this). That world would increasingly unravel as younger readers, the very ones that Cocca traces in her *Superwomen* study, began to seek out diverse models for their increasingly multiple selves.

I want to explore two contemporary comic stories that respond to this call for an authentic superhero identity but in strikingly different ways. When G. Willow Wilson (writer) and Adrian Alphona (artist) published the first volume of *Ms. Marvel* in 2014, the comic had for months grabbed the attention of the online comic-reading communities.[6] Although the story traded on the convoluted history of Captain and Ms. Marvel, Kamala Khan was entirely her own sort of superhero: a young female Pakistani American Muslim teenager from Jersey City. As early as November 2013 an online columnist applauded this new hero, writing, "As a teenager, I wish I could have seen depictions of struggling with identity, religion and adolescence that reflected my own, and in a way that made me believe I could be powerful rather than confused, marginalised and abnormal." This appeal to authenticity—in which the Muslim superhero acts, looks like, and reflects a reader's own sense of self—is precisely what the series editor, Sana Amanat, claims for Kamala Khan, who explores "the Muslim-American diaspora from an authentic perspective."[7] But in keeping with the trajectory of this book and its focus on the ethical imagination, I want to complicate these claims to authenticity in the first volume to this series (although the comic has grown well past it) by exploring the moral universes that *Ms. Marvel* both enables and constricts. By depicting a Muslim superhero who "reflects" a reader's own struggles, *Ms. Marvel* translates the particularity of the Muslim experience as a stereotypically American one, even as it opens up new vistas for Muslim identity and acceptance. To say this somewhat differently, the *Ms. Marvel* series allows non-Muslim Americans to recognize Kamala Khan as just like them. This is what the appeal to authenticity empowers, but it also constricts our capacity to imagine religious others *not like us* who might still be heroic.

A. David Lewis's *The Lone and Level Sands* (2005), the other comic narrative I wish to explore in this chapter, takes on the authentic self through modern tragedy.[8] Lewis and illustrator Marvin Perry Mann appropriate the title from Percy Shelley's "Ozymandias," a poem about the "King of Kings" who, perched on his sculpted pedestal, looks away in despair on his deserted and lost kingdom, where "the lone and level sands stretch far away." Lewis's narrative revisits the Israelite exodus from Egypt, now envisioned from Pharaoh's perspective. This is Egypt's story, and, even more, that of Ramses's own movement through "identity, religion and adolescence." Ramses is scripted as the tragic hero who must come to terms with an inherited flaw even as he learns to accept his role in a cosmic drama not of his own making. This is not the stuff of superheroes, but Ramses plays a compassionate, thoughtful, reflective villain to the hero Moses, and herein lies Lewis's power to reimagine religious, moral universes that are occluded by the superhero narrative. As Stanford W. Carpenter has argued, superheroes need "superior villains."[9] But so do we if we wish to stretch our moral imaginations. Lewis depicts comic tragedy as authentic struggle, in which Ramses need not be like his readers for them to imagine alternative modes of being (super)human.

Superheroes in comics, like their readers, are expansive, limiting, ambiguous, and conflicted. Superheroes can motivate alternative modes of human flourishing because they are and are not like us. But this is not how scholars tend to read these texts. We come across titles such as *Our Gods Wear Spandex*, or *The Gospel According to Superheroes*, or even the rhetorical *Do the Gods Wear Capes?* In my reading of these accounts, Knowles's *Our Gods Wear Spandex* is the most straightforward in articulating this common approach: "Superheroes now play for us the role once played by the gods in ancient societies. . . . Their powers, their costumes, and sometimes even their names are plucked straight from the pre-Christian religions of antiquity."[10] The generality of this claim is startling, as is the centrality of Christianity in the creation of our new gods. The very term "pre-Christian" centers this narrative directly on Christ as a religious hero of the past (before the advent of the Christian tradition), something the cover to Knowles's book makes strikingly clear. The cover alludes to common depictions of Jesus's last supper but with a Superman-like hero now in the place of Christ. As this man in a cape presides over a mixed multitude of modern superheroes (and perhaps the villain Judas as well), the moral message—rather than the historical and cultural context of meanings—is what matters for a clear linear narrative such as this one. Our gods really do wear spandex, even as they preside now over a modern meal of fast food burger and cola. All the complexity and cultural specificity of religious traditions are lost here; instead we have a simple mythic story transcending local contingencies and religious diversity. It simply does not matter whether Jesus's last meal included bread and wine within a religious ritual or a hamburger with fries among colleagues. Their gods gathered in communal fellowship; our gods eat and run.

But even this visual appeal to mythic origins grants too much to this straight line of inquiry. Knowles's account of comic superheroes, like so many others, focuses on narrative and very rarely engages in the visual apparatus of the comic book. This is an odd interpretive turn, for so much of comic scholarship focuses on the unique properties of this image-text medium. But when modern spandex replaces ancient robes, or when Captain Marvel becomes "the new Christ,"[11] the material features of our superheroes are no longer visually significant. The issue here is not whether these heroes look like us (at least in *Our Gods Wear Spandex*, they certainly do not). The concern with this form of scholarship resides in textual meaning and moral message. So we can turn to Geoff Klock's title *How to Read Superhero Comics and Why* and his honest confession of literary bias: "If this book does draw attention to the 'writer' more than the 'artist,' then, this is because of a bias that connects the narrative with the writer and because more often than not this book analyzes the more abstract 'story,' only occasionally providing detailed commentary on specific images."[12] If we want to learn how to *read* superhero comics, in the very narrow sense that this form of reading entails, then comics become just another form of storytelling, although one with some fanciful pictures. What these images *do*, or how they represent superheroes as modern religious figures, lies beyond this form of textual reading.

This kind of scholarship transforms modern superhero comics into moral lessons, ones that (most often) draw from Christian Gospel accounts of Jesus. Witness how Greg Garrett's *Holy Superheroes!* surveys the superhero genre. Like Knowles, he views a figure such as Clark Kent as a modern Jesus of

Nazareth. Superman, Garrett claims, can "teach us about religion, the idea of the elevated or enlightened being and the Christian concept of Incarnation." The multiple conflations here are almost dizzying—religion as a singular entity, enlightenment as a static concept, and the singular notion of incarnation. These moral truths come at the price of important distinctions and disagreements, but Garrett is willing to let all this go: "Our purpose in this book—as it should be in any attempt to study popular narratives to see what they can teach us about life, I think—is to notice correspondences to spiritual and mythological stories, to consider how those correspondences can inspire and instruct us, and not to get too tied up in the ideas that don't fit our purposes."[13] This blindness to material and spiritual detail is double-edged, for it trivializes both modern superheroes and their ancient forebears: "So, like Jesus, or like the Buddha, Kal-El [Superman] is an elevated human who represented a model for us, a model not only of strength, but of decency, not only of power, but also of moral authority." Like Superman, Jesus too "delivers some ultimate lessons about power."[14] This is certainly true, but Jesus also raises the dead, is angered by disciples who continually misunderstand him, suffers on the cross, heals and talks in parables, is in the beginning with the Word, and so on. Jesus is not a unitary or simple figure, either among Gospels or in any one Gospel or letter. But when scholars understand comics as stories to be read, when "comic heroes reflect universal principles of morality found in the Hebrew Bible and the New Testament,"[15] then we really should not get wrapped up in the details that misalign with our morality play. As mere aberrations, "ideas that don't fit our purposes" only get in the way of our moral education.

But this narrowness means that we discover in superhero comics, and certainly also in the Hebrew Bible and New Testament, only those models we know already. There really isn't anything learned here; it's just that our gods wear spandex, and theirs do not. This is not moral education but moral ideology, in which ethical lessons appear to be natural or even divine because they have always been so.[16]

What if we begin to imagine superheroes not as mirrors of our true, authentic selves but as others who we cannot "yet either understand or envisage completely" (as Dipesh Chakrabarty describes subaltern histories)?[17] To imagine in this new, far more destabilizing mode of inquiry, I want to suggest an alternative approach to *reading and seeing* superhero comics, one that draws on Marianne Hirsch's notion of "postmemory" and Robert Orsi's account of the scholar's positionality as "in-between." Through a reading of Toni Morrison's *Beloved*, Hirsch distinguishes her account of postmemory from what she calls Morrison's notion of rememory: "I see a range between what Morrison has called 'rememory' and what I am defining as 'postmemory'—between, on the one hand, a memory that, communicated through bodily symptoms, becomes a form of repetition and reenactment, and, on the other hand, one that works through indirection and multiple mediation."[18] Holocaust survivors often refer to something like this rememory, in which the *re-* in *rememory* "signals not just the threat, but the certainty of repetition." For Hirsch, this means memories transposed onto me by previous generations are never worked through, and so the worry arises that I can lose my sense of self in this repetitive process of rememory. But postmemory enables an "identification-at-a-distance," a form of "identification that does not appropriate or interiorize the other within the self but that goes out of one's self and out of one's own cultural norms in order to align oneself, through displacement, with another." This is like Roland Barthes's *punctum*, Hirsch claims—a "prick" or "wound" that "enables an act of recognition across differences."[19] By appropriating Hirsch's notion of postmemory, one that opens up space to recognize others not as like me but as different yet deeply human, we can look to forms of identification as nonappropriative—as valued otherness at a distance. Instead of seeking out superheroes as mirrored representations of the self, we should take up Hirsch's call for a negotiated mediation in which the self "goes out of one's self" in order to linger with the other. The value here is not to validate authenticity, in which the superhero confirms what I wish to find in myself. Instead, the pedagogical value of superhero comics is to move us beyond ourselves to discover new and strange modes of human flourishing. It is, as Chakrabarty argues, to discover both the limits and new possibilities of our own moral and intellectual worlds.[20] Instead of finding or rediscovering the self, we encounter a "prick" or "wound" in it, undermining the very notion of authentic selfhood.

This sense of openness, in which the self loses its security and claim to authenticity, is the kind of ethical stance Robert Orsi calls for in the study of religion. In his provocative essay "Snakes Alive: Resituating the Moral in the Study of Religion,"[21] Orsi criticizes Dennis Covington for safely constructing the religious other such that Covington's own values and position as liberal critic are never destabilized or open to critical inquiry. Covington had written a popular and exceedingly riveting book on snake handlers in southern Appalachia, and although he was not a religious scholar himself, Covington and his book, *Salvation on Sand Mountain: Snake Handling and Redemption in Southern Appalachia* (1995), presented a mode of ethnographic research in which one becomes an insider (Covington, for example, eventually handled poisonous snakes himself) only to retreat to the security of the familiar and safe. For Orsi, such a retreat does two unforgivable acts of religious engagement: "The other is silenced and securely returned to otherness and the world of the writer is restored and reauthorized rather than transformed."[22] Now Orsi has come under attack for his reading of Covington, and his article generated a heated exchange with Stephen Prothero, a respected professor of

American religion, about the position of the scholar in religious studies.[23] But Orsi's reading of Covington is less interesting than what he thinks a student of religion should do in the field of research: "The challenge becomes then to set one's own world, one's own particular reality, now understood as one world among many possible other worlds, in relation to this other reality and to learn how to view the two in relation to each other, moving back and forth between two alternative ways of organizing and experiencing reality. The point is not to make the other world radically and irrevocably other, but to render one's own world other to oneself as a prelude to a new understanding of the two worlds in relationship to each other."[24] This ethical positionality in encountering new moral worlds is one that Orsi calls "an in-between orientation, located at the intersection of self and other."[25] The other is never completely alien, as Chakrabarty argues, but lingering in this "in-between orientation" certainly alienates one's own self.

I want to appropriate Orsi's call to render one's self and one's own world problematic for all comic readers and not just for religious scholars. In reading comics, we should all take on this provisional stance in confronting the other and thus prevent the kind of easy moral closure to other moral universes. We should not see our superheroes in ways that only confirm and make hospitable once again our own moral assumptions. This is, as I stated earlier, moral ideology rather than moral education. Instead, we should *read* superhero comics as studies in alterity that decenter our moral worlds and render problematic our secure borders. But in this anxious space of in-between, one does not merely study the other to learn something new about one's self. An orientation in-between, on the contrary, suspends the language of authenticity and authentic selves for encounters with new modes of human flourishing. One has to lose the self to discover alternative heroes for the moral imagination.

Ms. Marvel (Volume 1, 2014)

The cover image to *Ms. Marvel: No Normal*, the first volume of the *Ms. Marvel* series, is both striking in its symbolic imagery and illustrative of the identity politics in these comics (see fig. 32). Scholars Chris Reyns-Chikuma and Désirée Lorenz notice the fashion (the rings and bracelets on her right arm) and the fierce determination of this new superhero (clenched fist, though they could have also highlighted Kamala's tightened lips), but they focus most of their attention on the three books carried in her left hand: a blue book on "U.S. History," a dark-brown text with the title "Hadith to Live By," and a light-brown work on "Illustration & Design." These three works, Reyns-Chikuma and Lorenz argue, are "signs revealing (parts of) her identity"; Kamala Khan is an American Muslim student who has career aspirations in fashion.[26] But one has to guess at these titles on the front cover because the title for the series, *Ms. Marvel*, covers over the words "U.S." and "Hadith" in those two works. This is not the case on the inside splash page, which removes the heading "Ms. Marvel" and displays the three book titles clearly and, because we know something is missing in this repetition, more centrally as well. This dual movement of revelation—in which the cover obscures while the inside splash image discloses—visually captures the dynamics of authenticity and identity in the *Ms. Marvel* series. In public, on the outside, as a cover, Kamala must negotiate her multiple identities that she knows live brightly and powerfully on the inside. *Her* history is probably not even told in her US history book, and her Muslim rebellion (her hijab is worn as a scarf, and unlike her older brother, she stays clear of the local mosque and the wise imam there) suggests a more troubled relation to hadiths that she may not wish to live by. But on the inside, where, according to this comic, the authentic self resides, such negotiations dissolve, and instead we confront fashion, grit, intelligence, and an unencumbered American Muslim identity. Clarity of inner purpose and identity replace the ambiguity and confusion of roles in public view. Kamala cannot expose too much of herself on the cover. And so together, cover and splash page mark personal identity as a revelatory dynamic of openness and concealment. These images not only reveal her identity, as Reyns-Chikuma and Lorenz usefully point out, but also articulate the movement of identity as a politics of exposing the authentic self within.

That authenticity resides within is a common perception of identity. The philosopher Charles Taylor has popularized this view in his *The Ethics of Authenticity* (1992), but Taylor always tied that inner sense to wider social frameworks of meaning. And so does *Ms. Marvel*, for Kamala has a more visceral, material engagement with identity than Reyns-Chikuma and Lorenz's linguistic, symbolic reading would suggest. The opening scene to the first volume—the only volume I focus on here in this chapter, although the series has continued and changed beyond it—depicts an encounter with food, with Kamala's magnetic attraction to the "Easy Greasy B.L.T." sandwich in the local food store (see fig. 33). For those who have experienced the allure of prohibited foods, Kamala's opening words, "I just want to smell it," are all too familiar. This is forbidden desire, not in the form of beliefs or principles but in the material sensations of smell and memory. The initial frame presents a close-up of the offensive pork product and then takes on a wider side-angle view of Kamala's intense look at the sandwich display, with her close friend Bruno behind the counter and her more traditionally dressed friend Nakia by her side. Kamala's fixation becomes the reader's also as we gaze with Kamala at the forbidden food.

Wilson and Alphona condense cultural and religious knowledge in a very tight space, exactly as Will Eisner argues comics must do, yet they compress

FIG. 32 Cover image of first volume of *Ms. Marvel: No Normal*. From *Ms. Marvel* by G. Willow Wilson. Copyright © 2014 Marvel.

FIG. 33 Kamala confronting infidel meat. From *Ms. Marvel* by G. Willow Wilson. Copyright © 2014 Marvel.

all this by appealing to and undermining common stereotypes. Note, to begin with, how Kamala categorizes bacon as that wholly other "delicious, delicious infidel meat" that attracts her by its forbidden nature. Smells entice, prod, and often disgust. Kamala will not taste the meat, but she hopes the very smell might cure her desires—the scent itself might satisfy, as though she really had tasted the forbidden article. If she could only smell the bacon, then perhaps that whiff might linger, in memory if not in aroma. Nakia has learned to control her desires, and she looks on with modest impatience, as if she has to once again pull Kamala back from the abyss. With her traditional head covering and the more recent taking on of her Turkish name, Nakia returns to her Muslim roots and practices by adopting her given name and refusing infidel meat. Here too, desire and material practices embody religious identity. In these and other ways, Wilson and Alphona undermine stereotypical views of Muslims in this opening scene. We see diversity, even in this younger generation, in which Muslims make choices, have distinctive yet appropriately fashionable dress, hail from different regions of the world, and have a religion that "happens" in public. And we learn all this through an encounter with food. Wilson and Alphona do not reduce Muslim identity to a set of beliefs and ritual practices; they imagine American Muslims with desires and yearnings, with names that reflect a proud heritage, and with appetites and witty senses of humor.

This material context for religious identity situates authenticity within embodied practices and visions, in which clothes matter, smells engage our desires, and food consumes as much as it is consumed. But this everyday encounter with lived religion also brands religious identity as colloquial, as part of the common teen banter of high-school jesting. Of course, material religion need not be this way; it can, like many of Robert Orsi's works, expose strong relations of love and power.[27] But as we have seen throughout this book, comics trade in stereotypes, and *Ms. Marvel* appeals to the sarcastic register of teen discourse. Bruno, the young man behind the counter (and one whom we will soon learn has a romantic interest in Kamala) provides the soft conversational tone of this religious encounter: "Either **eat** the bacon or stick to your principles. Chow or chow **not**, there is no **smell**." This quick reference to the Star Wars' character Yoda[28] draws Kamala's experience within the popular culture of teasing. Less dramatic than a blockbuster movie series, Kamala's predicament is light and casual, itself participating in sarcasm by referencing the "infidel" meat. This is not serious religion; that role belongs to Nakia alone. Here, Kamala's decision "to chow or chow not" really comes after no conflict at all; she never takes eating the bacon seriously, and so Nakia fails to understand why she torments herself in this way. It's not about principles—it's about the allure of the foreign and the forbidden. Foodways do indeed create the possibility of those desires, but this scene paints desire, and the desire for desire, as the experience of authentic selves. Bruno wrongly believes that Kamala faces a principled choice, for this is not how Kamala understands her food desire. Yet by positioning Kamala's desire as a kind of performative tease, one situated within the discourse of popular sarcasm, Wilson and Alphona fashion Muslim identity as vernacular American. High-school teens in Jersey City speak this language and understand the movements of cultural satire. Kamala too can do this. It's a familiar game of tease.

That familiarity draws Muslim identity into the orbit of American identity. Neither Kamala nor Nakia—nor Bruno, for that matter, the son of Italian immigrants—are outsiders to this common American culture. They are all American teenagers in Jersey City who happen to be Muslim or Italian. This opening comic scene, then, presents two movements of religion in America: it situates religious identity within material, embodied practices, but in doing so dramatizes identity as conventional, recognizable, and relational. There is really nothing awkward, strange, or foreign in Kamala's encounter with infidel meat. It is not just a Muslim dilemma; Jews, vegetarians, vegans, teens with food allergies, among a whole host of others, also experience just these kinds of pulls and limits. So Kamala's struggle for personal identity as both Muslim and American is also a recognizably American conflict. It happens within the context of everyday encounters, within the banter of teenager sarcasm, within the diversity of urban life. This is less about assimilation than it is about the recognizable experiences of supposed outsiders who are really like us. As soon-to-be superhero, Kamala and her struggles are our own. We need not imagine a life unlike the ones we currently lead, and we don't have to labor to appreciate a moral universe strangely foreign to our own. Chow or chow not, we know this world already.

This becomes clear in the role reversal on the next page, in which the beautiful, popular white students seem oblivious to ethnic identity. This is how blond and popular looks from the outside, but the comic now positions Kamala and friends on the inside of Jersey hip and cool. When Zoe and Josh burst into the corner store, they treat Bruno, Kamala, and Nakia as interesting, foreign objects. Their sense of entitlement matches their ignorance; they utterly fail to recognize others as embodied subjects. When Zoe compliments Nakia for her beautiful headscarf, she recognizes choice as only an aesthetic category. Obligations belong to a religion demanding conformity. As Zoe says to Nakia, "But I mean . . . nobody **pressured** you to start wearing it, right? Your father or somebody?" Nakia, with an offensive stare, responds that her father actually wants her to remove it, but Zoe reacts with blank incoherence: "Really? Wow, . . . cultures are so **interesting**." Kamala, to Nakia's amazement, is enthralled with Zoe, believing her flighty interests are sincere. Bruno hates her for her patronizing scorn (as Zoe tells Bruno, "I only buy stuff here to **tip** you, because I'm concerned about your **economic situation**"), and Nakia thinks "she's only nice to be **mean**." Kamala's desire to be white, as Wilson and Alphona will soon reveal, nourishes her continued fascination with superheroes. But this scene does more than set up Kamala's transformation into Ms. Marvel; it shows us how religion looks to outsiders who never engage the lived reality of religious practice. For Zoe, wearing a headscarf is either an aesthetic choice or an imposition denying individual autonomy. She can only see the headscarf within modern values of freedom and liberty. This too is Bruno's position—for him, decisions are rooted in principled discipline. But Nakia's religious identity travels beyond the structure of personal choice. As Kamala recognizes on the opening page, Turkish heritage and pride, rather than personal choice, ground Nakia's claims to authenticity. Nakia did indeed choose to wear the headscarf, but the language of personal choice fails to capture the sense of tradition, heritage, and religious culture that engage Nakia's identity.

Zoe fails to confront the unfamiliar as an opportunity to expand her moral imagination. She neither engages her own peculiar views of culture and religion nor problematizes her own moral reasoning. So despite the cultural dissonance on these opening pages, in which food and clothing mark religious observance and identity, everything remains familiar. This is true too for those readers who respond to *Ms. Marvel*. I noted earlier how online readers appreciated Kamala's difficulties, in part because those difficulties reflected their own negotiations with white American culture. Reader responses appear at the end of the first volume, and we encounter praise like this: "I'm extremely excited to read her backstory because I am also the daughter of Muslim immigrants. I feel very gratified to see a character who looks just like me and would have a lot of the same challenges and experiences in life and with her family, someone in whom I could really see myself."[29] This kind of readerly connection is important, for it broadens the superhero genre to reflect an increasingly multicultural and multiethnic America. Models such as Kamala respond to white privilege and identity and offer compelling images of belonging. But we have also seen in these opening pages how cultural and religious conflicts move beyond Muslim or Pakistani or Turkish identity. Kamala appeals as much to minorities as she does to any teen who struggles to fit into high-school culture. So we read the following kind of response as well on the back pages of *Ms. Marvel*: "I'm Mormon, not Muslim, but I love seeing positive portrayals of any religion. Religion is something that's important in my life and it's kind of fun seeing it be important to somebody else, however fictional, such as the Khan family."[30] Here Kamala stands in for all religious types, for her Muslim commitments echo more common religious obligations and struggles. Infidel meat signifies food choices in general, not a peculiarly Muslim concern. "Heroes are everywhere," as one reader writes on the back pages of *Ms. Marvel*. "They can be anyone, and they can be as broken or flawed or non-conforming as we are." Wilson and Alphona have produced a remarkable comic, in which a Pakistani Muslim looks and struggles like an American teenager.

This is the dual movement of *Ms. Marvel*: it situates authenticity within minority religious cultures, even as it images these cultures as quintessentially American. *Ms. Marvel* is an *American* story, even if those most privileged, like Zoe and Josh, fail to recognize this. The "non-conforming" outsiders have become the more legitimate, more authentic bearers of American culture. Yet this is more than the common teenage fantasy of someone like Jerry Siegel, who yearned for attention from the attractive girls. His story reads as the Jewish kid from Cleveland desiring the beautiful non-Jewish shiksa. Recall how this fantasy played out for Frimme Hersh in Eisner's *A Contract with God*; Hersh too sought comfort and respectability in his shiksa mistress from Scranton, Pennsylvania.[31] But neither Bruno nor Nakia nor Kamala seek out this kind of recognition. They neither demand nor require insider status, although Kamala learns this a bit later in her coming-of-age story. She wants to be like the white, beautiful Captain Marvel and so wear "the classic, politically incorrect costume and kick butt in **giant wedge heels**."[32] As the cover to the first volume already indicates, Kamala matures to adopt clothing and postures that match the kind of person she is rather than the inauthentic character she wants to be. The point is not to become or gain acceptance from the desired other, as it was for Siegel and for Eisner's Hersh; rather, the moral play here is about accepting oneself as the already authentic. Outsiders remain outsiders, but they embrace their "broken or flawed or non-conforming" selves as truly heroic. This is the fantasy of authentic presence, in which one need not reach out beyond the self to discover authenticity within it. Heroes may be everywhere, but *Ms. Marvel* pictures them within all of us.

As the daughter of Muslim immigrants so eloquently confessed, this kind of self-recognition and modeling is itself necessary and heroic. And Kamala reaches out to Mormons and others who see themselves, or a better America, in the lives of these teenage New Jersey kids. This is all for the good. But there is a moral cost in discovering a superhero who looks and struggles like me. Appeals to authenticity in this mode, in which I discover and accept the superhero within, never move beyond the self to confront the challenges of what Marianne Hirsch calls "identification-at-a-distance." For Hirsch, self-formation is not about finding the authentic self. Instead, it is a movement beyond "to align oneself, through displacement, with another." This "act of recognition across differences" seeks out a "nonappropriative" other who challenges my own self-recognition as heroic.[33] Clearly Zoe and Josh never engage in this kind of evaluative self-reflection. But neither do Bruno, Nakia, and Kamala. They function instead as stereotypical characters who model religious identity and authenticity for readers who seek out recognition. Kamala may indeed face cultural and religious challenges, but readers are not challenged to identify across differences. Their moral imaginations are rendered neither suspect nor problematic. Claims to authenticity do not work this way in the first volume of the *Ms. Marvel* comic series. We discover ourselves *in* Kamala or Nakia but not at a distance. Hirsch calls for a kind of troubling dissonance to trigger the moral imagination, even as Wilson and Alphona portray the imagined self as recognizably familiar. Accepting the self, rather than expanding it, is the model of authenticity in *Ms. Marvel*.

Such an expansive self could respond to Orsi's challenge to move "back and forth between two alternative ways of organizing and experiencing reality."³⁴ Here, the goal is not to render the other as nonconforming but to provisionally mark oneself as "nonappropriative." In *Ms. Marvel*, all the characters remain stereotypically themselves. They role-play to mark positions of subjectivity; they are closed rather than expansive, porous selves. Readers who continue through the *Ms. Marvel* series might object to this kind of static reading of the first volume, for Zoe learns in later volumes to appreciate Nakia, befriending her, it appears, by abandoning her sense of white privilege. But this repositioning remains undeveloped and arrives more as appropriation than it does as reflective displacement. As I read Orsi, the challenge is not to take on the other, as Zoe seems to do, but to accept an in-between state in which both positionalities surrender the comforts of authenticity. The characters in *Ms. Marvel* are not expansive in this way, and so this comic never challenges its readers to uncomfortably reside and linger in this in-between state of identity formation. As I will argue in the conclusion to this book, there are strong moral reasons to linger in this way when reading comics. But *Ms. Marvel* does not provoke this reflective stance. Like Kamala, readers may wish to just smell the infidel meat, with no real interest in actually tasting it. As either Muslim or infidel, it is chow or chow not. The in-between state of nonappropriative identity never arises to challenge the familiarity of authenticity within.

There are, to be sure, real goods to be had here. Accepting a Pakistani Muslim as a familiar American teen is no small thing, as is the expansion of American identity to include underrepresented groups. But this form of acceptance, in which the text mirrors rather than challenges a sense of self, does not provoke the moral imagination but instead confirms it. We find in *Ms. Marvel* what we have been looking for all along.

Discovering oneself in the *Ms. Marvel* series carries over to another food scene in which Wilson and Alphona depict religion in familiar images and tropes. Here, recognition works to draw sympathetic responses from readers who discover themselves in the stereotypes drawn on the page. The scene follows Kamala and Nakia's encounter with Zoe and Josh in the corner store. We find Kamala at home playing her beloved video games, describing her internet social group in incomprehensible language to her mother, who responds, "Fan

feek . . . what is a fan feek?! I thought you were up there doing **homework**"
(see fig. 34). Kamala's mother cannot even hear the words correctly—"feek"
instead of "fic," a reference to fan fiction—and so the social and cultural distance between generations contextualizes what will soon happen at the dinner
table.[35] Wilson and Alphona imagine this scene as one that features a typical
American family, only this family is an immigrant one from Pakistan. They
introduce us to Kamala's older brother, Aamir, who before eating prays in
subservience to Allah, as his working father, reading a newspaper like so
many other fathers home from work, mocks his faith as impractical: "Aamir,
if you don't stop praying long enough to put some food in your mouth, one
day you will **starve** to death." Kamala's father is dedicated to middle-class
propriety and hard work, believing that Aamir's effusive praying masks an
insincere desire to avoid a paying job. The mother, who draws Kamala down
for dinner, carries a spoon in her right hand, signifying her role as food provider and good cheer for her family. She calms the argument between son and
father, and we will learn in later volumes how she always suspected Kamala's
superhero pursuits and even quietly supported them. This dinner scene has
all the stereotypical markings of an American family. We have a son and a
daughter with strikingly different aspirations complaining about parents who
fail to understand their desires. The mother functions as peacemaker even as
she feels distant from who her children are becoming, while the father works
hard to provide, although he demands competing allegiances from his children: his son to hard work and a salary, and his daughter to good grades and
respectability. All of this is gendered, classed, generational, and frustrating
for a budding superhero.

Religion too has a stereotypical look in this scene. Aamir dresses in a
traditional white robe, with head covering and beard, all of which mark him
as the rebellious son in his parent's middle-class home. He remarks, "Money
earned from a profession that offends Allah has no merit. I refuse to profit
from **usury** . . . unlike **some** people." The father's response has a touch of secular disdain for holiness—his job at the bank makes it possible for Aamir "to sit
here at home **contemplating eternity**." Religious practice is a luxury, offered
only to those who have the leisure time to actually *do* religion. For those hard
at work, religion appears as a kind of extravagant privilege, and an insincere
one at that. And this is true only for boys; Kamala's father requires merely that
she receives good grades, plays nicely with her friends, and be presentable for
a future husband. In this scene, religion is the gendered practice of a private,
contrived, and luxurious faith.

There is, however, another form of religious practice, one we might label
cultural religion, lurking in the background of this dinner scene. On the wall
behind the dining table hangs a calligraphic image in Arabic. Readers cannot
view the entire text because Kamala's mother walks in front of it (those versed

FIG. 34 Dinner at Kamala's house. From *Ms. Marvel* by G. Willow Wilson. Copyright © 2014 Marvel.

in Arabic might be able to guess at the inscription). To the left of that image, where the mother's head obscures the Arabic, Aamir prays to Allah, and to the right the father reads his paper, while Kamala bides her time before asking to go out to a party that night. "Prayer is noble," the father admits, but not too much prayer. And this is the kind of cultural religion that American readers too have come to expect, in which religion is part of a background cultural landscape. The Arabic inscription is an aesthetic piece indicating cultural heritage but without the kind of public display associated with Aamir's faith (and so the mother obscures the calligraphy). The father admires religious practice but not at the expense of other legitimate commitments. Cultural religion happens at the dining table as aesthetic gestures of heritage; Aamir takes religion too seriously, and Kamala appears to leave much of Islam behind, only to recover it as she comes to accept her identity as Ms. Marvel. Readers who pick up *Ms. Marvel*, those daughters of Muslims or those others who love seeing portrayals of religion, will recognize what they see here. This is an American story far more than it is a Muslim one. That is a remarkable achievement for Wilson and Alphona, and I do not wish to minimize it. Both Muslim and Mormon readers will see Kamala's predicament, and her family, as their own. They do not have to travel far to remain at home with Kamala. This is, as Eisner insists, what stereotypes do in graphic novels.

Admittedly, mine is a somewhat disingenuous critique of *Ms. Marvel*, if only because the comic does so much to break down common stereotypes within the superhero genre. Again, I do not want to lose sight of that triumph, and I even wish to celebrate it. But comics, like religion, are rarely good or bad. Instead, they are often ambivalent, negotiating competing demands, allegiances, and economic realities. I think we honor Wilson and Alphona's craft more in taking that ambivalence seriously than in acclaiming only its successes. Throughout this book I trace these double movements in comics, in which the moral imagination is both stretched and confined through this graphic medium. By imaging Kamala as a Pakistani Muslim superhero, one who comes to accept her own cultural identity as an authentic resource, Wilson and Alphona stretch our imaginative worlds to envision new embodiments of the American hero. But in situating that hero within a recognizably middle-class suburban American family, in which religion is either extreme or an aesthetic accessory, Wilson and Alphona might win acceptance for Muslim Americans at the cost of challenging our moral borders. For it appears that readers accept Kamala only so much as she stylizes an American scene, perhaps through her "challenges and experiences" or simply because religion is "important." Kamala is not foreign, and this kind of domestication is both a blessing and a curse. The blessing is clear: we accept those like Kamala into our homes as one of us, expanding our circle of national belonging. But the curse is equally transparent: to belong Kamala has to become one of us—the unfamiliar has to be rendered familiar. The superhero arrives not to challenge our identities but to confirm them. The hero lies within, not beyond the self. And this too is what stereotypes do in superhero comics, in which the super in comics looks like us in both its expansive and limiting possibilities.

The search for the authentic self—the underlying narrative quest for Kamala in the first volume of the *Ms. Marvel* series—limits recognition to a form of appropriation, in which one absorbs the other into oneself. But there is another mode of recognition, one that travels across differences and lives in a more insecure state of the in-between. This is not an easy space to inhabit and linger, for it requires a suspension of judgment and discovery. The goal here is not to find the self but to expand and challenge it. Recognition, in this liminal context, is a social practice in which others challenge my place, location, security, and commitments. Now, this unease cannot go on indefinitely, but we should allow ourselves to linger there, if only for a moment, to explore alternative models and modes of being human. As I will argue in the conclusion to this book, that sense and feeling of lingering is part of the joy and moral challenge of reading comics. If we run too fast through them, taking in the stereotypical cues without pausing to reflect, we lose some of the moral pleasures of reading. *Ms. Marvel* suggests, rightly I believe, that readers should not be like Zoe—barging into the corner store, pronouncing her entitlement, treating subjects as though they were curious objects, and then leaving to return to a more hospitable place. We might be attracted or repulsed by others, but we should no longer look at them, as Zoe does, as mere curiosities. The ethical import of these comic images, in which the religious other becomes the American teen, is too consequential to merely dismiss as like or unlike me. Young Americans such as Kamala deserve more, as do the moral imaginations of those with increasingly expansive selves.

The Lone and Level Sands (2005)

Susannah Heschel has effectively deployed the notion of *counterhistory*, a term borrowed from such scholars as Amos Funkenstein and David Biale, to help explain how Jewish thinkers appropriate the sources of their antagonists in order to polemically offer an alternative narrative reading.[36] Something like this is going on in Lewis and Mann's rendition of the Exodus story, told this time from the perspective of the Egyptian court. *The Lone and Level Sands* plays off that well-known biblical account and subverts it by allowing readers to linger in the minds of those who lost that battle. This is an expansive narrative, one that retells the Hebrew God's battle with Pharaoh as a decidedly human, tragic story. In this sense, *The Lone and Level Sands* does not quite conform to Heschel's counterhistory, for this is less a "reading against" than a deeper, exploratory account of human limits, obligations, and failures. If anything, Lewis offers a counterhistory to *Ms. Marvel* and, for that matter, much of the superhero genre, because he turns to Ramses as villain to better assess the heroic. In the reading I offer of *The Lone and Level Sands*, this comic responds to Orsi's challenge to linger in between, and to Hirsch's call "to align oneself, through displacement, with another." By taking up the other side to the divine narrative, one that has proved so foundational to Western culture,[37] Lewis and Mann present a more textured, conflicted, heartening sense of liberation. Pharaoh is defeated, to be sure, but his acceptance of those failures opens a very different kind of moral universe. For readers moved by this tragic figure and his profoundly gracious heroism, moral textures and obligations collide to produce a fragile world of ethical actors. This is neither the space for those like or unlike me nor the context for discovering the authentic self within. *The Lone and Level Sands* challenges both dualistic and insular claims to identity, instead offering a more humble, tragic, and yet ever expansive account of human flourishing.

The opening prologue establishes two important themes that run throughout *The Lone and Level Sands*: familial ties and accepting one's place in the world. The pharaoh Seti has just returned from battle but on his own familial terms. Three timelines confront the reader on the opening page, with dates for the Gregorian and Hebrew calendars together with the year fourteen of the Nineteenth Dynasty in Seti's reign. Those calendar dates appear as backdrop to the larger panel depicting the fourteenth year, thereby returning the reader, like Pharaoh's army, to "an antique land." When we turn the page we see the first close-up of Seti as a kind, handsome, and regal pharaoh. He is muscular and lean, and although he speaks the language of state and warfare, he yearns for the comforts of home. Young Ramses greets his father with stately grace, but Seti quickly dispenses with formalities, taking his son Ramses into his arms—a public sign of affection that seems immediately out of place in this courtly setting. Indeed, at first Ramses appears worried, if not threatened, by how his father will react to his official welcome. But the gutter between that look of fear and the melting into his father's embrace suggests a quick jump toward his bosom and a more intimate, if shy, love. There are more important things, Seti teaches his son here, than statecraft and warfare.

This regal public affection contrasts sharply with Moses's agitated state on the very next page. He seems out of place too but distracted and, when compared to both Seti and Ramses, thin, frail, and unsteady. Seti calls him quiet and awkward, and Ramses considers him "withdrawn and mild-tempered." We soon learn that Ramses and his confidant Ta have news for Seti about Moses, who has inexplicably killed a Hebrew slave master. But before hearing those rumors, Seti warns, "we follow what paths are written for us" (*Lone and Level Sands*, 008). News, good or ill, reflects the roles we are destined to play out. If this is Moses's fate, then he too follows the only path open to him. *The Lone and Level Sands* is not about authenticity or discovering the self within; it is about finding, and thus accepting, one's place in a world already designed and written.

Clifford Geertz once famously argued that studying culture is about symbolic action, and on that linguistic model ethnographers write down what "is getting said." We are meaning-making creatures, and so anthropologists such as Geertz read cultures like a text, decoding "the said" for meaning rather than the embodied act of "the saying."[38] But in a world already written, "the saying" is an embodied placement within an established order. This is Seti's model too for his son: the "saying"—our embodied, often familial acts in the world— do not signify ("the said") but locate ourselves in an ordered and meaningful world. Moses will follow one path, and Ramses will follow another. To disrupt that order, even to willfully attempt to undermine it, is a futile gesture. This is, in part, the tragic dimension of Egyptian time, less a tragic flaw than the recognition of limited horizons and obligations.[39] We find ourselves here and no other. Readers of the Exodus story already know that Moses's God will upset this order, but Ramses will soon come to understand his role in a wider universe he barely understands. Ramses is alone in recognizing his place in this broader religious landscape, for his wife Nefertari and his advisor Ta do not accept fate in this way. But Ramses is wiser than his friend and his spouse, for he has adopted his father's good counsel. He is more the inheritor of his father's world than a builder of new ones. His path too has been written for him.

But accepting the gifts of his father does not mean Ramses merely follows a predesigned course of action. He lingers and broods, whereas others unreflectively play out their designated roles. The comic quickly moves from the young Ramses to his rise as pharaoh, now with son and grandson, and Ta as his trusted advisor. There are signs—omens only Ramses appears to recognize—of a new, more powerful God than his Amon-Ra. When a guardsman repeats Moses's message to Ramses—a note concerning the intimate talk between Seti and his son—the guardsman who had been sturdy and upright on the previous page now seems bewildered and unsure of his surroundings. This foreshadows, as readers will soon discover, divine possession in which the Hebrew God controls the words of others. Seti's son is shocked, for he knows this language too as the private talk of father to son. How could an Israelite know this? But Ramses looks straight at the now perplexed guardsman, and his reply is calm: "The Israelites . . . I . . . I will see them" (023). Those two ellipses, within which Ramses begins to recognize the import of this encounter, confer both spatial and temporal positioning. The quoted message from Moses—"Does your father still watch you sleep, little apricot?" (022)—could be known only by an intimate family member. Seti had called Ramses little apricot, just as Ramses and his son call their children by this affectionate nickname. Hearing these words repeated by an Israelite slave unwinds these inherited lines, displacing Ramses's sense of familial order. It is now unclear who this Israelite other really is and where Ramses as Pharaoh stands in relation to him. But the temporal displacement is just as disorienting. This message comes from Pharaoh's past, and it upsets the intimacy of a father's love for his son. It pierces that soothing memory of a father's protective watch, but it also suggests that other eyes were watching too. Moses had always been there—glancing from the side, invading that private, familial space, and perhaps experiencing the jealousy of a father's love. Those two sets of ellipses witness to these temporal and spatial displacements, and not just figuratively so. Ramses exists in between, and like the marked ellipses, is meant to linger there.

Lewis and Mann locate this sense of dragging, of not being entirely sure of one's place in the world, in Ramses's embodied movements. Seeking counsel from his high priest, Ramses sits bent over in his chair as he tells of this new god Yahweh (see fig. 35). The high priest Bekenkhonsu instinctively appeals to the divine narrative of worship, saying that they need to rededicate themselves to Amon-Ra and win back his love. Such confidence in human prayer and God's response only angers Ramses, for he recognizes something altogether strange and new in the Hebrew God. He turns his body away from Bekenkhonsu, closing his eyes as if to retreat from the priest's counsel. Ramses's body moves with anger and despair—anger that his priest cannot think beyond the comforting narratives of divine love, and despair that only he seems to recognize a new path being drawn. Bekenkhonsu speaks of things he cannot plausibly know: "A century is but a blink to a God. Time means nothing" (027); and Ramses, bending away in an embodied act of withdrawal, appears lonely and isolated in his skepticism. This he cannot show to the approaching guardsman, who warns that Moses and Aaron desire to speak with Pharaoh. Ramses stands erect and tall, as he does a few pages later when confronted by the Israelite slaves (031). There, with the priest Bekenkhonsu to his right, his wife Nefertari to his left, and the members of his court behind him, Ramses stands above his visitors with determined and impatient disdain. But clearly this is all a front, for readers know that behind closed doors, Ramses is far more uncertain. His body shows us this: it bears the weight of suspicions. As Pharaoh, Ramses portrays confidence and power, but as Seti's son, as little apricot, he has lost his footing. Yet this hero does not retreat to comforting narratives of divine favor, as his high priest too quickly advises. Instead, Ramses lingers in this unknown space and time, now unsure which paths are written for him.

This sense of bewilderment is not for Ramses alone. Lewis creates a double narrative in the following pages to confuse the temporal dimension of the narrative plot. In the wake of Moses's encounter with Ramses, Nefertari

FIG. 35 Ramses seeking counsel. From *The Lone and Level Sands* by A. David Lewis and Marvin Perry Mann. Copyright © 2005 by A. David Lewis and Marvin Perry Mann.

falls into a trance, and her confusion slowly infuses the reader's own, as she says, "I did not know whether to trust my eyes" (033). Envisioning battles and a female oracle, Nefertari soon dreams about her grandson Seti, who rules over Egypt, but she fears he may be the last of the pharaohs. Yet that dream effortlessly shifts to another vision in which Nefertari takes on the character of oracle who witnesses the present unfolding before her eyes. This we trust as prophetic vision, not of the future but of the present, as Ramses confronts Moses and Aaron on the banks of the Nile. Lewis and Mann use Nefertari's dream as a gloss to that meeting, a kind of interpretive overlay (in block panels) to this male scene of power. These dual registers, in which female oracles revision and interpret male authority, displace present time and a progressive, narrative structure. Ramses might appear alone, but there are other worlds, other visions impinging on his political realm. And this back-and-forth movement of time and prophecy is now part of the reader's awareness as Nefertari weaves in and out of oracular visions and current events. Lewis and Mann have manipulated the reader to experience Ramses's own sense of bewilderment. Much like Hirsch's call for "identification-at-a-distance," readers now align themselves, through displacement, with the other; we too are meant to linger in that in-between space of doubt and insecurity.

As plague after plague overwhelms Egypt and its people, Ramses stands in the middle of two competing narrative movements: one traces his own indecision and growing recognition of powers larger than his own, while the other counsels him to remain strong and defiant before Moses's demands. His counselors, Ta and Nefertari, are possessed by a spirit that demands strong leadership from Ramses. This is a clever counterhistory to the hardening of Pharaoh's heart in the biblical Exodus story. At first Ramses is unaware of these divine voices possessing his spouse and friend, but Mann employs possessed facial expressions, bent-over bodies, zagged font lines, and darker hues to indicate divine control. Nefertari challenges Ramses to defend his kingdom rather than attend to her sickness (see fig. 36), and Ta mocks his weakness by appealing to kingly pride. Ramses accepts both counsel as wise and appropriate, and against his own better judgment commands, "You heard my chief Vizier, son . . . hold the Israelites" (058). In between these two possessions of Nefertari and Ta, we once again see Ramses slumped over in his chair, alone in his disturbing thoughts. Here, physically and emotionally, Ramses sits alone in between divine pronouncements that overwhelm him. He accedes to his wife's request, and blindly follows Ta's stern commands. But in between, alone in his palace with Ta, he hesitates, asking, "Is . . . is this her fate?" (048). Ramses cannot understand Nefertari's sickness, and he struggles to recognize her written path. That brooding runs up against a divinity who, through possession of his closest advisors, demands punishment for the enslavement of his people.

FIG. 36 Ramses with Nefertari. From *The Lone and Level Sands* by A. David Lewis and Marvin Perry Mann. Copyright © 2005 by A. David Lewis and Marvin Perry Mann.

FIG. 37 Ramses recognizes his son is possessed. From *The Lone and Level Sands* by A. David Lewis and Marvin Perry Mann. Copyright © 2005 by A. David Lewis and Marvin Perry Mann.

Most readers of *The Lone and Level Sands* know how this story goes and how it ends. Lewis and Mann know this too and so emphasize not the freedom of a people but the way Ramses comes to accept the fate assigned to him and those he loves. I want to emphasize once again that only Ramses recognizes these forces controlling his destiny. He is the lone character who questions, lingers, and meditates on events beyond his own control: "Is this what is written? Am I . . . am I destined to lose you, my queen? Have I steered us wisely? Could only catastrophe for Egypt be what is written? And if so—what cruel author assigns us this fate?" (073–074). Ramses's other servants, including Ta and Bekenkhonsu, hold tenaciously to their impotent world-views. Not even Moses questions or reflects on his role in this cosmic drama. A force beyond all their comprehension, one directed by that cruel God, now takes over Pharaoh's kingdom. When Ta lashes out at the enslaved Israelites, Ramses questions his own leadership; when Bekenkhonsu appeals to the Egyptian gods, Ramses knows there are other forces at work that command his movements.

But it is only when the evil spirit possesses his grandson Seti does Ramses come to recognize the road he must follow (see fig. 37). He had wished "to be rid of" Moses, Aaron, and "their whole brood," but his high priest and son had advised against it. Yet when confronted with the possessed Seti, Ramses "found out how truly infectious the Hebrew blight would be" (076). Like Ta before him, Seti appears in dark hues, and his speech bubble contains words with jagged and heavy font. This time, Ramses recognizes that voice: "I knew this tone of voice, this possessed intonation. This voice came twice before. Once from a guardsman, and again from my Vizier" (076).[40] But Ramses neither challenges this oracle nor follows his own leanings. He accedes to Seti's request and "[gives] no order for the Israelites to be released." For Ramses, Yahweh's message was clear: "I had but only one recourse" (077). He enables his son to command his armies and to struggle against the Israelite God. He knows this is of no use, but he has learned well from his own father that "we follow what paths are written for us." His son devised a plan to butcher all the Egyptian cattle and store the meat for cooking, preventing Yahweh from slaying what they had already killed. Ramses, in tones distant but accepting, knows too how this will end, remarking, "It was a good plan. It was a decisive plan—and it was all for naught" (078–079). Ramses cannot write new endings, but he can learn to accept those written for him. Although he can understand neither how the narrative works nor the cruelty of the prose, he must, like all tragic heroes, accept defeat as his own.

Haunted by nightmares, Ramses turns inward to question his own place in an unintelligible world. This is the movement of self-reflection and displacement that draws Ramses into the orbit of Orsi's challenge "to render one's own world other to oneself as a prelude to a new understanding of the two worlds in relationship to each other."[41] Ramses's own sense of place is no longer stable, even if only as a prelude to a still distant understanding. But he recognizes, even at this point, that something has dramatically altered his place in the world: "Moses and Aaron awaited me in the throne room. But there was a difference in their return. Perhaps in me, or perhaps in them. The scales of Shai had certainly shifted" (083). In defiance, Ramses seeks order from his universe and, much like Frimme Hersh to his god, commands Yahweh to confront him as an equal: "I needed control restored. . . . Face me, Tyrant. . . . Stop hiding behind your emissaries . . . , your plagues. Face me!" (086). This, of course, Yahweh will not do, in part because power lies in silence too. In this ultimate sign of rebellion, Ramses has finally capitulated to the Hebrew God. Even Bekenkhonsu recognizes Yahweh as the more powerful deity, and Ramses follows the only path open to him, admitting, "Yahweh is mighty. I have led my people wrong. You are free to go . . . Go and worship Yahweh" (090). In his final acknowledgment of a higher power, he relinquishes his title to Pharaoh as he bows down in defeat. "My name is Ramses," he says.

It appears at first that Nefertari's awakening is Yahweh's reward for Ramses's defeat. But readers know this is not how the story ends, and Ramses comes to learn this too: "My Queen . . . your voice it's . . . No, No . . ." (96) (see fig. 38). The same darker hues and jagged fonts that mark divine possession structure Nefertari's demand that "the slaves must still remain." And in a clever reference to Shelley's "king of kings," Nefertari calls her husband "Ozymandias," a reference that Ramses appears to accept, for he replies, "As my queen wishes. The Israelites will be held." To be sure, Ramses understands the futility of this gesture, but he also recognizes divine possession in Nefertari's voice and his impotence to disobey it. He must carry out his destiny, and his look is one of neither anger nor defiance but calm, purposeful acceptance. This he must do. As Ramses tells his incredulous advisor Ta, who questions Ramses's order to recapture the Israelites in the desert, "We do not [want the Israelites back]. But we have no other choice. No other path. It is what we are supposed to do" (132).

Confronting Moses's world, and his God, has uprooted Ramses's own sense of place, but it has also returned him to a greater awareness of self. This is not a return to authenticity, the movement that so captivated the creators of *Ms. Marvel*, but a heightened awareness of justice, place, and power. *The Lone and Level Sands* engages the moral imagination and the ethical dimensions of unfamiliar worlds. That exploration occurs in the in-between clash between two competing visions of the good: the ordered power of Pharaoh's Egypt, and a possessive god who demands freedom for the Israelite slaves. These two worlds Ramses now holds together, but he is not altogether lost. He has rendered his own world other and foreign but in doing so has arrived

FIG. 38 Nefertari possessed. From *The Lone and Level Sands* by A. David Lewis and Marvin Perry Mann. Copyright © 2005 by A. David Lewis and Marvin Perry Mann.

FIG. 39 Ramses pleads to the Hebrew God. From *The Lone and Level Sands* by A. David Lewis and Marvin Perry Mann. Copyright © 2005 by A. David Lewis and Marvin Perry Mann.

at a new, more expansive understanding. It is particularly eloquent, I think, that in the end Ramses accepts Yahweh's power and his own mortality. But now he has come to see the world through the eyes of a Hebrew slave, and his cry to Yahweh is from one who suffers inexplicably: "What more would you have of me?? I have played my role! My land, my family, my people—we have paid the price slated for us! Is it over?? Why do this? What sick pleasure comes from our suffering? Revenge for the Hebrews? Sheer Entertainment? You could have freed them without harm to us! You could have prevented their enslavement in the first place! Damn you, why?? I am mortal. I never thought otherwise, never believed the priest's declarations! If the divine truly chooses the Hebrews, then I have no recourse. I never have. Then, why . . . why manipulate me so?" (145) (see fig. 39). This declaration of injustice, as I read it, is an act of postmemory: "identification that does not appropriate or interiorize the other within the self but that goes out of one's self and out of one's own cultural norms in order to align oneself, through displacement, with another."[42] Mann's images of Ramses highlight his solitude in the desert, yearning upward to a God who, as we all know, confronts Pharaoh's rage with silence. Like Frimme Hersh in Eisner's *A Contract with God*, who also leans back to project his anger upward toward his God, Ramses must accept silence as God's final act of power. But in that raging silence, Ramses takes on the position of the destitute slave—who cannot understand one's place but who also refuses to accept it. Like the Hebrews who were destined to leave this land, Ramses has had enough; his "lineage will endure," and "Egypt will flourish." Indeed, the final page of this thoughtful graphic narrative notes how Egypt will become "the sixteenth most-populous country in the world" (146–47). Yet that future Egypt has been transformed by a pharaoh who has come to recognize the limits of his power, the insecurity of control, and the inexplicable condition of human suffering. He has achieved these insights and a new sense of what it means to be pharaoh by rendering his world foreign to himself. This is the work of the moral imagination.

Conclusion

Dipesh Chakrabarty argues that historians tend to include minority histories into well-known and well-worn rational narratives such that they expand Enlightenment values and democracy to incorporate "yesterday's revolutionaries who become today's gentlemen." This rational game of inclusion maintains the recognizable narratives and archives of historical inquiry. But one can also imagine these minority communities as subaltern in the ways they develop "a degree of intractability with respect to the aims of professional history." Subaltern histories reveal the limits of western historical narratives; they reveal the "disjointed nature" of the present and illuminate new possibilities of human flourishing.[43] I have read the *Ms. Marvel* series as a minority history but *The Lone and Level Sands* as a subaltern one. There is much to admire in Wilson and Alphona's inclusion of a Muslim Pakistani American woman into the pantheon of superheroes. Expanding our sense of the heroic and exploring dimensions of inner subjectivity in minority communities is honorable and welcoming. But extending the superhero canon to include Kamala Khan does not undermine the discursive norms that govern the superhero archive. It certainly expands the visual and material representation of the heroic, but it neither interrogates nor subverts the practice. Chakrabarty warns of the imperialist and colonizing instincts of historical inquiry, and those forces play out too in the *Ms. Marvel* series. Searching for authenticity governs Kamala's story as it does many other superhero narratives. The rules are the same, now just expanded to cover a broader religious and cultural landscape. As I see it, this is what assimilation looks like in superhero comics.

Although broader inclusion is a democratic good, and one that I both admire and honor, the price paid for admission is religious conformity. Kamala Khan's Islamic beliefs and practices, however Muslim, are distinctly American. Religion happens at the dinner table, and we see it more as aesthetic accessory than material, embodied heritage. This is not the case in *The Lone and Level Sands*, in which possession, divine worship, and controlling powers dominate a religious landscape that soon becomes unfamiliar. Ramses only dimly recognizes the world of his childhood as he confronts a god who unwinds familiar paths. He cannot absorb Moses's God into his own moral universe: this is not a story of inclusion but one of displacement. Ramses faces not only the limits but also the new possibilities of his cultural heritage. As Ramses imagines a new Egypt arising from this tragic encounter, he accepts the "disjointed nature" of his present. Chakrabarty calls this an historical moment "out of joint with itself,"[44] and Orsi labels it an "in-between" encounter with the self and other. I call it the space of the moral imagination, in which we are called and challenged to explore ethical possibilities that lie beyond our comforting narratives of inclusion. In this reading, superheroes are super not because they reflect back to us our higher selves. They are super in their capacity to challenge our mortal and moral limits while revealing unfamiliar worlds of human flourishing. Jerry Siegel had it wrong: new powers will not move others to recognize me. Those powers dismantle the self, rendering my very self unfamiliar by imagining alternative models of being (super)human.

CHAPTER 4

The Nativist Imagination in Religious Comic Stories

In her transformative essay "How Native Is a 'Native' Anthropologist?," Kirin Narayan challenges appeals to native informants and ethnographers as authentic sources of knowledge.[1] Anthropologists tend to mark "ordinary people" and those "insiders trained to collect indigenous texts" as natives in a society under scrutiny, all the better to extract "the inside scoop" for a foreign community. Yet anthropologists too would claim native status if they were cultural insiders who could "forward an authentic point of view to the anthropological community."[2] These claims to insider status, as Arjun Appadurai argued, represented the ideology of authenticity, in which "proper natives" on both sides of the ethnographic divide could claim pure access "without distortion or residue."[3] Narayan seeks a more hybrid model of identity, such that "multiplex identities" like her mother's offer "many strands of identification" that frustrate claims to authentic selves and native perspectives. Indeed, how we label ourselves and others—as insiders, natives, outsiders, informants, American, Bavarian, and so on—too often condenses more fluid identities. These porous selves with rich cultural heritages become monstrous outsiders in more conventional stories about identity, and so Narayan—sounding very much like Leela Prasad as discussed in this book's first chapter—warns that "adopting a narrative voice involves an ethical stance."[4] To claim the insider voice of the native, either as ethnographic subject or anthropologist, is to appropriate the moral value of truth telling. Insiders reveal authentic knowledge and experience to those nonnative outsiders who can only sympathetically listen by proxy. Yet as Narayan eloquently shows, such native or insider status is problematic at best, and it most likely distorts the way we are always insiders and outsiders to multiple communities. Our lives are simply too complex to be reduced to a single identity; we need to account, Narayan argues, "for the complexity of an identity in which multiple countries, regions, classes, and religions may come together."[5]

Enacting this kind of hybrid identity as a bulwark against claims to native authenticity helps to contextualize the ethical challenge for this chapter, because I want to engage this more tangled sense of self by reading two comics that claim insider and native status. Craig Thompson's *Blankets* (2003) and Joann Sfar's *The Rabbi's Cat* (2005) are both coming-of-age stories in their own distinctive ways: the character Craig narrates his childhood experiences within an American Christian family, and the cat offers an insider's glimpse at French Algerian Jewry. But both Craig and the rabbi's cat are distinct outsiders in their own communities. Craig abandons the strict dualistic theology of his parents' evangelical Christianity, and the cat, seeking a bar mitzvah of his own, rankles a rabbinical establishment that can only ridicule those religious animals that are something other than human. Sfar is masterful in his parody of Jewish identity, but his mockery of Jewish and animal stereotypes is still rooted in nativist logic, as is Thompson's account of Christian fundamentalism. Both texts speak from the perspective of the insider, reinscribing the nativist appeal to authenticity, but do so as outsiders to the very traditions they know so well from personal experience.

This all sounds like Kamala Khan's position within the *Ms. Marvel* universe discussed in the preceding chapter, in which she struggled to find her authentic self within the white middle-class culture of suburban New Jersey. But I want to show how *Blankets* and *The Rabbi's Cat* play with hybridity while never enacting it. This constitutes less a failure of the moral self than a felt recognition that we are continually haunted and scared by the native. To imagine more plastic, hybrid selves is to abandon the pull of (admittedly) problematic appeals to the native, but those nativist roots make strong claims on embodied lives. *Blankets* and *The Rabbi's Cat* reveal how appeals to nativity relentlessly inhabit our moral worlds and our imaginative capacities to reach beyond the familiar. In *Blankets*, Thompson champions a spiritual and moral sensibility over and against the rigid confines of native religious practices but then claims a more authentic, and native, devotional voice liberated from irrational religion. Sfar, while taking pleasure in cultural and religious diversity, still reinscribes nativist boundaries to ward off temptations to cross over and inhabit alternative modes of being. Adopting a nativist voice, as Narayan asserts, really does involve taking an ethical stance, and it is a tone that continually haunts desires to move beyond home. Thompson and Sfar reach beyond the confines of the familiar yet inevitably take on nativist postures when they do. This searching beyond the frame may appear as voyeuristic stereotype (*The Rabbi's Cat*) or as stretching to access what always remains beyond one's grasp (*Blankets*), but the pull of native roots grounds their ethical imaginations. These are moral quests and stories that expose the staying power of the native informant.

Blankets (2003)

Told in narrative prose and visual image, Craig Thompson's *Blankets* is really a quite beautiful story of the young Craig growing up in an evangelical Christian home in Wisconsin. Thompson interweaves his family experiences with vignettes of Sunday school and bullies at day school together with subtle allusions to childhood molestation by his male babysitter. Craig remains emotionally distant from all of this until he meets Raina at a Christian summer camp, and she invites him to join her and her friends in mocking the camp's hypocrisy. While most of his high-school peers drink beer and dream about girls, Craig wants to draw and daydream, and he finds his muse in young, flirtatious love. As he develops sexual and emotional maturity, Craig finds in Raina the passionate and embodied other to the Christianity of his youth; she opens a world of material splendor denied to Craig by his strict parents and cruel teachers. As Thompson tells this autobiographical tale, he is the true Christian who wishes to "praise God with [his] drawings."[6] Only Craig's pastor takes him seriously, recognizing in him a spiritual and intellectual gift for ministry. But in a passage that I will explore later, Craig cannot accept the minister's more liberal sense of biblical revelation; for this spiritual searcher, either the Bible is the word of God or its "TRUTH was cancelled out" (*Blankets*, 549). To replace that either/or of revealed truth or human error, Craig extricates Christian morals from Christian religion: "I still believe in God; the teachings of JESUS even, but the rest of Christianity . . . its Bible, its churches, its dogma—only sets up boundaries between people and cultures" (533). This is Craig as insider, who has experienced the strict teachings of his evangelical parents and teachers and who appeals to a truer spirituality to counter a divisive, controlling religion. The native affirms a more authentic Christian sensibility.

Blankets is not the first religious autobiographical coming-of-age story in comic form. The most prominent and influential work of that kind is surely

Justin Green's magisterial *Binky Brown Meets the Holy Virgin Mary* (1972).[7] As Art Spiegelman notes in his introductory remarks to the reprinted version of *Binky Brown*, "Justin turned comic book boxes into intimate, secular confession booths and thereby profoundly changed the history of comics." Indeed, *Binky Brown* reads like a neurotic confession from a guilty Catholic who struggles to contain his sexual urges. Green highlights the confessional nature of his comic on the memorable opening splash page, in which the young Binky, holding pen in teeth while scribbling on paper with his father's blood as ink, admits to having left Catholicism in 1958: "I daresay many of you aspiring **revolutionaries** will conclude that instead of focussing on topics which would lend themselves to **social issues**, I have zero'ed-in [*sic*] on the petty conflict in my **crotch**! My **justification** for undertaking this **task** is that many others are **slaves** to their **neuroses.** Maybe if they read about one neurotic's **dilemma** in **easy-to-understand comic-book format** these tormented folks will no longer see themselves as mere **food-tubes** living in **isolation.**" *Binky Brown* is best remembered for its penis rays that damage all that stand in the way of their sexual blaze. Phallic potency is everywhere as Binky attempts to break away from Christian taboos. But the opening confession also reveals deeper yearnings for liberation from enslavement to neuroses, from the Vietnam war that Green admits lies heavy in the background (*Binky Brown*, 53), from the oppressive isolation of Catholic sexual and material denial, and from bodily desires and fantasies. Influenced by the contrarian spirits Lenny Bruce, Philip Roth, and Robert Crumb, Green crafted an autobiographical comic as catharsis—an exposure of what he would later recognize as his obsessive-compulsive disorder. This literary move to self-liberation would have a critical influence on Spiegelman's own witnessing in *Maus*, as it also would on later graphic artists who sought comic relief.[8]

We should understand Craig Thompson's *Blankets* within this literary history and context; but even more, we should recognize his appeal to native experience as a trope that continues to haunt these graphic depictions of adolescence. Although Binky finally overcomes "the primeval morass of superstition and guilt fostered by well-meaning institutions like the Catholic church" (40), his journey began as a child who absorbed those Catholic teachings and firmly believed in them. In short, he took Catholicism almost *too* seriously. The devil, God, sexual passions, dirty flesh—these were all-too-real for the young Binky. Green's confessional tale might free those other "tormented folks" because he speaks from the inside, from one who has fully experienced the slavery of a neurotic Catholicism. Neither Green nor I wish to imply that this confessional story reveals a Catholicism as it really is, always, for all. But Green does appeal to authentic experience as one who, like other Catholic American youth in the 1950s, read the educational comic *Treasure Chest*, with its "religious dogma, puzzles and narrative comic stories about the heroic lives of saints and brave Catholic altar boys behind the Iron Curtain" (51). The normative appeals to heroic saints and Catholic bravery only magnified the guilt and shame of Binky's sexual urges. But those passions, now labeled as neurotic, were real, authentic, and shared by other tormented souls. This sense of authentic self-exposure, in which coming-of-age is a form of cathartic taking-stock, is perhaps Green's most important legacy for understanding Thompson's *Blankets*. For here too we find an author appealing to an insider experience of Christian authority while finally breaking free from its oppressive regimen. In redeeming the native self—the one who has always been the authentic insider—the comic authorizes its own claims to authentic experience and religious journey.

Craig is a lonely child, often picked on in school by classmates and teachers, abused at home by his creepy male babysitter, and sternly reprimanded by his demanding father. No wonder, then, that he sees only a menacing secular world full of danger and threats. Dreaming of escape from this earthly nightmare, Craig finds solace in this Sunday school version of heaven: "But it doesn't have to be scary if you are a CHRISTIAN and have asked JESUS into your heart; because when you die, you'll go to HEAVEN" (*Blankets*, 49). Craig could now look down in scorn at a world of pain, abandonment, and failure in which he was only "passing through" (53). Thompson depicts this young man as compulsively driven to find clarity and purpose; he seeks firm and eternal answers for a sick soul who now understands his drawings as nothing more than secular escapism. Devoting himself entirely to God, Craig frantically destroys all his artwork ("the most secular and selfish of worldly pursuits") as a "burnt offering before God" (58). Devotion can travel along only one road, and by sacrificing his art Craig dramatically vanquishes his memories of childhood. But this sacrifice to God is really an abandonment of self, for Craig physically vomits these images of his youth (see figs. 40 and 41). Craig's body shakes violently, becoming a whirlwind of lines as his demons escape his body—another form of escapism that recalls Jesus's calling the demons out in the Gospel of Mark. Yet burning these memories, or really, setting them free, fails to protect Craig from his nightmares. He clings ever closer to God, wishing to be liberated, like his youthful demons, from the painful scripts of bodily existence.

This physical and emotional intensity, at once painful and sacrificial, marks Craig as the native Christian evangelical who yearns for truth, eternity, and God's loving embrace. He cares little for his educational studies, preferring instead to become "engrossed in the book of Ecclesiastes," from which he learns that "Pleasure is Meaningless, Toil is Meaningless, Wisdom is Meaningless, Everything is Meaningless" (56). But this denial of worldly goods is less a cultivated and thoughtful practice than it is the mundane and continual experience of futility—a complete loss of the self and its artistic labors. During this cavernous experience of abandonment Craig wretches his demons skyward as a plea for help. I draw attention to this violent and violating experience because it functions to authorize Craig's religious authenticity. He has sunk low, literally to his knees, to sacrifice a world of youthful pain and betrayal for an eternal one in God's love. In this religious experience, Craig has much in common with William James's depiction of the sick soul, who feels the "pity, pain, and fear, and the sentiment of human helplessness" all around in this weary world. As James presents him, Tolstoy mirrors Craig's own torment: "One can live only so long as one is intoxicated, drunk with life; but when one grows sober one cannot fail to see that it is all a stupid cheat. What is truest about it is that there is nothing even funny or silly in it; it is cruel and stupid, purely and simply." Tolstoy can only overcome this "feeling of dread" by turning toward God, a turning that "came from my heart."[9] This profound religious experience is Craig's own in *Blankets*, and it brands him as an authentic Christian. He has experienced the pain of worldly suffering and abandonment and through that trial has risen up to seek God's love and Jesus's salvific presence. Thompson portrays his young Craig as the Christian insider who knows through his own tormented experience the goods of heaven. He is the native informant, one of the intimate faithful who deserves our trust as an authentic voice.

That voice is a lonely one, even within the Christ-centered atmosphere of church winter "snow-camp." The other kids wear the Christian garb—large

FIG. 40 Craig's shaking body. From *Blankets* by Craig Thompson. Copyright © 2003 by Craig Thompson. Used by permission of Drawn & Quarterly.

FIG. 41 Craig releases his creative images. From *Blankets* by Craig Thompson. Copyright © 2003 by Craig Thompson. Used by permission of Drawn & Quarterly.

cross necklaces and "What would Jesus do?" jackets and shirts—but only Craig takes the Christian ministry seriously. In the cabin bunk beds at night, male bravado demands the recounting of sexual conquests, but Craig, under the covers with flashlight, continues to read his Bible. That devotion meets only scorn and ridicule from the other boys—"Shit, Thompson. You reading the Bible? Aren't we forced to read that thing ENOUGH here?" (80)—but Craig slips out to find solace in an abandoned game room. An older Craig looks back at his younger self and recognizes that lonely boy, but now, as a teenager, he has "learned to spot the other outsiders" (88). Thompson draws the young Craig as small and desperately alone; one image reveals a close-up of Craig holding his knees to his chest and then yields to a view from above to show Craig's agonizing smallness (see fig. 42). Craig is both alone and lonely, a singular soul who demands unyielding commitment: "I'm sorry, God, for sneaking out of the cabin and lying and not reading the Bible and not witnessing to people and picking on my little brother. . . . Please forgive me" (87). Release will indeed arrive, but not from God: Craig meets Raina some years later at camp, and with her discovers a spirituality far more forgiving and sexually liberating. As we will see later, Craig explores bodily and artistic pleasures to overcome the anxiety of his lonely religious devotion. But Thompson can depict this bodily awakening as genuine because he has so thoroughly rooted the young Craig in evangelical Christian culture. Craig rejects neither a hollow religious creed nor an easy Christian ministry; he abandons the passionate witnessing of Christian suffering, and he does so as a native insider.

Like the main character in Justin Green's *Binky Brown*, so much of what Craig rejects in Christianity involves the sexual body. As a child he "was always DISPLACED" from bodily comforts (291), a reference that Thompson associates with the babysitter's sexual assault. But that harassment only confirms the Christian teaching he absorbed as a child that denied bodily and material pleasures. One of his Sunday school teachers informs her young students that life in heaven is full of praise and worship, "EXCLAIMING His name for all ETERNITY" (137). This Craig finds captivating, for his drawings would finally count as scripts of devotion. But his teacher can imagine only voices of praise, and she mocks Craig's obsession with comics as rather silly: "I mean, 'COME ON, CRAIG.' How can you praise God with DRAWINGS?" But Thompson makes clear that such Christian derision for comics has deeper inscripted roots, for God has already created a world full of material goods, and so "He's already drawn it for us." Mimicking a well-rehearsed critique, Thompson shows that art is simply a reproduction of nature, and so Craig's aesthetic skill is merely poor imitation rather than praiseworthy devotion. The Christian trajectory, as Thompson depicts it here, always moves away from the physical and embodied world to another place of disembodied glory. Craig's

FIG. 42 Craig as a young Christian talking to his God. From *Blankets* by Craig Thompson. Copyright © 2003 by Craig Thompson. Used by permission of Drawn & Quarterly.

young love for Raina recaptures the beauty and pleasures of material existence and confronts these Christian denials of earthly bliss. As Craig finds his muse in writing sweet, lovely words, Raina's letters renew his "faith in the notion of making marks on paper" (142). Recall that in chapter 1 we discovered how Thompson tethers inscription to Dodola's body in *Habibi* (2011), such that calligraphy both sacralizes and sexualizes the feminine form. That later work appropriates Thompson's script in *Blankets*, for here too the act of marking the body ties writing to sexuality. The physical act of creation—in writing the body, if not reproducing it—is more than bland mimicry or uninspired copying. Material inscription is a physical act of (sexual) pleasure and creative expression.

Yet Craig's Christian education registers these gratifications as sinful self-absorption. An outsider at school, Craig can hardly wait to return home and read the perfumed love letters from Raina. The sexual allure of inscription captures Craig's youthful lust: "Most revealing was her handwriting—including the indentions traced on each page from the page above. (She must have been pressing her pen hard.) An alluring line looped her 'l's. Her 'f's were 'l's that instead of linking with the next letter, fell" (146). Craig relates these intricate, sexualized close readings of script as he slowly reaches for his penis, admitting this "was the ONE and ONLY time I masturbated my senior year" (147). But almost immediately after spilling his semen on a blank page, Craig feels the great weight of Christian guilt and sexual repression. Thompson portrays semen as inscribed marks on the page, matching Raina's own tracings (see fig. 43). But on the blank page it lies alone and distant from the touch of other physical pleasures, as if semen were an unwanted material discharge. It doesn't belong, either as product or as spilled marking. Craig understands this, and so he crumples up the paper such that none of the semen escapes and throws it away in his trash bin. But like the now wrinkled paper, Craig's body collapses to the floor, buckling under the burden of sinful desires. He has created unwanted script—seminal drawings that fail to praise a demanding God. Seeking pleasure in embodied practices—in drawings, in handwritten letters, in physical touch—Craig lies prone and beaten, unable to accept his own body as site for physical ecstasy. This insider to the Christian evangelical tradition has become an outsider to his own body and childhood.

If comic stories follow the narrative script of beginning, middle, and end, then Thompson devotes his middle to the struggle between a sexually repressive Christian spirituality and Raina's liberatory eroticism. Craig is caught between these two magnetic attractions, yielding ultimately to the erotics of material script rather than the denial of embodied pleasures. As I have argued, this transition surfaces as authentic because Craig knows these Christian denials from aching personal experience. Although readers may not condone his choices, Thompson still presents them as worthy of our admiration and

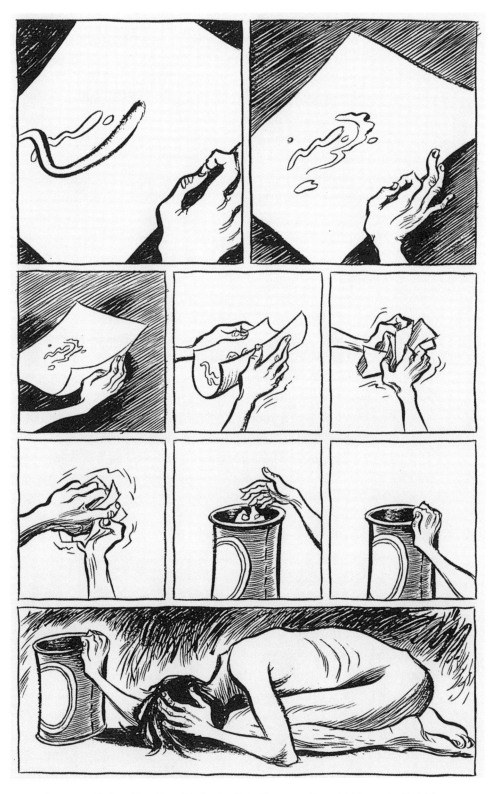

FIG. 43 Semen as spilled marking. From *Blankets* by Craig Thompson. Copyright © 2003 by Craig Thompson. Used by permission of Drawn & Quarterly.

respect. Craig's maturing spirituality, one that accepts the scripted body as productively carnal, claims religious authority because it derives from insider experience. His is not a critique from nowhere, and it is not a judgment from the Sunday classroom.

Thompson grounds Craig's conversion in personal religious struggle. When he first visits Raina's house for a two-week visit, he enters her bedroom and sees walls covered with images and paintings (see fig. 44). While he waits for Raina to read a bedtime story to her younger sister, Craig takes out his New International Version Bible and reads about a woman who touched Jesus's garment in the Gospel of Luke. Lying on Raina's bed, Craig feels ashamed that he did not treat Raina's garments with holy respect and thinks "that instead I should be removing my sandals (socks?) and averting my eyes" (201) (see fig. 45). The biblical story comes alive and condemns Craig's cavalier attitude to holiness. But the bed too becomes the sacred rival to Jesus's presence, and here Thompson focuses the reader on one particular image on Raina's wall. As Craig reveals, "Transplanted to the other end of the room, I realized that keeping watch over the bed was the same portrait of Jesus that had hung in my parents' room" (201). That image is the well-known 1940 painting *Head of Christ* by Warner Sallman, a portrait that a good many American Christians would immediately recognize.[10] But Craig sees this image only as "keeping watch over the bed." When Thompson illustrates Craig first entering Raina's bedroom, Sallman's *Head of Christ* is squeezed among a cacophony of unrelated pictures, including those of rock stars, naked bodies, family members, and teddy bears. In fact, Jesus looks away from that bed, as Sallman wanted him to, toward a heavenly light from beyond. But Craig has eyes only for

FIG. 44 Raina's bedroom. From *Blankets* by Craig Thompson. Copyright © 2003 by Craig Thompson. Used by permission of Drawn & Quarterly.

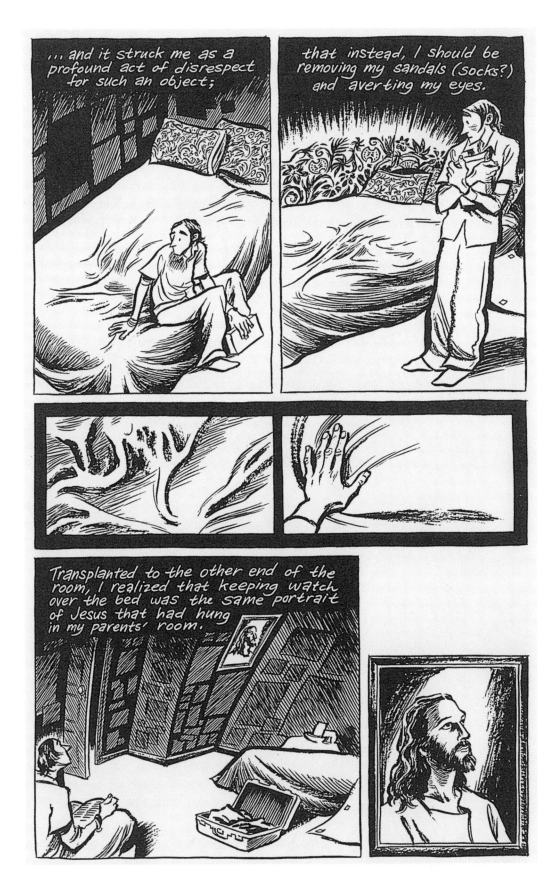

Jesus, and this gaze captivates the struggle between Jesus's watchful presence and Craig's own bodily desires. The choice lies between the allure of sexual pleasure and the light of Jesus's frame.

This tension runs deep in Craig's personal history and traumatized conscience. Thompson immediately follows the scene in Raina's bedroom with another intimate portrayal of a young Craig staring blankly and reluctantly at Sallman's *Head of Christ* in his parents' bedroom (see fig. 46). Once again, Thompson begins with a close-up of the young lad, only to then project his loneliness by drawing the entire bedroom from above. And here Sallman's Jesus really does keep watch over the bed as the lone picture on the wall. His parents enter and sit beside Craig on the bed's end. His mother is in dark shadows, gazing blankly downward in despair, while his father looms large, with outsized clenched hands, grimacing away from his child. Craig's bus driver had found a drawing of a naked woman, an image his mother now holds to show the reader (but not Craig). The image itself is a rather innocent and plainly bland portrait, but his parents worry that Craig has drawn a body "without any clothes on"—a naked body, his father repeats—and his mother, as the carrier of the Christian tradition in this family, reauthorizes the tension between sexual pleasure and Jesus's frame: "The body is beautiful, Craig, but not like that. God creates us, but sin has made us impure" (206). The narrative continues to impress Christian guilt, and soon Sallman's *Head of Christ* reappears, watching over a young Craig.

> Mother: How do you think what you did makes us feel?
> Craig: MAD?
> Mother: No. Sad.
> Father: Ahem.
> Mother: Because God gave you a talent and we don't want you to use it for the Devil. [Head of Christ is *now in view*.] How do you think JESUS feels?
> [*Craig sobs.*]
> Father: Huh?
> Craig: Sob . . . S . . . SAD?
> Mother: Yes, SAD. Because it hurts Him when you sin [*image of Sallman's Jesus crying*]. (*Blankets*, 206–7)

Craig then runs to Jesus on the wall to desperately seek forgiveness. But he hears someone entering the room and, turning toward the door, witnesses his own drawing of the naked woman morph into Raina's body. As readers we now understand this scene a bit differently: Craig had relived this childhood trauma while gazing at the *Head of Christ* in Raina's room. As a boy and then maturing teenager, Craig fails to escape the compressing dynamics of sexual

FIG. 46 Sallman's *Head of Christ* in parents' bedroom. From *Blankets* by Craig Thompson. Copyright © 2003 by Craig Thompson. Used by permission of Drawn & Quarterly.

bodies, Christian sin, parental and religious authority, and erotic inscription. When Raina interrupts Craig's traumatic memory, she asks if he is alright. Craig's response perfectly captures his own religious and embodied paralysis: "Oh Yes. Just dazed" (209).

As a coming-of-age story, *Blankets* leads us through Craig's childhood bewilderment to sexual and embodied liberation. That first night Craig wanted to touch Raina, but with Jesus above him—the image is Sallman's *Head of Christ* but with Jesus now in dark silhouette looking away from the light—Craig turns away in sinful despair. Even as Jesus looks away, Craig cannot help but feel his sacred gaze upon him. Some two hundred pages later, however, Thompson devotes twenty full spreads to their sexual embraces in rather lovely and romantic drawings. In awe of the experience and of Raina's beauty, Craig reverently "covered her body with the quilted blanket she had made me" (thus the title for this graphic novel), and after kissing her lightly on the forehead turns away only to be confronted once again by Sallman's *Head of Christ* (see fig. 47). But rather than receiving the light from above or turning away with saddened tears toward the fallenness below, Jesus now directly accepts Craig with an approving smile, and the shirtless teenager basks in the grace of belonging: "I realized that I didn't want to be ANYWHERE else. For once, I was MORE THAN CONTENT being where I was" (431–32). Admittedly, I find Jesus's confronting smile far too sentimental for my tastes, but Thompson clearly wishes to mark this conversionary moment for his youthful self. Craig finally appears at peace with his body and his love. And so is Jesus, for he looks directly at him rather than to his God above. Craig is beginning to discover a material spirituality, however mawkish, that condones bodily pleasures and the erotic touch of encounter. Perhaps there exists a Christian spiritualism beyond heaven or hell, praise or sin, enlightenment or the body. As Craig gazes in wonder at the smiling Jesus, candles flicker out, channeling upward luminous smoke shaped as light and airy drawings (431). These etchings hover between Craig and Jesus (who now returns his gaze toward the heavenly light), suggesting that the intoxicating smoke transfixed Craig's vision, and the smiling Jesus stands as a playful mirage. As Freud would have it, that external religious authority has become lodged in Craig's own superego, but he now appears as a comforting presence rather than as a disappointed, saddened parent. This is a personal, confessional story of survival and acceptance in which the airy lines of drifting smoke capture Craig's escape to body and place. His body is now the site of spiritual nourishment. He has come of age.

This too links Thompson's *Blankets* to Green's *Binky Brown*—the maturing self is one who grows out of a repressive, controlling Christianity. Gaining a more sophisticated wisdom requires the abandonment of religious ritual and tradition. As Thompson draws his graphic novel to an end, he has an older, wiser Craig return home for his brother's high-school graduation. Walking

FIG. 47 Imagining Jesus's approving smile. From *Blankets* by Craig Thompson. Copyright © 2003 by Craig Thompson. Used by permission of Drawn & Quarterly.

through the countryside, Craig admits to his brother that he "could never tell Mom and Dad that I'm not a Christian anymore" (531). But this disclosure is not entirely honest, as we learn in Craig's fuller confession that "I still believe in God; the teachings of JESUS even, but the rest of Christianity . . . its Bible, its churches, its dogma—only sets up boundaries between people and cultures. It denies the beauty of being HUMAN, and it ignores all these GAPS that need to be filled in by the individual" (533). Craig worries that to admit this to his parents would only break their hearts. Thompson owns this as autobiography, for he admits that *Blankets* is his public confession too in an interview with *Mother Jones*: "*Blankets* was the vehicle with which I came out to my parents about not being a Christian." And Thompson appears to share his character Craig's rejection of Christianity in order to affirm Jesus's ethical humanism.

> *Mother Jones*: Do you still consider yourself a Christian?
>
> Craig Thompson: No, I don't consider myself a Christian at all.
>
> *MJ*: Was there something in the church's teachings that turned you off?
>
> CT: It was slow and instant at the same time. The slow part happened all throughout my high school years, where I was really obsessed with Jesus and his teachings, but really disenchanted with the church and its dogma. . . . So I clashed with a lot of the teachings, and a lot of the Bible, actually. But I loved Jesus and his ethics. . . .
>
> *MJ*: That attitude could come in handy for a struggling cartoonist.
>
> CT: Yeah, definitely. I think there is some overlap in terms of artistic desires and Christian desires.
>
> *MJ*: So have you also said goodbye to Jesus, or are you still down with him?
>
> CT: I'm still down with Jesus. I like to think of him mostly as a social revolutionary who mixed with bad crowds and hated the rich. [*Laughs.*][11]

To be down with Jesus means to accept a social ethic divorced from ritual, tradition, and church dogma. It is to accept guiding principles that allow for individual creativity and reflection. In this, Thompson's artistic desires match his religious-turned-ethical ones, for just as the comic frame marks the boundary for creative expression within, so too do Jesus's teachings—without church, dogma, and even Bible—frame a more spiritual, individual assertion of "the beauty of being HUMAN." Craig the character and Craig Thompson the author have moved beyond Christianity to an ethic of expressive fulfillment and social justice.

But the Craig in *Blankets* and probably also the Craig Thompson who created that comic have not fully abandoned the Christianity of their youth. In the very last section, called "Footnotes," Craig believes that in maturing beyond his family he is also moving on from Christianity: "Upon moving out of my parents' home, I made a conscious effort to leave my Bible behind. It was the book of ECCLESIASTES that prompted me to do so" (545). We read in this chapter of Craig's intellectual development and his thoughtful critique of biblical authorship and authority. His pastor, impressed with Craig's worldly learning, hopes he will debate these issues in seminary school. But Craig is appalled by the pastor's apologetic defense of textual emendations by scribes who might have believed in a more covenantal account of progressive revelation: "GROWTH PROCESS? This I couldn't accept. I had been taught the words of the Bible came straight from the mouth of God. If indeed they were subtly modified by generations of scribes and watered down by translations, then for me—their TRUTH was cancelled out. It suddenly struck me as absurd that something as divine as God's speech could be pinned down in physical (mass-produced) form" (549). This, I submit, is the religion of his parents, in which an either/ or sensibility of truth or falsehood, saved or damned, sin or salvation prevails over more pluralistic, open, and porous boundaries. Ecclesiastes for Craig is either the word of God—pronounced once and for all in miraculous immediacy, without scripted translation, without being watered down, and without scribal interpretation—or mass-produced, material garbage. One can even hear echoes of this dualistic frame in Thompson's appropriation of Jesus as "a social revolutionary who mixed with bad crowds and hated the rich." This sense of assured closure that Thompson recognizes in his parents is still very much a part of Craig's spiritual ethic: the Bible is either TRUTH or a material absurdity. And in this too Thompson shares a good deal with Justin Green before him, for both are rooted in religious cultures that they can only partially abandon. Green is certainly more accepting than Thompson is of these competing pressures, yet for both, the force of "I had been taught" weighs heavily on their spiritual progress. Some things cannot be stripped and washed away from the self; these religious sensibilities are constitutive of who they are and so limit the kinds of beings they wish to become.

Perhaps a more constructive way to imagine nativity emerges here, one that appeals less to authenticity than to a coming to terms with the desires, judgments, and religious scars that shape and bind the self. What's more, Thompson's *Blankets* understands these entanglements well. Witness Craig's early childhood trauma with his male babysitter, when Craig is too young to fully understand his experience and powerless to warn his younger brother (31) (see fig. 48). That trauma continues to haunt Craig, and we see this when he first visits Raina and marvels how she protects her younger sibling: "They looked out for each other. . . . But I'd been too weak to look out for my own little brother" (291). Familial guilt of this type rarely disappears altogether, and Craig carries it forward in ways that bind him to his past. Thompson locates this sexual and familial trauma in the body, particularly in Craig's body, and in his fear of growing up. As Craig has it, "I couldn't fathom that the soul trapped in my child body would be TRANSPLANTED to it's [sic] grotesque adolescent counterpart" (293). The mystery of transitional puberty reveals the adult body as foreign and grotesque because Craig marks it as the very site of childhood sexual trauma. With "LUMBERING, awkward FLESH, body odors and foul mouths, curdled ACNE, first sproutings of facial hair, and swollen sex organs," those "older people were such foreign beasts—especially HIGH SCHOOLERS" (292). Thompson blames his Christian upbringing for its pervasive and toxic denial of the material body, but certainly that anxiety has several traumatic roots. The body leaks—emitting noxious smells, sprouting new growths, ejaculating semen—to leave trails of the grotesque. This is not a frame to abandon so much as a material, disfigured boundary to anxiously inhabit. For Craig, the transplanted body marks an inescapable continuity, in which the child literally becomes that adult body—a body that physically and emotionally absorbs its representational history of anxiety and abuse. This, indeed, is what a growth process really means for sacred texts and the bodies of our desires. Rather than a maturity that abandons religious constraints, it is a more developed acceptance of the traumatic scars that mark both the page and the moral self.

For these and other reasons, Sallman's *Head of Christ* always looks over Craig, even as Sallman's Jesus looks up toward a purer space. It may at times signal a form of abandonment of Craig's youthful desires and embodied frame, but it nonetheless stands in judgment over him. The registers here move between the stern denial of bodily pleasures (in his parents' bedroom) and the approval of, if not gratifying assent to, the emotional and material splendors of embodiment with others (in Raina's bedroom). But these movements never abandon that image or that Christian inheritance: Craig neither escapes Jesus's visual judgment on his body nor wishes to do so. He stands naked before Christian authority and accepts his place either as the sinful worshipper of naked female bodies or, lying next to Raina, as the satisfied lover who finally secures a home. The judgment may be stern and repressive or accepting and liberating, but it is a judgment under the Christian gaze. Craig's flashbacks—to his babysitter's sexual advances and to his parents' bedroom under the watchful protection of Christ—serve to recast narrative time as haunted presence. Some things, and some images, are inescapable and lodged too deep to abandon; they are native in this reimagined sense of acquired inheritance. In some ways Craig never leaves home and never grows out of his site of nativity but just resituates his inheritance within a painful narrative of acceptance.

When Craig admits to his brother Phil that he has left the Christian church, they both recall a giant cave that they discovered as children, one that

FIG. 48 Memories of childhood trauma. From *Blankets* by Craig Thompson. Copyright © 2003 by Craig Thompson. Used by permission of Drawn & Quarterly.

FIG. 49 Ascending snowflakes. From *Blankets* by Craig Thompson. Copyright © 2003 by Craig Thompson. Used by permission of Drawn & Quarterly.

disappeared only a few days after they discovered it. Thompson draws images of Raina as Craig realizes that memory "is so dream-like—too eerie and beautiful and cryptic [like Raina, the images suggest] to be true" (538). But Phil grounds that memory in historical truth—"No," he claims, "I was there"—and that assurance roots Craig's memory in something "real" (539). Memories deceive, as did the smoking candles when Craig witnessed Sallman's Christ smiling upon him. Yet being with others as witness to joy embodies, literally, those fleeting moments of ecstasy. Here the body is a carrier of those painful traumas marked by a physical past, and these scars are just as real as those transcendent experiences. Nativity, in a very real sense, is being born into, and never really leaving, this scene of marked, embodied presence.

Thompson renders comic drawings as precisely those marks of real presence, however momentary, haunted, or stained. Returning home with Phil, Craig whitewashes his memories of Raina as he attempts to move beyond his first romantic encounter. Thompson portrays this mental erasure as the literal whitewashing of an image, with Raina and Craig huddled together in a tree nook—the very image Craig painted for Raina on her bedroom wall (342). But as he slowly spreads white paint over his beloved drawing, undoing the inscription to the original "blank wall" (340), Craig fails to erase the image entirely—a short line, reminiscent of his spilled semen on the blank page, leaves an indelible trace of presence. And this is how Thompson concludes his graphic novel, as testament to the very realness of the comic book: "How satisfying it is to leave a mark on a blank surface. To make a map of my movement—no matter how temporary" (581–82). This very last image explodes with lines and energy toward the darkened sky as snowflakes appear to reverse course and fly upward out of the frame (see fig. 49). But they do not escape that frame; the drawn snowflakes are bounded by a structure establishing their very existence as markings on the page. A mark on a blank surface is also contained as a native presence; it moves along a page and perhaps even projects beyond it, but it stains within borders of identity.

This is, I want to suggest, a more appropriate and ethically sensitive way to think about nativity and the native informant. The native is situated, to be sure, within enclosures of culture, family, religion, and embodiment. She is marked in these and many other ways. But like the snowflake, she also presses beyond those confining architectures of being, demanding a "growth process" that rejects biblical prescriptions and dualistic fairy tales of heaven and hell. To be native is to be caught in this ever-present movement of searching beyond the boundaries of one's recognizable existence. We cannot escape those borders entirely, but we should imagine the ethical worlds beyond them. This is why Thompson's *Blankets* leaves a mark on a blank surface; he has mapped the contours of the ethical imagination. The native is and should be us.

The Rabbi's Cat (2005)

Even as Thompson's *Blankets* appeals to a problematic nativist logic in its claims to authentic exposure and experience, the graphic novel continually yearns to move beyond and out of the constricted boundaries that define Craig's youth and, as I suggested earlier, the very contours of the graphic medium. That arresting image of snowflakes moving skyward mirrors Craig's own inner trajectory and bodily desires—to finally let go of a tormented past and escape to lighter, less encumbered air. But Craig is rooted firmly in the snow below, tethered to the lower frame and even moving beneath it (note the gap appearing where his legs should be). As the tree branches swoon upward, giving the appearance of the snow following in that direction, Craig is tied to the stable ground, unable to even jump heavenward.

This sense of desire and yearning beyond the frame, beyond the confines of our grounded existence, is also the subject of Joann Sfar's *The Rabbi's Cat*. In many ways this graphic novel is so much more pluralistic, exploratory, and open than *Blankets*, and yet Sfar's pluralism requires all his characters to stay in place, never moving past the frames of their closed worlds. This is especially surprising given the novel's conceit of a talking cat—perhaps the most recognizable trope of hybridity and boundary crossing. But as I hope to show in my reading of *A Rabbi's Cat*, there are structural and normative reasons why the cat loses his capacity to speak (French in the original, English in the version I read here). *The Rabbi's Cat* is a meandering tale of a once-speaking cat who tells all about his host family—the rabbi and his daughter Zlabya—offering delightful stories of Algerian Jews and their sometimes comic, sometimes traumatic encounters with a colonizing French elite. The other characters that capture the cat's imagination—the rabbi's students and congregants; the nephew Rebibo, who leaves for Paris to make it on the big stage; and the rabbi's exotic cousin Malka—all fill out a story of continuity and change. If there is a narrative thread in this comic, it is the rabbi's fear that he will be dismissed and replaced by the man who captivates his daughter Zlabya. When he understands that they both can coexist together, he comes to appreciate other ways of being Jewish in the world. All this the cat narrates in sarcastic and mocking tones. But there really is no story here; unlike *Blankets*, I find little to distinguish a beginning and middle from an end. This is but one reason why the cat gains and then loses his ability to speak: the plot never goes anywhere because no one in this comic really leaves home. Here we discover a pluralism by convenience rather than by confrontation; it is a comforting pluralism in which everyone stays in place to live the familiar patterns of native culture.

Sfar's characters imagine these other worlds and sometimes even play within them (like the cat and the rabbi's nephew Rebibo), but they never fully inhabit these other cultural spheres. Unlike Craig in *Blankets*, they peek through but never actually yearn to stretch beyond the comforting borders of their familiar. The cat who speaks challenges these secure walls separating cultural and religious worlds, but he cannot remain in this liminal space. In the end he too must return to his feline world, satisfied and secure as the rabbi's now silent cat. Sfar pokes fun at many of these worlds, the cat's included, to reveal a kind of innocent and playful insularity. I want to look closely at the cultural stereotypes at play here and at the ways they never really engage or move beyond the frame. Although Sfar deploys them in a gentle, mocking tone, stereotypes in *The Rabbi's Cat* function to safeguard one's own cultural-religious worlds: other folks do these things (the stereotype reveals), and so we are just fine doing what we do here. This is all remarkably light and airy and makes for a good comic read, but it never takes seriously why someone like Craig might yearn to travel.

Each page of *The Rabbi's Cat* contains six square panels, all of the same type and dimension. Inside those frames we read of cats who can speak, daughters who desire to become fashionably French, and tough Jews who walk with lions. But the bounded frame remains ever present and constraining. This is a different kind of nativity than the one we encountered in *Blankets*. In *The Rabbi's Cat* the native is comforted with being-at-home, always, in a recognizable and reassuring pluralism. Characters simply never have to worry if the snow might, just this once, fly upward to unknown universes. Even the cat, in the very last frame of this novel, looks approvingly at his rabbi, who once again leads his congregation in prayer. The native might voyeuristically peek at other worlds, but she never yearns or is motivated to reside elsewhere.

The opening page of six panels introduces what will become central themes in *The Rabbi's Cat* and in my analysis of it. The cat narrates his story as the rabbi's pet, and he offers self-indulgent wisdom that appropriates the trope of chosenness: "Jewish people aren't crazy about dogs. A dog will bite you, chase you, bark. And Jews have been bitten, chased, and barked at for so long that, in the end, they prefer cats. Well, maybe not all Jews, but that's what my master says. I am the rabbi's cat. I don't disturb him when he reads."[12] This story takes place in Algeria in the early part of the twentieth century, and the yellows and reds in Sfar's images settle this community in the earthy textures so often associated with the Maghreb. Even the stylized script advances a more down-to-earth, relaxed atmosphere, as Algerians of all types, Jews, and many others walk the streets with a calming ease. Yet in the background to this contentment in cultural authenticity lies a clear hierarchy of value. Jews like cats more than dogs, and they do so because of their lachrymose view of history; they have been bitten by so many dogs over so many years that it seems reasonable that they would seek comfort in cats, who leave them alone to study. Here, Sfar's light tone, one that stylistically matches his font, playfully alludes to stereotypes of Jews and their history. Jews study, and have always wanted to, but dogs (the goyim) continually hound them and never let them be; they prefer the serene comforts of being home, under candlelight, with a book and scroll. The cat understands this, and so Jews (at least most of them) prefer the calm quiet of feline companionship. By placing these observations in the cat's voice, Sfar can play at how Jews appear to others. The cat serves as the translator (his linguistic knowledge reinforces his authority) who reveals what Jews really are from the inside. As we will see later, the cat's status is problematic, especially when he desires to be counted as a Jewish insider—and wishes to have a bar mitzvah. Yet already on this opening page the cat holds a privileged place; he is, after all, the rabbi's cat, and he can think, if not speak, in the English (originally French) language. The cat "talks" even before he swallows the house parrot, although after he swallows the parrot, others can actually hear a recognizable, linguistic voice in speech bubbles. The cat, then, speaks to *us* on this first page, offering readers access to this world of Algerian Jews.

But he is not a trustworthy narrator. He asserts self-congratulatory preferences (Jews enjoy cats more than dogs) and justifies them with questionable readings of history, but then he deflects responsibility for his unwarranted claims by demurring, "That's what my master says." Even more, the cat deceives. We learn this some pages later when he lies about his parrot meal, again evading responsibility. "Is it my fault if the parrot decided to split?" he says. "What can I tell you?" (*The Rabbi's Cat*, 8). But we are already aware of this scamming on the very first page when the cat, much like the hated dogs, will not leave his master alone. The rabbi strains to read the open page on which the cat sits—we see his exertion in his large white eyes as he stretches closer to the page, peering over the cat's tail as it casually hovers under the rabbi's nose. As for the cat, he is unmoved by his rabbi's work, and we have only to turn the page to see the cat wreak havoc with the rabbi's papers and then see the rabbi dragging his pet away in response as one would unwanted trash. This is clearly not a cat who leaves his rabbi alone. If we imagine a narrator as a kind of native informant, then our native is unreliable. His words might tell one story, but the images reveal something else. And although we hear a certain playful sarcasm in the cat's speech, we should wonder just how native this native cat really is.

All of this, I believe, reveals how Sfar deftly enshrouds concerns about the native within satirical speech to undermine notions of nativity. The soft yellow and red tones, together with the cursive script, suggest an opening into the rabbi's world. But instead we see and hear only what the cat reveals to us, and that is less the rabbi's world than it is the cat's perverse staging of it. As the title to this graphic novel advises, this is a story about the cat, about a cat who describes a world only he inhabits. There are indeed others in his world—the rabbi, the rabbi's daughter Zlabya, and Malka of the Lions—and the cat ventures off into unknown territory, but he narrates as one who does not see what lies directly in front of him ("I don't disturb him when he reads").

Sfar draws a world partially hidden to the cat such that his boastful story does not quite line up with the yellow and red tones of Algeria. The rabbi's cat is an insider only to his own world but not to the world of others.

This dynamic tension between text and image in *The Rabbi's Cat* opens a distinctive pluralism that rubs nicely with but not against the cat's solipsism. In an insightful article on notions of the sacred in *The Rabbi's Cat*, Leah Hochman explores how texts and images rarely interact with each other and how even the cat's narration stands aloof from his own speech. According to Hochman, Sfar presents "word and image not in dialogue but in competition with each other," and this bifurcation runs throughout the graphic novel: "As characters debate Jewish practice and mysticism, historicism and myth, the novel displays multiple, unconnected narratives (image, dialogue, narration) that appear on the page simultaneously."[13] These disjointed movements in stylistic form mirror the ethical orientation of Sfar's pluralism, in which multiculturalism is always in view but is rarely engaged directly or in reflective contrast to other orientations. And here the cat is not the exception but the rule: for the central as well as incidental characters in this graphic novel, other cultural worlds are closed even when glimpsed from afar.

Take this one of many examples in which the rabbi interacts with an anxious congregant. One morning, fearing the letters just received in the mail will bring only bad news, the rabbi sets out to an open café to relax, drink some coffee, and read these letters in quiet. He is, however, rudely dismissed by the waiter, who notes coolly that the restaurant serves neither Arabs nor Jews—multiculturalism in Algeria goes only so far, a sign that pluralism remains a distant ethical principle. The rabbi and his cat walk to an open square and drink from its water fountain, but they are soon accosted by "a Jew" named Birkat Hacohanim (the priestly blessing—the name itself of a well-known blessing). Having left the closed establishment for the open square in which "the sun belongs to everyone"—a direct response to the waiter's racial nationalism—the rabbi faces this question from his congregant: "My question is this: Ashkenazim [Jews from northern Europe] wait five hours before drinking milk after eating meat, while we Sephardim wait only three hours. Imagine, God forbid, that I had to eat with one of these Jews from the cold and I felt like having milk four hours after the beef stew or God knows what meat they serve in that Poland of theirs" (51). Note the mocking caricature of those northern Jews: they live in the cold, are far more strict than "we Sephardim" in the south, and probably eat strange and barely edible food. Although they are considered Jews, the Ashkenazim remain outsiders to this more parochial "we," and they seem distant and obscure, living in diasporic lands ("in that Poland of theirs"). The rabbi, perplexed that such a question would arise in Algeria, fails to understand the dilemma, and so Birkat Hacohanim makes his question clear: "Would I have to conform to this polar Jew's ways out of respect for him?" For this Jew, the "polar" one is barely living by Jewish law; Birkat Hacohanim maintains little respect for the Ashkenazi dietary practices but thinks he ought to be polite in the polar Jews' company. There are two cultural food practices in play: the Sephardi custom of waiting three hours to drink milk after a meat meal and the other custom of enduring five hours before dairy. To Birkat Hacohanim, that other dietary custom always remains other; he will politely "conform" to the Ashkenazi rule but only because he travels in a foreign land, and he will only meet the Ashkenazi custom halfway. One gets the sense that he would tiptoe lightly in that northern cold, returning as soon as possible to the comforts of his people.

Of course, Birkat Hacohanim will never travel north, and the rabbi already knows this. "Do you know any Ashkenazim, Birkat Hacohanim?" the rabbi asks. When the negative answer arrives as expected, the rabbi reasonably wonders, "So why do you ask the question?" Sfar certainly pokes fun here at the rabbinic game of *pilpul*—often extended and tortuous legal disputes among rabbis that may have little relation to worldly experiences. Such queries, which might be fascinating for legal theorists, are altogether arcane for practical purposes. In perhaps the most outlandish satire in this comic, the cat himself appropriates the strategy of *pilpul* to outflank and dispute the rabbi's own rabbi when discussing the nature of God (11–18). But the question is only speculative, because Birkat Hacohanim will never encounter these polar Jews; he stays only within his circle of "we Sephardim." The possibility of a cultural and religious conflict with these Jews from Poland is simply that—a concept of the other that never practically engages or critically challenges Birkat Hacohanim's dietary practices. He knows there are other ways of doing Jewish, but he ridicules these differences rather than appreciating the diversity they signify. His is a closed nativity in which others remain outsiders to his local cultural practices. Pluralism remains, but it remains as a picturesque ideal that one never really encounters. Again, this explains why each page in *The Rabbi's Cat* produces six panels. Structurally, nothing changes, even when Arabs, Jews, polar Jews, and "we" Jews emerge within the frames to disrupt this universal singularity. There is no point in worrying about how they eat if we do not and will not know any of them. Let the Ashkenazim stay in the north in their Poland; we Sephardi Jews will continue to wait three hours to eat dairy after a meat meal. And if we do travel north, let us not completely abandon our ways but respectfully adopt theirs up to a point so that we do not fully justify "God knows what" kind of cultural practice. Such a nativity lacks a basic curiosity for cultural difference.

When these Algerian Sephardim do encounter other cultural worlds, those foreign landscapes are still recognizably their own. Sfar's portrait of Malka of the Lions articulates this kind of safe pluralism beautifully. The rabbi's cousin is legendary as a nomadic wanderer who "only likes women of the desert" (53). Malka boasts of his storied pasts in which he saves women from the ferocious lion, but this is all masculine bluster to earn a living; the lion plays along as Malka's trustworthy sidekick, and Malka himself is a devoted husband who, we learn in the second volume to *The Rabbi's Cat*, has grown weary and worn as he ages, mostly ungraciously. But to the young women, he conjures up a romantic escape. Still, their passions are tempered by a desire to become good wives rather than adventurous travelers. These young women are not alone in their fantasy of Malka as the mysterious, strong, attractive oriental Jewish male with gun and lion in tow. The waiter who had earlier dismissed the rabbi from his café now dutifully takes Malka's order, terrified of the gun and lion but also of Malka himself, who "has a particular way of looking at you that makes you not want to say no to him" (70). Here is a tough Jew—not a polar one but one who still travels within the rabbi's family. They speak to each other as loving cousins who rarely have the pleasure of each other's company. The rabbi confesses to his cousin about fears of being replaced as communal rabbi by a "pale-faced rabbi" with "horrible features like freckles and Polish teeth. He'll smell like a corpse and conduct prayers in my place" (71). Like Birkat Hacohanim, the rabbi too harbors cultural stereotypes of northern European Jews. Malka, playing his role to perfection, responds immediately with, "If that's so, I'll cut his throat myself."

Although with his lion and gun he might look the part, Malka is a pussy cat. He carries a big stick, but he will not use it. He cares deeply about his family, and he knows and even participates in the Sephardi Jewish customs. Although he lives an exotic and wandering life, Malka is at home in the rabbi's house because he is, in truth, one of them. He may not wait for three hours to drink his milk after catching a wild animal for dinner, but he will say prayers over the deceased and defend the rabbi's daughter when she wishes to marry the Parisian rabbi. This is a safe pluralism because Malka never disrupts the cultural continuity and authentic sensibilities of the rabbi's house and home. Malka plays at adventure, but he is not adventurous. He is the alluring other who lives by his own rules but allows others to live by theirs.

This is precisely how Sfar paints the relation between the Jewish rabbi and the Muslim sheikh singer. They too, as it turns out, are related and often meet up as they visit their saint's grave (see fig. 50). The cat has a hard time with this, wishing to acknowledge the saint as a Jew rather than an Arab "called Sfar" (83), but the sheikh and rabbi share the very same ancestor. They maintain a spiritual bond, and the rabbi wishes they could simply "live in a cave and mind our own business. I bring my books, you bring your songs" (85). Lyrics and texts, sound and sight—they all coexist together without the anxiety of mixing and disrupting boundaries. The rabbi calls the Muslim singer his brother, and they dance and pray together, "one facing Jerusalem, and the other Mecca," as the rabbi learns he has passed his French language exam and so can stay on as communal rabbi. He will not be replaced by a smelly Jew from the north. This is a safe pluralism in which two cultures meet and interact but do not challenge or explore: "The sheikh took his aud and lent the rabbi a tarbuka drum and they danced and sang and laughed, and they couldn't have been more drunk if they'd been drinking" (87). This kind of pluralism works when nothing is demanded or required: the sheikh can sing his songs and pray to Mecca, and the rabbi can read his books, borrow his friend's drum, and sing joyously as he prays to Jerusalem. I do not know if facing Jerusalem means that one's back is to Mecca, but this is how Sfar imagines and draws this scene, and it fits this gentle pluralism. The rabbi and sheikh peacefully coexist and even enjoy each other's company, but they do not face one another. That kind of stance would require a more disruptive and energetic moral imagination.

A disruptive pluralism is one in which people take other cultural or religious practices seriously enough to question and reposition their own. It is one in which people linger in the ways discussed in the previous chapter and situate themselves in the liminal space that Robert Orsi calls an "in-between orientation."[14] In the end, they may very well decline these other modes of being human, but the live possibility remains, even if it is not robust enough to adopt as one's own. But this disruptive pluralism is not the one encountered in *The Rabbi's Cat*. Instead, we discover a softer, gentler pluralism that accepts difference at a safe distance. The rabbi and sheikh sing and dance together, but each prays to his holy land by turning away from the other. Birkat Hacohanim, for his part, imagines how he would act in the northern lands, but he will never travel there to face a practice he mocks from the safety of his familiar. The cat too dismisses a more complicated history when he argues with the sheikh's donkey about the saint's true religious heritage; he cannot envision a Sfar who is not also a Jew (and so, in the cat's imaginary, not an Arab). I noted that Sfar employs yellows and reds to evoke the Maghreb sensibility, but Sfar transforms those earthy colors into shades of blue when he shows the rabbi and sheikh dancing, praying, and singing. The reader has come across a lighter form of these blues only once before, in an earlier dream sequence. Although the blue tones here with the rabbi and sheikh evoke the nighttime darkness, the tinted allusion to that previous dreamscape is a tantalizing reminder of this playful and carefree pluralism. Like dreams, it dances and floats above reality. Many of our dreams, however, arise from anxieties felt but not fully recognized. In this sense, anxiety dreams touch something real, and they can often be revelatory. If this safe pluralism is more dreamlike than real, what anxieties does it expose? How does Sfar portray cultural and religious unease?

Let us return to Birkat Hacohanim, our poor Algerian Jew obsessed with cultural practices he will never encounter in his lifetime. When the rabbi asks "So why do you ask the question?" he is really inquiring about cultural and religious anxiety: Why the restlessness, why the disquiet over something so

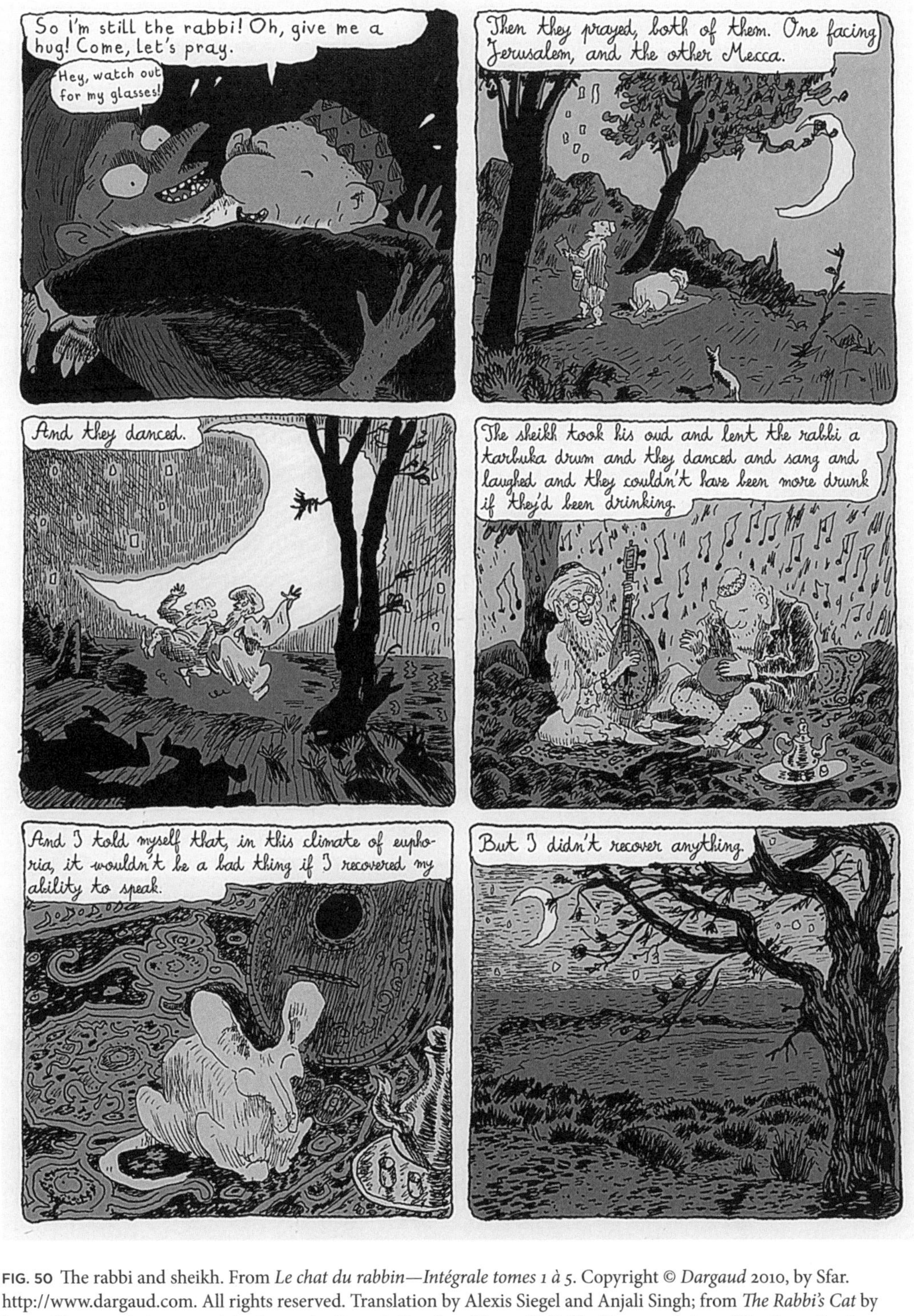

So I'm still the rabbi! Oh, give me a hug! Come, let's pray.
Hey, watch out for my glasses!
Then they prayed, both of them. One facing Jerusalem, and the other Mecca.
And they danced.
The sheikh took his oud and lent the rabbi a tarbuka drum and they danced and sang and laughed and they couldn't have been more drunk if they'd been drinking.
And I told myself that, in this climate of euphoria, it wouldn't be a bad thing if I recovered my ability to speak.
But I didn't recover anything.

FIG. 50 The rabbi and sheikh. From *Le chat du rabbin—Intégrale tomes 1 à 5*. Copyright © *Dargaud* 2010, by Sfar. http://www.dargaud.com. All rights reserved. Translation by Alexis Siegel and Anjali Singh; from *The Rabbi's Cat* by Joann Sfar, translation copyright © 2005 by Penguin Random House LLC. Used by permission of Pantheon Books, an imprint of the Knopf Doubleday Publishing Group, a division of Penguin Random House LLC. All rights reserved.

extraneous and remote? Birkat Hacohanim is clearly bothered by another Jewish practice that is not his own, but he can alleviate his anxiety only by doing what all the characters in *The Rabbi's Cat* do when confronted by otherness: mock through stereotype. For Birkat Hacohanim and the rabbi, northern Jews hail from some distant, cold land, and they both conjure up the Ashkenazi as filthy and uncivilized. When the rabbi travels with his daughter and her young husband back to France, he "bundles up" with scarves and coats, imagining a frigid climate. Sfar calls this chapter "Exodus," and this biblical title nicely captures how the rabbi understands his predicament as he lashes out at his son-in-law: "Do you think this is making me happy, this exodus? Do you imagine I'm pleased to see my daughter's husband take her to the land of Eskimos?" (104). When looking out at the Seine River, the rabbi can feel only pity for the "poor things, they don't even have the sea" (102–3). The stereotyping works to disempower and delegitimize the other. Jews from the north are boorish; Paris is cold, sad, and diasporic to the Algerian homeland. The rabbi's cat does not tell the tale of the colonized returning the gaze to the colonizer, even though the tortuous history between France and Algeria remains steadily in the background of this story. Instead, this story illustrates a native in a foreign land: the rabbi cries on the boat to Paris because "we're leaving Algeria," and he brings a heavy suitcase of books to continually drag him back to his familiar rituals and study (101). Even when these characters leave home they never *really* leave home. The other is always the imagined, stereotyped other, not the confronted, face-to-face other.

Russell McCutcheon has criticized Orsi on just this point: Orsi's others are always the safe others, those attractive foreigners we wish to face and engage. But what about those more violent, deadly, and downright evil others we must respond to or risk the security of our own lives?[15] Do they deserve the same sort of abiding respect and concern? Orsi, in my reading, has a thoughtful response to this critique, but McCutcheon helpfully raises the issue here between imagined and real others: some others appear more attractive and more like acceptable others. In *The Rabbi's Cat*, the others arrive as those exotic yet safe others of our imagination.

This is as true for Birkat Hacohanim as it is for the rabbi, the rabbi's cat, and indeed for all of Sfar's characters in this graphic novel. When Zlabya boasts to her girlfriends about Malka's legendary escapades, she tells how he entered a desert tent to save a frightened woman from the lion. That woman, claims Zlabya, stood completely naked, but this comes as no surprise to her friend, who says, "Non-Jewish women are always naked."

"Totally naked?" asks Zlabya.

"Yes, and covered in soap," answers her friend (55).

Now I see the humor in this, and I will not deny that Jews often think of non-Jewish women in this way. But to stereotype others like this is to mock them into submission. They no longer threaten—their beauty, charm, and desirable perfumes repel rather than attract the male, who, in this story, remains the object of their desire. Deploying stereotypes as an act of ridicule only denies and suppresses a felt vulnerability. Zlabya and her girlfriends might feel superior in their decency and natural scents, but when the rabbi's cat wishes to inform his mistress of what really happened in that tent, Zlabya shuts him up (56). When stereotypes function as derisive commentary, they silence others and fashion dreamscapes at a safe distance. The desire to recognize the unfamiliar, to see the beauty of the Seine River, or even to respectfully consider the culinary practices of others fades from view as stereotypes alienate and often dehumanize the foreign; indeed, they help create the foreign as that which must remain forever external and remote. In *The Rabbi's Cat*, stereotypes work to establish boastful insiders and silenced, distanced, and nonthreatening outsiders.

As declawed outsiders, they reveal the anxiety of the native informant. That anxiety, I am arguing here, arises from the native fear of difference; if France is not completely other to the rabbi's Algeria, if Polish Jews are not uncivilized compared to the Sephardim, and if non-Jewish women are not indecent when measured against the natural beauty of Jewish women, then perhaps the native has no ground to claim a privileged status of authentic being. When Narayan asks, How native must a native anthropologist be?, the answer here is: native enough to establish a privileged difference. The characters in *The Rabbi's Cat* enact that privilege through stereotypical portrayals of others who threaten their native existence. This kind of othering never gives that in-between orientation a chance to expose uncomfortable affinities; indeed, it denies those affinities by disembodying others as inhuman. And this is Orsi's response to McCutcheon: those others, even the most violent ones, remain human others, and appeals to a privileged status of authority, rationalism, or native humanism violate that common humanity. Although the stereotypes in *The Rabbi's Cat* are far less cruel and are often amusing, they still demean others in order to vindicate native superiority. Mocking goyish women as voracious harlots serves to justify the more obedient, submissive, and dignified Jewish lady. Although perhaps she is not as savory or exotic, she tempts by being coy, natural, and supportive. Northern "polar" Ashkenazim, for both Birkat Hacohanim and the rabbi, are barely human in their filth and stench. It is not merely that their ways are not our ways; it is, instead, that we should harbor disdain for their cultural and religious practices. Stereotype as parody reveals the anxiety of dislocation; the native fears rather than lingers with an imaginative ethic of disruptive pluralism.

The nativist logic captured here exposes the allure of cultural authenticity as a returning home to the safety of the singular and the familiar. Stereotypes work to avoid this anxiety of difference by conjuring a safe pluralism in which others never compete for my allegiance and recognition—they eat "God knows what meat" up there in the north. Birkat Hacohanim will never touch that meat, and he will certainly not smell it like Kamala Khan does, but more importantly, he doesn't have to. It's enough to mock others to better justify and authorize his own familiar practices. Sfar empowers his characters to make light of these others, and he clearly has fun doing so. But this is serious play, one that forbids the in-between orientation of boundary crossing. The cat learns to speak, but he also loses that ability as soon as he takes God's name in vain. There are some borders you simply do not cross.

Sfar's characters don't just stereotype others in ways that establish strong, uncrossable borders; these characters also embody those stereotypes, and none more so than the rabbi's nephew Rebibo. When the rabbi is in Paris with his daughter Zlabya to meet his son-in-law's parents, he also wishes to see his nephew Rebibo, who the rabbi imagines as a famous stage singer of Sephardic heritage. Yet when he finally catches up with his nephew, Rebibo has given up on all that. I will return later to the restaurant scene in which the rabbi calls Rebibo to pay for his meal (on Shabbat, no less). I want to highlight at this point the discrepancy between the Rebibo with the singing career after three years in Paris and the Rebibo who lives in the Rabbi's imagination. Rebibo answered the rabbi's call because he works on Shabbat—it is one of the few days with a big turnout, he tells his uncle. Taken aback, the rabbi explains that he knows storekeepers who close their shops on Saturday but make up their business twofold the rest of the week. Rebibo has no time for this, telling him, "Your Jew doesn't work in music, Uncle" (119). This banter continues as Rebibo and the rabbi walk the streets of Paris and ends when the rabbi finally confronts his nephew as street performer. Rebibo changes into his work clothes—the costume of a dancing, singing Arab from Algeria with a shoeshine box under his arm. He sings for his crowd, making a fool of himself as he turns shining shoes into sexual parody:

This pretty lady she came up you see. She said, "Oh, you polish with so much energy. I'll give you more money, shine something else for me." Back and forth, back and forth, Algerian-style. For her I went the extra mile. Ah, she liked the result, let me tell you. The little Parisian lady gave me plenty to do. But I did it too much, my brush is all bent. Can't polish no more, now my money's spent. I can't work for no pretty French lady—yeah, I'll just have to go back to Algeria. (121)

The crowd adores Rebibo's act, but as the cat tells it, "My master is in shock" (122). The rabbi laments that Rebibo must play the Arab fool, and Rebibo's retort works as commentary on the role of stereotypes in *The Rabbi's Cat*: "Because to play a Jew you have to have a Polish accent, and I don't know how to do it. Playing a North African Jew just doesn't work, people aren't interested, it's too complicated for them. The public, Uncle, doesn't like things that are complicated" (122). For this public, Jews hail from Poland, not North Africa, and they speak with Polish accents. To suggest otherwise—to engage in a disruptive rather than a safe pluralism—would be to complicate and thus undercut the affirming stereotypes in play. This might be good ethics, but it is bad business—a reality confirmed when the rabbi and Rebibo audition together for a stage act but are rejected out of hand by a producer who hires Rebibo to do more Arabian shoe tunes (131–33). Rebibo must play the stereotypical game of the familiar, the recognizable, and the farcical. But even as Rebibo inhabits that humiliating role at work, it comes to define his personal life as well. Madly in love with a Catholic singer, he knows she is "banging half of Paris in addition to me. So when she doesn't come home at night I get drunk and if it goes on much longer I'll end up blowing my brains out" (124). Demeaned at work and at home, Rebibo is not even around when his Catholic singer returns home, completely drunk herself, and collapses on the plush chair.

Rebibo cannot break out of this burlesque parody as he plays in and lives caricatures of degradation. He never made it big in Paris; he became the fool others imagine him to be. The rabbi also ventures into the life he imagines others experience, but he does so as Jewish voyeur into the goyish world. In some ways he remains the foil to his nephew Rebibo, who has come to mimic the stereotype he plays. The rabbi too plays at being other, but he can and certainly will return to the warmth of his familiar customs in Algeria. This sense of slumming it, in which the rabbi tastes the allure of a world he will never inhabit, is how I read the restaurant scene that I alluded to earlier, in which the rabbi must call his nephew to foot the bill. On a Friday night, unable to sleep comfortably on the hard wooden benches of a local church (he refuses to stay at his son-in-law's house because the parents do not observe the Sabbath), the rabbi heads out to an elegant restaurant to eat a dinner he cannot afford. He orders what he considers to be "the least kosher meal in the universe," in which the food stands for everything forbidden: "Do you have ham? And blood sausage? That thing made with pig's blood you serve that to your customers?" When the waiter approves, the rabbi continues: "So give me some ham, some blood sausage, snails, seafood, and swordfish, which is a fish without scales, and oysters—and please check that they're really alive. And a glass of milk with the ham. And a good wine named after a church or a Virgin Mary" (116). This is less a meal than a hardened protest, one that hearkens back to Frimme Hersh's brash anger at his God in Eisner's *A Contract with God*. The rabbi ceremoniously breaks this contract, but he cannot enjoy his trespass. As he digs in, he speaks to his God: "Tell me that I've deprived myself of these foods for sixty years and that it served some kind of purpose. Tell me you'll be sad if I break your Law" (see fig. 51). The rabbi's God, like Frimme's, remains silent, and looking forlorn and beaten, the rabbi admits, "Just this once, I'll have eaten all this, Lord. Tomorrow I'll go back to fearing you" (117). This is not altogether true: the rabbi still fears his God (he even offers a blessing over his nonkosher meal), because even in this decisive moment of interchange he never crosses over. As a voyeur he peeks over the edge, but he remains tethered to the world he knows. He cannot become what he imagines others to be. He is a native in a foreign land.

When the rabbi finally returns to Algeria, he bathes in familiar surroundings that confirm his recognizable practices as authentic. I find this closing scene both moving and troubling, for it at once suggests the comforts of heritage together with the easy pluralism that marks this graphic novel as morally soothing. Before leaving Paris, the rabbi does meet with his son-in-law's father, who, as a self-proclaimed Westerner, cheats on his wife, never steps foot in a synagogue, and smokes on the Sabbath (137–38). Rather than reacting with disdain, the rabbi comes to respect his son-in-law's father, and he tells this story to his congregants back home: "Dear friends, I met a Jew who ate pork all the time. And on Shabbat, he smoked. And he never prayed. Kahal Hakadosh [Holy community], I looked at him and I thought, you don't respect the Torah, which is the instruction manual of existence. You don't know it, but you must be less happy than me. I looked at him carefully, and quite honestly, I don't think he lived less well than I do" (142). For most of *The Rabbi's Cat*, Sfar portrays characters who demean others, but here we have a glimpse at what lingering in that in-between space might look like. Rather than dismiss those others as foreign and exotic, the rabbi turns to his own practices and wonders aloud, "If we can be happy without respecting the Torah, why should we exhaust ourselves to apply all these precepts that make life so complicated?" Good question, his congregants admit, "Come on, Abraham, tell us why, we're waiting." This is the moment when a safe pluralism could become disruptive; it could move the rabbi and these Algerian Jews to reconsider their own practices in the light of other, equally good habits and ideals. Even were this community to reaffirm their Torah, they would engage in a more vibrant, reflective practice in conversation with others.

But this is not what happens in *The Rabbi's Cat*. Rabbi Abraham has no answer to his Jewish brethren. "Well, the truth is, I don't know," he admits. And then, in a radical closure to other ways of living a good life, he shows that he cares only for the native simplicity of accepted practice: "Come on, let's do the kiddush, because if you're late for dinner your wives will chew me out" (142) (see fig. 52). All this reflects the safe pluralism that travels throughout *The Rabbi's Cat*: let their ways be theirs because we have ours, and the one never challenges to disrupt the other. As the rabbi deflates the enormity of this confrontation with his colloquial "Come on," his cat looks down approvingly from the upper balcony (actually, I think he is purring contentedly with his eyes closed). All remains as it should be, with the rabbi blessing the wine and

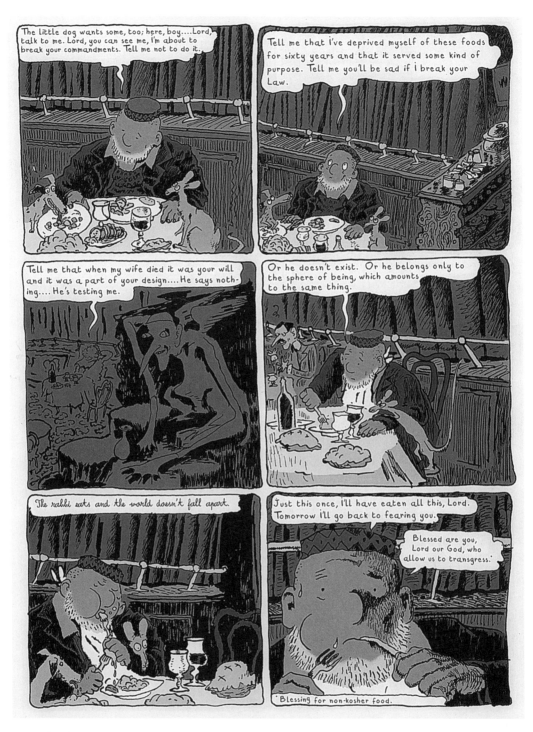

FIG. 51 The rabbi eats nonkosher meal. From *Le chat du rabbin—Intégrale tomes 1 à 5*. Copyright © *Dargaud* 2010, by Sfar. http://www.dargaud.com. All rights reserved. Translation by Alexis Siegel and Anjali Singh; from *The Rabbi's Cat* by Joann Sfar, translation copyright © 2005 by Penguin Random House LLC. Used by permission of Pantheon Books, an imprint of the Knopf Doubleday Publishing Group, a division of Penguin Random House LLC. All rights reserved.

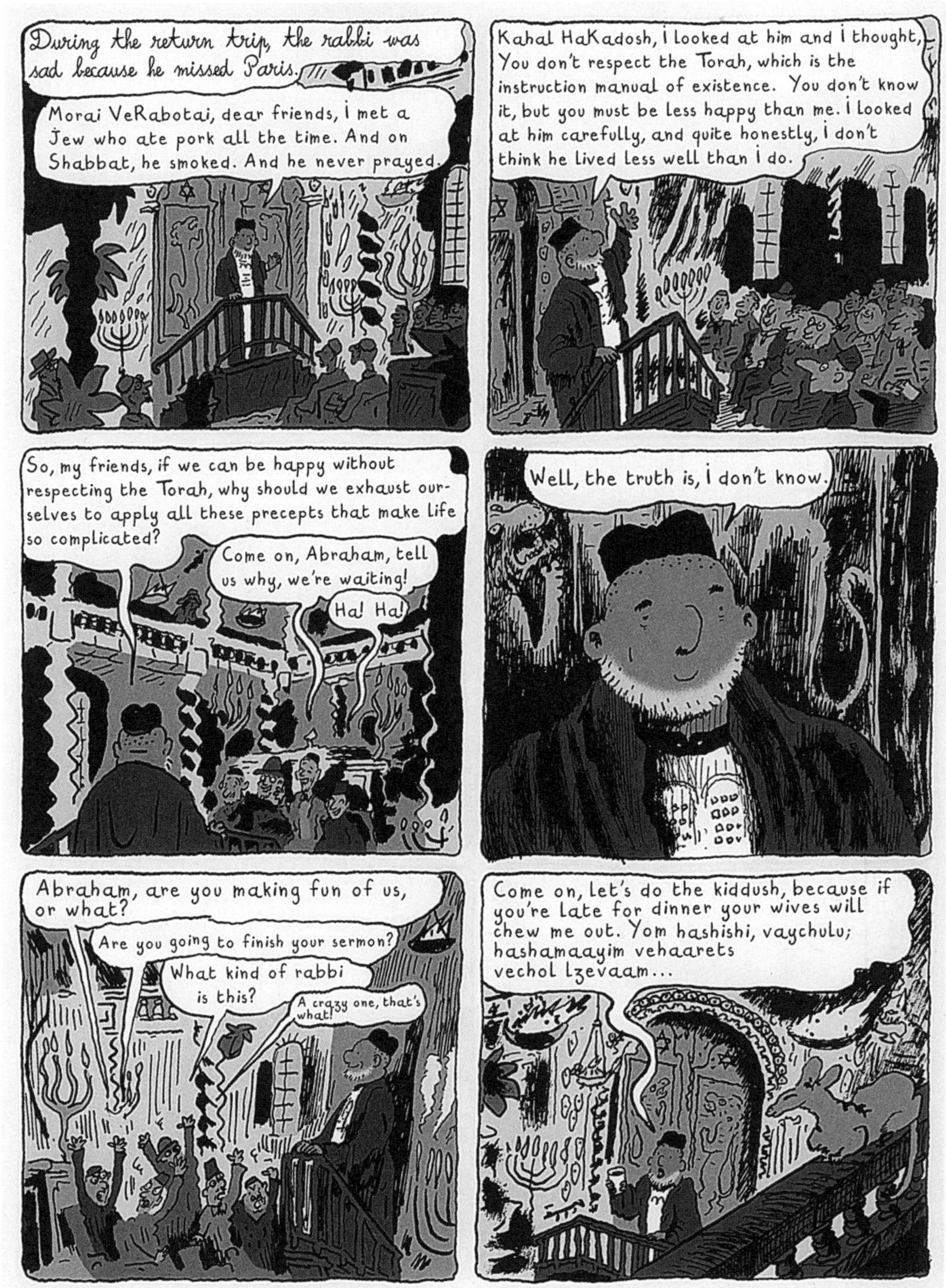
During the return trip, the rabbi was sad because he missed Paris.
Morai VeRabotai, dear friends, I met a Jew who ate pork all the time. And on Shabbat, he smoked. And he never prayed.
Kahal HaKadosh, I looked at him and I thought, You don't respect the Torah, which is the instruction manual of existence. You don't know it, but you must be less happy than me. I looked at him carefully, and quite honestly, I don't think he lived less well than I do.
So, my friends, if we can be happy without respecting the Torah, why should we exhaust ourselves to apply all these precepts that make life so complicated?
Come on, Abraham, tell us why, we're waiting!
Ha! Ha!
Well, the truth is, I don't know.
Abraham, are you making fun of us, or what?
Are you going to finish your sermon?
What kind of rabbi is this?
A crazy one, that's what!
Come on, let's do the kiddush, because if you're late for dinner your wives will chew me out. Yom hashishi, vaychulu; hashamaayim vehaarets vechol lzevaam...

FIG. 52 The rabbi and his congregation. From *Le chat du rabbin—Intégrale tomes 1 à 5*. Copyright © *Dargaud* 2010, by Sfar. http://www.dargaud.com. All rights reserved. Translation by Alexis Siegel and Anjali Singh; from *The Rabbi's Cat* by Joann Sfar, translation copyright © 2005 by Penguin Random House LLC. Used by permission of Pantheon Books, an imprint of the Knopf Doubleday Publishing Group, a division of Penguin Random House LLC. All rights reserved.

the cat apparently blessing the rabbi. It is a tranquil, cozy picture of the native in authentic ritual practice. The rabbi stays home because he will not venture out to leave his familiar.

Conclusion

Kirin Narayan challenges these images in *The Rabbi's Cat* by situating identities in complex and shifting relationships. She writes of "enacting hybridity" and the ways that anthropologists must "acknowledge our shared presence in the cultural worlds that we describe."[16] Most of us belong to multiple entangled societies, and we often move as participants in cultures not of our own making. This is a powerful account of identities in exchange, in which informants can turn on their interviewers and subject them to critique and scrutiny (as Narayan's informant, Swamiji, did to her). Narayan shows how telling stories can expose these shifting perspectives and relational positionalities, and I think she is right that persons "have many strands of identification available, strands that may be tugged into the open or stuffed out of sight."[17] She rejects appeals to the native as blatant and problematic claims to authenticity, and she dismisses threatening postures that silence others by relocating them to the outside, beyond pure knowledge and experiential truth. The title of her paper announces her polemic as hardened rhetoric: "How Native Is a 'Native' Anthropologist?" Never enough, one can hear Narayan contend, because it suggests a stable, fixed objectivity that forever recedes from view. The point is not to become native but to recognize hybrid forms of identity in relation. Identity is neither what one achieves nor what one owns; it is a continuing process of being in relation, and even in opposition, to others and to oneself.

In her lecture at the Graduate Theological Union (GTU) Convocation, Ann Taves appropriates Narayan's critique that "a fixed distinction between 'native' and 'non-native' anthropologists is simply unworkable." Taves recognizes how faculty at theological schools (such as GTU) "routinely move back and forth between the worlds of theological education and the secular academy" and find themselves enacting hybridity in the very ways Narayan describes in her article. With Narayan's critique as a model, Taves maps out a geography of shifting identities by "adopting a performance metaphor that carries with it the idea of movement between roles that can be learned or cultivated." She adopts Thomas Tweed's theory of crossing and dwelling to help rethink Narayan's attunement to selves in motion.[18] All this puts her in a position to resituate Orsi's appeal to those in-between orientations: "In shifting from a spatial to a performance metaphor, I want to suggest that the in-between 'place' described by Orsi and others is better understood as a role that can be cultivated than a location or even a movement, through [*sic*] the role may involve cultivating the ability to move across boundaries or the ability to hold different perspectives in tension."[19] Narayan attempted to rethink anthropological discourse as a narrative about hybridity and shifting relations; Taves channels that story into a cultivated role of boundary crossings. We do not inhabit a place, Taves warns, but rather advance a series of migrations. The role of the anthropologist, theologian, or any self is to take on this diasporic challenge of dislocation.

Joann Sfar's *The Rabbi's Cat* shows us how a soothing pluralism, in which alternative worlds are sequestered within clear, demarcated, bordered panels, often fails to cultivate the hybrid selves in motion that Narayan and Taves imagine. But Craig Thompson's *Blankets* reveals the weight of native experiences and traumas, such that moving across boundaries is sometimes a supernatural act of transgression—like snow rising upward beyond the panel borders. Taves and Narayan both suggest that living in this in-between space of hybridity or role reversal is a more authentic mode of human personhood. As such, theirs is both a descriptive and normative claim about how we should live in a world of shifting boundaries and perspectives of increasing cultural complexity. Sfar illustrates the pleasures of the familiar, but this requires the protection that comes from caricaturing others so that their foreign ways remain so. *The Rabbi's Cat* offers but one response to the modern complexity imagined by Taves and Narayan: return home to the splendors of the routine, to the commonplace, to the well traveled. The rabbi and his cat engender a rather innocent view of the familiar, but there are also more sinister modes of staking claim to the native, especially when race and nation become the objects of our affection. We see this in the waiter's quick dismissal of the rabbi in the café, but we recognize this too in our current political times.

I believe *Blankets* has the last word here, because this comic gestures toward worlds beyond our capacity to inhabit them. Unlike Sfar's characters, who invoke stereotypes to subdue and alienate those worlds, Craig yearns for their strangeness, even as, or perhaps because, they are forever beyond his reach. Thompson grounds his pluralism in a more chastised vision of self-cultivation, for there are some scars that never recede from view. Boundary crossing does not always mean leaving home; the rabbi Abraham, even when eating the most nonkosher of meals, could not reject his Jewish God or even enjoy playing the role of the *goy*. He was stuck in between. To be sure, he did not linger there, but he understood Thomas Tweed's point that dwelling is as much a human need as crossing. For Craig in *Blankets*, works of art open imaginative, erotic worlds that gesture to possible erasures of past traumas, even if they could never wholly cover the stain. This, I think, is the ethical challenge of the native: how to accept the scarring of embodiment as the inevitable, exposed mark to those other worlds—beyond the bordered panels—that arrive to disrupt our familiar.

CHAPTER 5

Graphic Violence and the Religious Self

In 1978, the popular Hindu comic series *Amar Chitra Katha* published *Tales of Durga*—a series of three short comics based on a sixth-century Sanskrit text. The series explored the martial features and warrior traditions of this Hindu goddess.[1] In the first of these comics, Mahisha (the villain in this story) seeks immortality, and he makes a pact with Lord Brahma that he will die only "at the hands of a woman" (*Tales of Durga*, 2). As he attacks the Devas and their god/king Indra in heaven, he quickly wins the battle and ascends to Indra's throne. The Devas seek justice from Lord Shiva, and together with Lords Vishnu and Brahma they produce an "intense light" to form Durga, "a female form with a thousand arms" (6). She races to confront Mahisha with "a blood-curdling roar," and her response to Mahisha's quick dismissal of "a mere female" foreshadows his doom: "No! I am no mere female! I have come to fulfil [*sic*] Brahma's boon. *You* wanted to die at the hands of a woman, didn't you?" (9). As their intense battle rages over some six comic pages in bright reds, yellows, and blues, Durga shows both her martial skill and her brutal savagery. Karline McLain, who explored this particular comic in her insightful *India's Immortal Comic Books*, describes the final scene in this way:

"Here our heroine leaps upon the charging buffalo's back [Mahisha], stabs him with her trident, and decapitates him with her sword, all while retaining a serene half-smile."[2] Blood spills from the buffalo's neck as Mahisha's human head lies to the side, and the Devas bow in salute to Durga as the "upholder of virtue." It is a comic scene of triumph, but it is also grotesque and violent.

What does this representation of religious violence do for imagining virtue and the moral self? How should we honor spiritual beings who enjoy and enact violence? What does it mean to *see* this violence in religious comics? These are a few of the questions I wish to explore in this chapter as I look at English-language comics that engage in violent representations of religious communities, worlds, and selves. This graphic portrayal of violence has been a stubborn feature of the American comic tradition, and although these images have circulated for some time, a critical turning point occurred in 1954, when a conflation of three interrelated events irrevocably changed the comic industry: (1) postwar America increasingly worried that comics were "harmful to impressionable people," a view championed by Frederic Wertham's influential *Seduction of the Innocent* (1954); (2) Congress held a two-day hearing on comic violence in April 1954, which Senator Robert Hendrickson described in chilling terms: "Today and tomorrow the United States Subcommittee on Investigating Juvenile Delinquency, of which I am the chairman, is going into the problem of horror and crime comic books"; and (3) in reactive response to this public and political pressure, "a comics-industry trade group" known as the Comics Magazine Association of America (CMAA) established its own Comics Code in September 1954 in order to self-regulate violent images in American comics.[3] The more horrific and creative energies of the comic industry were channeled underground by this concern for gratuitous violence, and those comics seeking broader acceptance were now appealing directly to middle-class consumer tastes. This did not mean, however, that violent images, especially religious ones, disappeared altogether, even if the anxiety over those images still lingered. Although *Tales of Durga* had, according to McLain, softened and "sanitized" Durga's violent nature when compared to traditional Sanskrit sources, it still marketed violence for a Hindu diasporic community—many of whom now lived in America—increasingly uneasy with graphic religious bloodshed. Referring to the goddess Kali, whose epic, savage battles are the focus of the second and third comics in *Tales of Durga*, McLain notes how "many modern middle-class Hindus—not to mention non-Hindus in India—are uncomfortable with the extreme martial nature of the Goddess."[4] The only connection that many Hindu Indians living in America had to the Sanskrit tradition came through the *Amar Chitra Katha* series—a series directly marketed to this diasporic group. But it is not just the "extreme martial nature" that disturbed some Americans in the 1950s or those readers of *Tales of Durga* in the 1970s. One of the scriptwriters interviewed by

McLain suggests a different kind of discomfort shared by comic readers: "To be honest, at that point of time I was uncomfortable with this theme. I'm not a worshipper of Mother Goddess, who to me appeared bloodthirsty."[5] It's not just the violence but the lust and enjoyment of it. Durga's half-smile as she decapitates Mahisha signals a desire to violate others, and even an indulgent pleasure in doing so.

Religion and violence have long been the focus of ritual studies on sacrifice[6] and of psychological accounts of formation, popularized by Freud, that return us to a primordial, oedipal state of desire and murder. One need not work through *The Oxford Handbook of Religion and Violence* (2013) to know just how widespread and how deep this relationship is.[7] I would like to focus, however, on a particular mode of religious violence, one that takes up Cynthia Baker's provocative account of defining others in the Jewish and Christian traditions. In her arresting book *Jew*, Baker argues that Christians used this term in order to define the other to their emerging sense of self-identity: "The most persistent meanings and force of the term *Jew(s)* derive, then, from an antique Christian worldview in which *the Jews* functions foundationally as a kind of originary and constitutional alterity, or otherness. *The Jews* serves as the alpha to the Christian omega." Note the violent borders of identity in Baker's critical appraisal of Christian identity politics in her claim that: "*Jew* is Christian cultures' signifier for the fraught, debased, material primordiality *out of which* spiritual and moral stature must *arise, from which* it may *free itself*, and *back to which* it is always in danger of *falling* (a threat or condition commonly labeled 'Judaizing'). Hence, *Jew(s)* becomes a key element in formulations of Christian identity through narratives of origin, aspiration, and liberation, as well as of abjection, rejection, and otherness."[8] In Baker's reading, Christians must arise, liberate, and free themselves from an other who threatens their identity as Christians. But this violent portrayal of religious selves is more than an us/them duality of boundary maintenance; it is a continual fear and threat of reversals, one that constitutes the self as violent. This is what we see in *Tales of Durga*: a recurring desire to violate others in order to found and secure the religious self. Durga must continually battle and decapitate Mahisha, both in the comic images and in the Hindu moral imagination. It is a scene that readers of these comics return to again and again. This repetition compulsion, to return to Freud, vivifies those images for Hindu and non-Hindu readers alike. And this is how and why religious comic violence challenges the moral imagination.

I take up this challenge by looking at three comics that traffic in religious violence: Jack Chick tracts of the last thirty years, Douglas Rushkoff's *Testament: Akedah* (2006), and Grant Morrison's "The Coyote Gospel" (1989), the fifth volume in his *Animal Man* series. All three comics begin with a foundational moment of religious violence, but they treat this brutality in distinct ways. For the evangelical Chick cartoons, the other is violence: savage brutality marks the core of religious others, even as peace and love inform the Christian self. In Rushkoff's dazzling *Akedah* comic, part of his larger *Testament* series, we are all caught up in a religious, violent war enacted in every generation by gods and humans alike. We must take on this violence in order to recognize powers that dehumanize us, and so we return to our authentic, liberated selves. In Morrison's award-winning *Animal Man #5*, "The Coyote Gospel," we are embodied violence: it is both inescapable and productive of self-formation. By engaging these three texts in this order, we move from violence beyond the self to define the other (Chick), to violence that enraptures all of us (Rushkoff), to violence that is constitutive of self-hood (Morrison). But in all three texts we *see* violence emerging to create male religious selves, and I wish to explore how this mode of seeing a violent (masculine) story—and not just a violent image—informs and challenges our moral imaginations.

Jack Chick Tracts

By some measures, the Jack Chick cartoons—and this label is important, as I argue later—are the most popular religious cartoons in America and have been since they began in 1974. Over 750 million tracts have been sold worldwide in some 100 different languages, and their staunchly evangelical tone and unapologetic critique of others continue to offend Catholics, Mormons, Muslims, and Jews (among others), even though Chick died in 2016.[9] Born in 1924, Chick converted to a strident form of evangelical Christianity in 1948, at the age of twenty-four, after listening to Charles Fuller's radio broadcast *Old Fashioned Revival Hour*. Since 1961 Chick Publications has produced and marketed religious materials to both sustain Christian identity and convert those from outside their evangelical community.[10] Martin Lund helpfully summarizes the main and continual message in these tracts, which is that "no matter how good you have been in your life, you are a sinner and therefore hell-bound unless you accept evangelical Christianity as promoted by the Chick brand."[11] All Chick tracts showcase the same basic format: they are five by three inches in size and in black-and-white (except for the covers); they run twenty-four pages in length because "it's the minimum page count that the US mail considers a book and allows to be mailed at the cheaper book rate";[12] they all conclude with back-cover instructions to accept Jesus as one's personal savior; and each costs seventeen cents (although one must buy a packet of at least twenty-five online). On the Chick publications website, the byline is forever in view and to the point: "Witnessing made easy . . . Chick tracts get read! (Equipping for evangelism for over 50 years)."[13] And indeed they do; as the opening page of their catalog attests, "The **cartoons** draw them in, the **emotional story** holds their attention, and then they are brought face-to-face with the **gospel**." They are consumable products in the American religious marketplace.

But Chick cartoons are not merely read; they are also *seen* and digested as visual media. The Chick website and publications refer to their pamphlets both as tracts and cartoons. The term *tract* often refers to political and religious promotional material, and the story goes that Chick utilized this pocket-sized format after hearing that communists distributed their propaganda "by passing out minicomic tracts to the ignorant masses."[14] Chick tracts offer a concise, clear message of damnation and salvation, with each page consisting of two square panels of equal proportion. But the label "cartoon" best captures the visual dynamics of these tracts, because they seduce through clear, intelligible stereotypes. Scott McCloud distinguishes cartoons from comics by focusing on their "simplified conceptualized images," and this is what we see going on in Chick's works.[15] I want to focus on three such cartoons in this section, and their covers are all alike: they traffic in stereotypical images on the left side, as the right side (in white ink over a black background) seeks to draw the reader in through pithy but provocative titles such as "Men of Peace?," "Is Allah Like You?," and "Gun Slinger." They each pose a problem or question that only faith in Jesus can resolve. These are not comics in the sense of an extended image-text with intricate plot development and visual splendor. These are lowbrow cartoons designed to attract and arrest. "No 'seeker-friendly' compromises," the Chick catalog informs us, "just straight old-fashioned salvation by faith."

Yet the visual dynamics of these cartoons are anything but "old-fashioned." The white lettering on an empty black backdrop articulates the Chick message that accepting or rejecting Jesus is indeed black or white. Each cartoon addresses the reader with an ultimate decision, "with a simple step-by-step invitation to accept Christ." But if Jesus saves, then men of this world (and it's mostly men in Chick's world) deceive through ignorant boasting. The images do this work for Chick as they manipulate stereotypical depictions of others. Note, for example, the three men on the cover of "Men of Peace?" (see fig. 53). One holds delicate flowers, a second flashes the peace sign with his right two fingers, and the third hails with his right hand as the symbol of the crescent and star—a common and popular symbol for Islam—arises (apparently) from his left hand. They all carry heavy and crooked noses, wear head coverings that suggest religious orthodoxy for some and dangerous terrorists for others, and have overly large teeth and shifting eyes. These Middle Eastern men thus take on violent stereotypes of untrustworthy Arab Muslims. And that's the point; Muslims appear peaceful, but who knows what they hold in those hidden left hands? Darby Orcutt argues that Chick deploys "cartoon characters with whom readers can readily identify and plac[es] them into visual narrative worlds that readers easily and unconsciously 'fill in' and thus experience as immanently 'real.'"[16] This explains why Chick tracts are so immersive, Orcutt explains, but he misses the sinister use of stereotypical images that appeal to notions of filth, deceit, terror, and the diabolical. These cartoons are read, to be sure, but the visual images inform *how* they are read.

Not all Chick tracts begin with foundational moments of savagery, but the three I discuss here certainly do, as they depict "lost" souls as fundamentally violent. This sense of violence often goes unnoticed by scholars who revel in their status as popular exemplars of Americana and who seem to believe that cartoons are entertainingly cartoonish:

> The best part about Chick tract collecting is the pleasure in reading the tracts themselves. They are serious for those who believe them, hilarious for those who don't, and entertaining for everyone. The "Chick Universe" is a place where God and Satan are at a continual state of war. Chick reveals an invisible world of angels and demons as they fight it out around us, as well as many conspiracies we would otherwise never imagine. The Masons, the Vatican, the witches—it's us against them. With Chick tracts, everyday is Halloween and Christmas combined. Who doesn't enjoy at least one of those two holidays?[17]

Lighten up, Kuersteiner implies here, and enjoy that Chick tracts offend everybody. But the violence depicting "them" is more than offensive: Chick cartoons visualize others as essentially violent, just as they imagine Jesus and his followers as true men of peace. And that violence hearkens back to medieval and Renaissance invectives against Muslims, Catholics, and Jews.[18] I am not suggesting that these violating images actually support acts of violence, as some literary theorists and historians might claim.[19] Instead, I want to look at what these images and texts do to enable the readerly imagination to locate violence *in* the other and so constitute the other as violent. This is not a representation we should enjoy; it is, instead, an image of religious violence that undermines moral, and certainly Christian, imaginative faculties.

"Men of Peace?" (2006) opens with a terrorist attack in London, as a man in black abandons an equally dark suitcase at the counter of an elegant hotel (see fig. 54). His all-black suit, together with his dark beard and sunglasses, distinguish him from the other workers and guests at the hotel—all of whom are white, beardless, and innocent (one woman even holds the hand of her young son). As the next panel on the same page depicts the explosion just outside the Big Ben tower, the gutter lying between the panels does its work; the reader now recognizes the "them" who has terrorized and killed "us." The following page makes explicit what we already know, as the terrorist from "Muhammad's Faithful" calls a television station to declare, "Your **wicked**

FIG. 53 Jack Chick covers. Copyright © 2010 by Jack T Chick LLC.

city is feeling the **wrath of Allah!**" ("Men of Peace?," 3). The sequence of events—this "step-by-step" approach—visualizes Muslims as vengeful murderers. The station call arrives *after* the explosion from a man who, without a head covering, still projects the same facial features as the three Muslims depicted on the cartoon's cover. Clearly these are not men of peace. The white television producers, however, appear weak and cowardly: they show anxiety, fear, ineptitude, and fragility. We are, they state, in deep trouble!

This two-page spread establishes the scene of religious violence: barbaric others arrive to kill innocent whites and inept bureaucrats who seek only to protect Western civilization. Who will save us from this cycle of violence and weakness? Before we get there (and we all know that we will get there), this Chick tract turns, as so many do, to a more folksy middle-class family that recognizes the terrorists for who they are, and unlike the business executives at the television station, they are willing to stand up to the Muslim savages by accepting "Lord Jesus as [their] Saviour" (21). The "us" imagined here is neither the wealthy elite nor the poor and downtrodden. They are white Christian suburbanites with stable families, earning enough to live comfortably in single-family homes with multiple rooms and televisions. Muslim terrorists have come to destroy *this* kind of security and well-being. Religious violence arrives from elsewhere to violate a particular class of space, freedom, and decency. In this sense Orcutt is right to see how this white suburban family stands in for the imagined reader. We are moved to see ourselves in the room with Gramps and Jenny as they watch "[London] **burning**" in horror. Whereas the initial two-page spread occurred within an imagined sense of terrorism, as the story unfolds the cartoon depicts recognizable spaces and conversations of middle-class family life. Although readers will be asked in the end to make a decision, as Jenny must do, to accept Jesus as savior, the decision has already happened here, as the images draw the reader in, and we see ourselves in the living room with Jenny and Grandpa, "brought face-to-face with the **gospel**." Violence is the other and comes from outside the Christian community.

This is a holy war, Gramps informs Jenny, one that the Prophet Muhammad initiated long ago with "his god." This Chick tract has already targeted Muslims and weak bureaucrats, but here Chick goes after the educated elite. Jenny knows Muhammad to be a great man because she "**learned** about him in college" (6). But there is folk common sense to be found outside university culture, and Gramps embodies small-town wisdom. Jenny stands in for simple-minded liberalism, judging her grandfather to be intolerant and condescending; of course there are a few bad apples, but you ought not to judge a religion by the acts of "fanatics." Yet to the grandfather, the fanatics are good Muslims who blindly follow their prophet and the will of Allah. So what readers witness in "Men of Peace?" is not the terrorizing work of a few

FIG. 54 Jack Chick, *Men of Peace?*, terrorist attack. Copyright © 2010 by Jack T Chick LLC.

"bad men" but the natural and even holy work of Muslims devoted to their idol god. The London attack should not shock us, because it simply exposes the violent and subhuman features of Muslim worshippers. Visually, the three men on the cover, who only appear to be men of peace, now stand in for an entire religious community. This is what "they" look like: violent men who worship an idol and wish to carry out its will.

As the cartoon story develops, things get a bit weird. As it turns out, Muhammad's wife Khadija was really a wealthy Catholic widow who infected the prophet's worldview (13), and upon her death, "Allah and his 'Angel Gabriel' changed Muhammad into a religious dictator. **He showed NO mercy!**" (14). Like the men of peace, Gabriel is not really a compassionate angel, and Muhammad becomes the first Muslim terrorist. Chick graphically depicts Muhammad beheading a wealthy man as he imagines the fortune soon to be acquired, even as the prophet forces the man's wife, Safiya (a wife that he will soon take for himself), to watch his decapitation. Horrified, Jenny approves of Muhammad's soul being "damned for all eternity" (16–17), but she too has something in common with Muhammad. As the cartoon informs us, "**Both** you and Muhammad **rejected Jesus**" (18). To her grandpa, Jenny is just as lost as Muhammad, and here the violence inscribed in Muhammad and his Muslim followers adheres to all those who deny Jesus. The decision itself is violent, as Gramps asks her, "Well, Jenny, now that you understand, **you must decide**. Will you **believe** Him or **reject** Him like Muhammad did?" (21). Violence in any form is really violence against Jesus. As promised, the Chick tract brings Jenny and the reader "face-to-face with the **gospel**," either a Christian crusader or a terrorist, one who awaits heaven or one damned to hell, a worshipper to be saved or one forever lost. This is old-fashioned, black-and-white salvation by faith.

But if violence goes all the way down for those who reject Christ, why do Chick tracts, as Lund recognized, end with the hope of saving faith rather than good works? In "Men of Peace?" the concluding message appears to undermine the import of violence: "Going to heaven is not a matter of GOOD or BAD, it's a matter of SAVED or LOST. No matter how **bad** you've been, Jesus **died** for you and wants to save you **right now! Let Him!**" (22). If Muhammad had just accepted Christ as his savior, he too would be in heaven. "Yes, Jenny," her grandpa tells her. "The Lord Jesus Christ died for **all** our sins—**even Muhammad's**" (20). Violence ensues from lost souls who reject Jesus's saving grace, but it does not determine one's status before Jesus. In this sense, violent acts do not inform or count against one's soul. But this means that violence against those barbarous others also stands outside God's judgment. Violence does not count when it matters most: salvation in heaven. Grandpa remains calm before the horror in London because life and death are not ultimate concerns: the decision lies elsewhere and beyond this material world. The violence enacted by others on Chick's Christian world, and the violence imparted on those deemed subhuman and barbaric, enact a holy war between the damned and saved. Its meaning lies within the evangelical view of ultimate, faithful decisions. To reject Jesus—as Muhammad did and the reader presumably did too—is to live a violent life of capitalist indulgence, hate, rape, and murder. True men of peace are saved by God not because they are peaceful but because they have accepted Jesus as their only savior. That is what it means to be at peace; violence is not truly a human concern, and that is why it defines the damned others.

This ultimate dynamic between good and bad, saved and damned, lies at the heart of the "Gun Slinger" tract (1997).[20] The cover to this cartoon is, in many ways, functionally similar to "Men of Peace?," for both portray individuals appearing as something they are not. The plot is straightforward enough: the owner of the town saloon, Bart Dawson, hires a gunslinger to kill the preacher who has wrecked the drinking and general "hell raising" in town (see fig. 55). He is bad for business. But when the gunslinger meets up with the preacher in church and hears the good word that "no matter how **BAD** you are, Jesus can forgive you" ("Gun Slinger," 14), he repents and, though hanged for his crimes, is welcomed by Jesus "minutes later in heaven." This is not the fate of the marshal who has arrived to capture the gunslinger. He has no need for Jesus, for as "the most honest, law-abiding man in this **whole territory**" (19), heaven is easily secured. But upon his death he goes immediately to hell, and as the marshal looks out to the reader in shocked pain, crying out, "**Wait!** This **CAN'T** be! I was a **GOOD** man! I **UPHELD** the law!," someone in a black cloak responds, "But you **NEVER** received Christ as your Saviour" (21). Gunslinger exemplifies Lund's summary of Chick tracts, that is, "No matter how good you have been in your life, you are a sinner and therefore hell-bound unless you accept evangelical Christianity."[21]

This saved/damned decision clearly articulates the basic theme of the cartoon . . . if one just reads the text. But this cartoon includes images too, and the visual markers suggest how race and religion interweave to subtly inform *how* one reads Chick tracts. The gunslinger wears only dark clothes, and his face is originally the darkest of the characters in this tract. But his face lightens up considerably when he hears the preacher's good news (see fig. 56). And the preacher delivers even more good news when he meets the gunslinger for the last time in prison and tells him, "You're **not** terrible anymore, Tom. You are now a **child of God!**" (16). Compare all this to the depiction of Jesus who, although lacking in facial features, still projects a completely white face and all-white robes, whereas those in hell wear dark black robes reminiscent of the Ku Klux Klan. The African American artist Fred Carter illustrated a number of Jack Chick tracts, and there are numerous cartoons within Chick publications that move beyond American racial barriers. But this is not one of them. "Gun Slinger" is a racialized text because it traffics in racial stereotypes that locate blackness in evil and violence, and whiteness in salvation and faith. To be sure, this is a black-and-white cartoon, but the illustrator still can utilize shades of gray to nuance facial expressions. This too is a choice, if not an ultimate one then at least fateful for how readers *see* race and violence in this tract.

This is also the case for the marshal, but his facial features disclose pleasure in just punishment. He looks on with satisfaction as the gunslinger hangs in the gallows, in contrast to the preacher who closes his eyes in horror, Bible clutched strongly in his left hand (see fig. 57). A close up of the marshal's face reveals his joy in lawful retribution as he exclaims, "**At last!** Terrible Tom got **exactly** what he deserved" (18). This is how servants of the law—those who seek to do good works fairly, honorably, and justly—look in their fervor for righteousness. Chick quotes from Romans 3:10 ("There is none righteous, no, not one") to subvert this mistaken vision. Yet the context for Romans 3:10 is

FIG. 55 Jack Chick, *Gun Slinger*, a darkened gunslinger. Copyright © 2010 by Jack T Chick LLC.

FIG. 56 Jack Chick, *Gun Slinger*, a saved and whitened gunslinger. Copyright © 2010 by Jack T Chick LLC.

very specific: Does the Jew hold any advantage over the non-Jew? To this Paul responds in Romans 3:9, "What then? Are we Jews any better off? No, not at all; for I have already charged that all men, both Jews and Greeks, are under the power of sin, as it is written: None is righteous, no, not one."[22] Here too, the gunslinger appeals to common stereotypes of Jews seeking righteousness before the law. This is what Cynthia Baker recognized when discussing the term *Jew* as a violent marker of otherness to better assert Christian self-identity. My point is simply this: when readers *see* faith in this Chick cartoon, they see whiteness, and when they see law, they see Jews. This is not a violence that destroys buildings and murders innocent civilians, but it is violence nonetheless. It violates Chick's basic principle that we are all one before Jesus.

This issue of violence and the other is the focus of the last Chick tract I wish to discuss briefly here, "Is Allah Like You?" The cartoon begins with an

FIG. 57 Jack Chick, *Gun Slinger*, the whiteness of faith. Copyright © 2010 by Jack T Chick LLC.

act of violence: Ahmed is quietly reading his Qu'ran when his son acciden-
tally bumps into his mother, who then splashes water all over Ahmed and his
holy book. His response is violence embodied, as he yells, "**You idiots!** That
water defiled my Qur'an! I'll beat you **both** for this!" ("Is Allah Like You?," 3).
A similar racial dynamic is in play here, as Ahmed is far darker in skin tone
than his wife and children, and this is clearly not the first time he has harmed
them. His dazed and bruised child offers the context for the cartoon's title
as he says, "You're so mean, Papa. Is Allah like you?" (4–5) (see fig. 58). The
answer, if I can cut to the chase here, is, only when Papa is a Muslim. But as
Ahmed learns of the New Testament and God's loving grace, he realizes his
Qur'an and its God have deceived him. Ahmed seeks forgiveness from his
family, promising never to hurt them again, and Ahmed's son concludes this
cartoon with the punchline, "Daddy, I was wrong. . . . Allah is **nothing** like
you!" (22) (see fig. 59). The son's face does the work of embodying violence
in religious others. When, beaten and hurt, he looks to his father ("Is Allah
like you?"), he actualizes the gratuitous and cruel violence of a father devoted
to Islam. But surrounded by the white halo of salvation ("Allah is **nothing**
like you!"), the son emanates the peace and security of Jesus's love and grace.
In the one he is darkened; in the other he is whitened. This is what violence
looks like in others not like ourselves: they are dark, beaten, abject, and lost.
They *are* violence, now embodied in the blackened skin of those who have
rejected Jesus's lordship.

When Chick tracts bring a reader "face-to-face with the **gospel**," that
gospel looks distinctly white, suburban, folksy, personal, and divisive. Readers
are not asked to imagine others like themselves or to see virtue in those others
but are instead moved to a judgment about *one's own* salvation. Jenny's decision to accept or reject Jesus is much like Muhammad's, but it is *hers* to make.

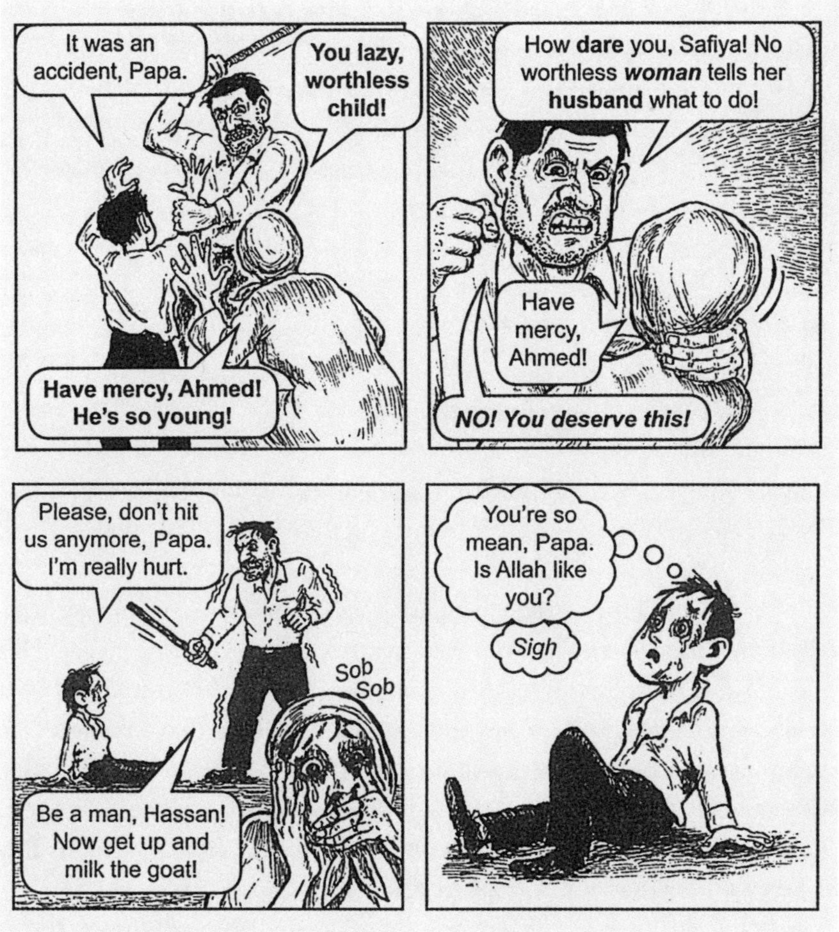
It was an accident, Papa.
You lazy, worthless child!
Have mercy, Ahmed! He's so young!
How dare you, Safiya! No worthless woman tells her husband what to do!
Have mercy, Ahmed!
NO! You deserve this!
Please, don't hit us anymore, Papa. I'm really hurt.
Sob Sob
Be a man, Hassan! Now get up and milk the goat!
You're so mean, Papa. Is Allah like you?
Sigh

FIG. 58 Jack Chick, *Is Allah Like You?*, Muslim violence. Copyright © 2010 by Jack T Chick LLC.

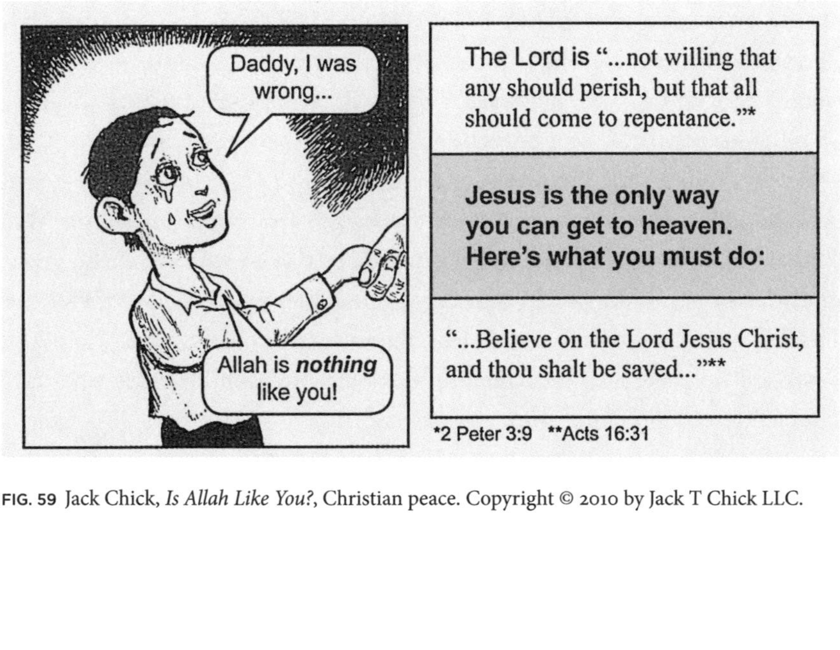
Daddy, I was wrong...
Allah is nothing like you!
The Lord is "...not willing that any should perish, but that all should come to repentance."*
Jesus is the only way you can get to heaven. Here's what you must do:
"...Believe on the Lord Jesus Christ, and thou shalt be saved..."**
*2 Peter 3:9 **Acts 16:31

FIG. 59 Jack Chick, *Is Allah Like You?*, Christian peace. Copyright © 2010 by Jack T Chick LLC.

As a reader, Chick tracts are about me. So I do not arrive "face-to-face" with anything outside of my own religious imagination; the decision to accept Jesus is mine and mine alone. Chick's world is a starkly closed one that never exposes readers to a difference beyond the black-and-white distinction of us and them. And so it is all too easy to dismiss others as less than human, or even beyond recognition. This is not a seeing of the other, but a failure of vision. I have argued that the visual dynamics of these cartoons establish others as violence incarnate. But Chick tracts also harm readers who must restrict their imaginative faculties from searching beyond their safe worlds of ultimate decisions. To believe or reject is to be for or against, and this divisive politics of religion harms our moral imaginations. Instead of envisaging worlds of different shades, the beauty of texture and nuance slides into the straight black-and-white frames of "old-fashioned salvation by faith." This is Chick's graphic violence, and it is harmful to the religious self.

Testament: Akedah (2006)

Writer Douglas Rushkoff and artist Liam Sharp's *Testament: Akedah* (2006) is a story about idolatry and iconoclasm.[23] It is a self-proclaimed mythological account of foundational violence: a war between the gods who use humans to further their own ends. That battle between Moloch and the Hebrew God in Genesis recurs again and again, in every generation. But we need not subsume our identities or our lives to this divine narrative; Rushkoff suggests we can rewrite our stories, change the founding code, and so liberate ourselves to become who we seek to be. Idolatry is the passive worship of false gods; iconoclasm breaks that faithful chain and reimagines by rewriting our own stories. David Morgan calls iconoclasm a "strategy of replacement," one that "mount(s) a spectacle, a theatrical staging of violence that would enact an ideological transfiguration of the past." In this way, iconoclasm and idolatry go together: "the conviction of idolatry is driven home by the destruction of the offending gods, whose power restrains the civilization of the subject until it is broken. Idolatry represents the blindness, resistance, and ignorance of the nonbeliever or child. Iconoclasm enacts his or her liberation."[24] This is how Rushkoff understands his graphic novel *Akedah*, volume one of his four-part *Testament* series that continues with *West of Eden* (2007), *Babel* (2007), and *Exodus* (2008). Rushkoff understands the power of these idol gods (as all iconoclasts do, according to David Freedberg),[25] and a power that strong can be undone only by an aggressive liberatory act. Violence lies at the heart of Rushkoff's mythological vision, in which human liberation is a fierce act of religious destruction and rebirth.

The comic book *Akedah*—the biblical Hebrew term for "binding" that functions as the traditional Jewish shorthand for Genesis 22—rewrites Abraham's sacrifice of his beloved son as a liberation story from false worship. Rushkoff is remarkably candid about this, and he opens his introduction to *Akedah* with this revisionary pressure in view: "The Bible may have actually been better off as a comic book" (in *Akedah*, this is all in bold, all in capital letters). The suggestion is obvious: the *Akedah* comic lying in the hands of the reader might actually liberate and transform the Bible into what it *should have always been*. Rushkoff understands the boldness of this claim. Perhaps few of his readers know of his professional life as professor of media studies at City University of New York, Queens College. They probably don't know of his website[26] or his many books and articles on media and technology. So Rushkoff must legitimate his credentials to his readers: "I'm saying this in my day-job persona as a halfway respectable media theorist—a guy who has written books and novels, taught university classes and made documentaries about the impact of new technology on the way we relate to stories."[27] He has also written a book about Judaism—*Nothing Sacred: The Truth About Judaism* (2003).[28] Rushkoff's *Nothing Sacred* may have moved him to do this comic series, for his reading of Judaism substantiates much that we see in the comic narrative. Here I want to point out the very title of this comic, *Akedah*, as itself a claim to Rushkoff's authority as textual interpreter. This is inside, Jewish language: most readers, perhaps even most Jewish readers, do not know Genesis 22 as the *Akedah* but as the sacrifice of Isaac, or the binding of Isaac, or just as the twenty-second chapter of Genesis. To call this story *Akedah* is to self-consciously appropriate an internal, religious, and Jewish story. I, for one, use the term *Akedah* only when speaking to insiders aware of this title or to those I want to impress with my Jewish knowledge. This latter point is how I read Rushkoff—his authority lies not only in his university training but also in his knowledge of *Jewish* texts.

Those texts are mythological, Rushkoff claims in *Akedah* (and, as we will see, in *Nothing Sacred* as well), because they are a false medium that transports us into blind passivity. He compares our relation to biblical texts to "watching TV or a movie and imagining ourselves as the characters on the screen." The scripts have been written for us, and we all just insert ourselves into these ready-made narratives (you should hear the media theorist behind this account). We all "get lost in the seamless reality and get taken along for a ride," and "we're either afraid or forbidden to inhabit the places where temporality, interpretation and sequence are up for grabs." Rushkoff describes us (although I think he excludes himself from this description) as entertained readers of someone else's narrative. This is all very comforting and fun, but this is "how populations are kept in control." Rushkoff's authority as truth teller is important because his claim rests on the way media works. "We get a good night's sleep"[29] because media dulls our critical capacities and thereby appeals to our unconscious desire for order and security. This too is what idols do: they transform selves into passive worshippers of false narratives. It is a violence of control and enslavement. But this is not our story, Rushkoff now tells us, and so we must rewrite the Bible as comic book to break the spell. The media theorist has become the liberatory iconoclast.

But not all media work this way. Rushkoff appeals to something like Weber's notion of charismatic decline to describe how new media arises as the iconoclastic destroyer of older media idols. But soon this new media declines, much like its predecessor, seeking only to defend its authoritative claim on our lives; iconoclasm devolves into idolatry. The printing press transformed a sacred document into a "mass-produced book," but now that book has become oppressive and authoritative as closed text. Rushkoff believes we are in a new era of the "open source tradition" that radically questions sacred truths (thus the title of his book on Judaism, *Nothing Sacred*). This iconoclastic tradition reimagines that printed text as alive and forever open to interpretive creativity. We can change the code: "The emergence of interactive technologies like the computer has revived the open source tradition, providing the opportunity to again challenge unquestioned laws and beliefs and engage with our foundation myths as participatory narratives, as stories still in the making."[30] Genesis 22 is not a settled text—it is one we can again return to and rewrite as our own *Akedah*. As we will see, the comic images interweave scenes from Genesis with contemporary stories about sacrifice. This visual dynamic uncovers the basic mythic patterns that undergird foundational stories—the Genesis battle still rages on in the modern world.

But Rushkoff's point is more radical still: the open-source tradition really isn't a modern invention. He believes the Bible was actually the first open-source text, but readers have sought to protect its divine, fixed status: "I've found some less than receptive audiences for these observations. When I wrote a book [*Nothing Sacred*] presenting the Bible as an 'open source' collaboration, I was blacklisted by fundamentalists of more than one religion. They just didn't want their story messed with—even though I had been able to prove it was written with that very intent!"[31] In my reading of *Nothing Sacred*, Rushkoff does not prove so much as assert the "core beliefs" he discovers in the Bible: iconoclasm, abstract monotheism, and social justice. Above all, Judaism is a "breakthrough concept" that can awaken us from our slumber. That tradition "has been built to change and to cause change," and so what we require is less revolution than "renaissance—literally, the rebirth of old ideas in a new context." Open-source Judaism *is* Judaism, Rushkoff claims: "A Jewish renaissance, too, will demand that we dig deep into the very code of our religion, then reexperience it in the context of full modernity. It will require us to assume, at least temporarily, that nothing at all is too sacred to be questioned, reinterpreted, and modified. . . . And, perhaps ironically, we'll be engaging ourselves in Judaism's most time-honored tradition."[32] Rushkoff's open-source developers are religious iconoclasts who return us to the core of religious practice and the original intent of Jewish texts. In this sense, it is simply not true that nothing is too sacred to be questioned. Rushkoff's appeal to a code assigns a fundamental core structure to religious narratives, and such core structures can be recognized, brought to light, and manipulated. The code lies already in these texts and in our narrative worlds; we just have to be enlightened enough to retrieve and remodulate them. Modern code "hackers" are "today's equivalent of the Hebrews"[33] and, like their predecessors, must violently reject the idol worshippers who oppress them.

The battle raging within the Genesis 22 text—which as Rushkoff sees it is between those who sacrifice their children to Moloch and those, like Abraham, who replace child sacrifice with circumcision—has its interpretive corollary in the way "scripture-thumping mind controllers" prevent us from connecting to "the real power of these myths."[34] The Genesis text was able to transform a deep human need for sacrifice into a "relatively harmless ritual" that still responds to modern desires and anxieties.[35] The point here is that the Bible itself is transformative, but religious elites have protected it as "a dry and sanctimonious tome"; an open-source text has devolved into a closed book. This is why "the perfect place to tell what I've come to believe is the 'real' story of the Bible may not be that leather-bound tome the Gideons put in hotel dresser drawers, but comics." We need to see the Bible anew as a radical, iconoclastic, open-source text that calls for readers to write new code. As "a band of cyber-alchemist revolutionaries," we can recode reality itself, "and then *we'll* be the superheroes."[36]

The comic book *Akedah* functions as camouflage "to expose the essential mythic battle underlying Western Civilization." That battle is a violent one enacted by the gods, and we see this in the comic's opening scenes of Genesis 22. A weathered Abraham grabs his sleeping Isaac, a young boy who looks terrified. Sarah too is bewildered as she looks on in horror at Abraham's quick dismissal. "Don't interfere. It must be done," he says (*Akedah*, 9). This is male violence, and male sacrifice. The biblical women watch aghast from afar as the males enact this repetitive barbarity. But Isaac is unsure, and as his father saddles his donkey he looks back toward either his mother Sarah or the reader, or perhaps both. Liam Sharp has nicely illustrated this scene and the perceived distance between the boy who will be slaughtered and the father who slaughters. Medieval Jewish readers had challenged this reading of an uneasy Isaac, for they identified far more with Isaac's plight, being themselves children of a different kind of medieval violence. But Sharp remains closer to the biblical sensibility that this is indeed Abraham's burden. The following pages draw out Rushkoff's reading of Genesis 22: Abraham's servants who accompany him to Mount Moriah question his devotion, but they are unsure which god Abraham desires to appease. As Rushkoff sees it, the Canaanite god Moloch seeks Isaac as a child sacrifice. To be clear, there is nothing in Genesis 22 that would suggest that Moloch, a god associated with child sacrifice, is the God who commands Abraham to sacrifice Isaac on Mount Moriah. Rushkoff has read Jon Levenson's *The Death and Resurrection of the Beloved Son*,[37] but in this work Levenson does not establish Moloch as a rival god to the Hebrew one, for *both* the Israelite and the Canaanite worship "involve child sacrifice, and both seem to have had some frequency in ancient Israel."[38] But in Rushkoff's comic, a battle looms between Abraham's "old" god Moloch and his "new" Israelite God. The servants, now waiting for Abraham and Isaac's return, do not know if "his new God tests him" or if "his old one wants him back" (10).

The visual imagery on the recto folio (right side of the page),[39] however, answers their question decisively: this is Moloch's demand (see fig. 60). Rushkoff might still believe, as the eighteenth-century philosopher Immanuel Kant once famously argued, that Abraham has misunderstood this divine request, for no moral god would require a father to sacrifice a son. But Kant's moral law is not in play here, and we see this in Sharp's depiction of the fiery Moloch. Now readers know it is Moloch and not the Hebrew God who demands the child sacrifice, and for the first time we witness the angry, even grotesque, face of Abraham, who appears ready and willing to worship Moloch. Note how Moloch's right fingers cross the black panel borders as he creates the billowing fire on Mount Moriah. Rushkoff explains this overreaching as follows: "Overseeing all this action—from beyond the confines of either narrative line [the biblical and modern sagas]—are the gods. They live outside sequential time and, accordingly, are always depicted beyond the panels. If they try to interfere in the linear action by reaching into a panel, their arm or breath transforms into an element like water or fire."[40] Sharp and Rushkoff use panels to great effect here, for the three linear panels just underneath Moloch's face situate the god beyond the panels (11). Were those narrative borders located below, where we see Abraham, Isaac, and the mountain, it would appear as if Moloch were hemmed in by the page itself. But these three panels offer visual depth, and the god engulfed in fire now inflames the lower world, demanding Abraham's beloved son. The image on the verso folio (on the turned, left side of the page)[41] reveals that both Isaac and Abraham worship Moloch; they both know that it is *this* god who demands sacrifice, although Isaac has not yet understood the full nature of his offering (12) (see fig. 61).

Isaac's anxious question, "Where is the offering?," is one that draws nicely from Genesis 22:7 and appeals to both the father and the reader, for sacrifice is a violation that occurs in every generation. According to the editors of *The Oxford Handbook of Religion and Violence*, sacrifice remains "an enduring theme in the study of religion and violence" and may even be the only

FIG. 60 Moloch demands sacrifice. From *Testament: Akedah* by Douglas Rushkoff and Liam Sharp. Copyright © 2006 by Douglas Rushkoff and Liam Sharp.

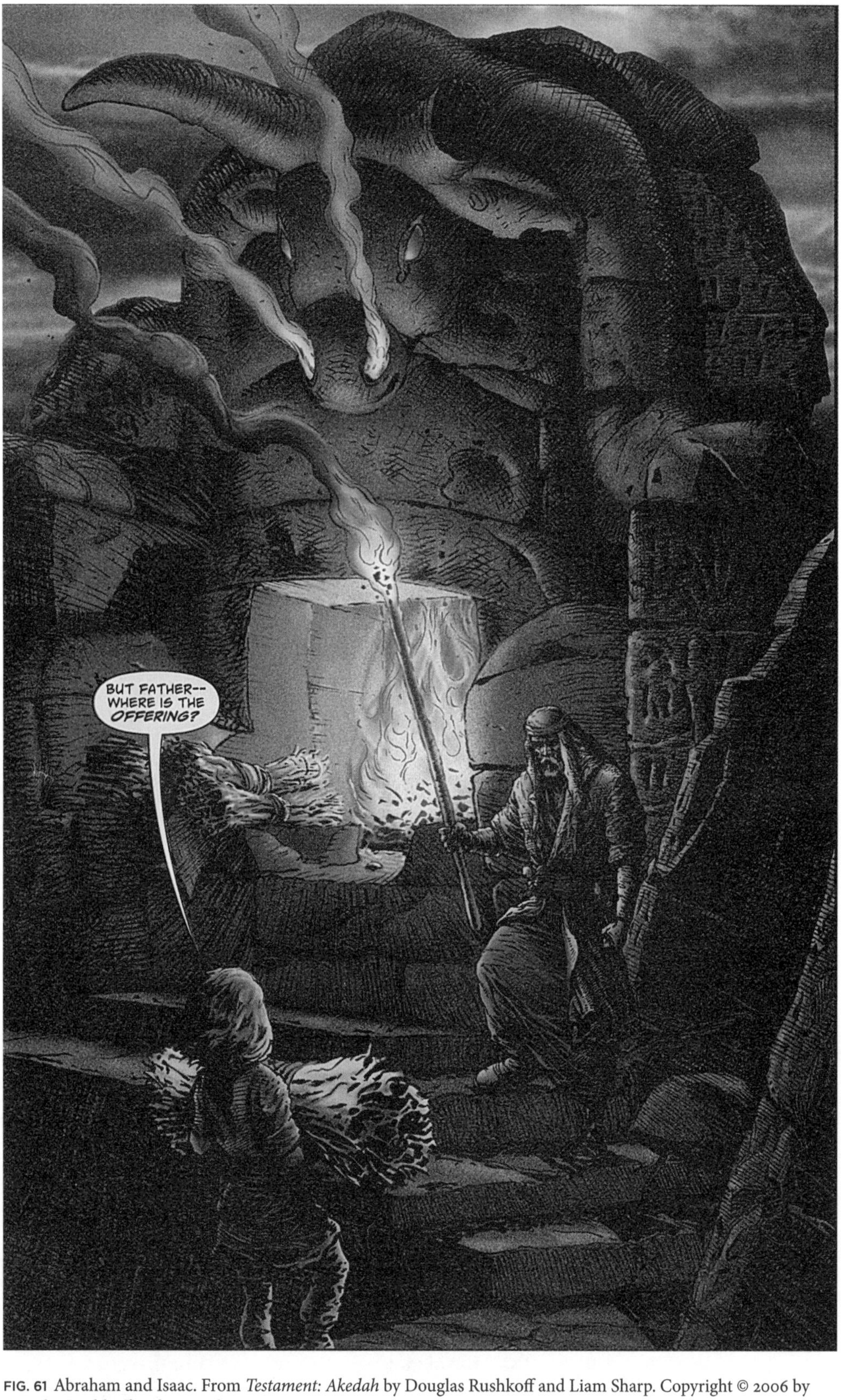
BUT FATHER-- WHERE IS THE OFFERING?

FIG. 61 Abraham and Isaac. From *Testament: Akedah* by Douglas Rushkoff and Liam Sharp. Copyright © 2006 by Douglas Rushkoff and Liam Sharp.

"intrinsic" act of violence in religious experience.[42] "Where is the offering?" is a perennial question, one that still holds power in the modern world. Rushkoff insists on this point: "The Bible is happening right now, in every moment. That's right: We still engage in child sacrifice—every time we send our youngest citizens off to another world. We still practice idolatry through our worship of the almighty dollar (in God we trust)."[43] When readers envision the Genesis 22 story, as they do here in the comic *Akedah*, they should recognize their own anxieties played out in this mythical story. And this is precisely the effect of the recto folio opposite the Genesis scene, in which Rushkoff and Sharp depict the modern analogue to Abraham and Isaac (13) (see fig. 62). Here too we see the father awakening his son from a deep sleep, and again we gaze at the boy's fearful eyes as he realizes the time has come to "get on with it." (We learn over the next few pages that the boy must implant a digital homing device to enable the government to quickly track its citizens so that they can be enlisted for war, and much else.) To establish these two sagas as parallel stories, Sharp illustrates both Isaac and the boy Jake arising within an open tent with similar shades and folds. Jake becomes one of the "cyber-alchemist revolutionaries" who refuses to implant the device (and soon his father will join this group as well), but Rushkoff and Sharp make clear that all this "takes place in Bible time—exposing how these sagas and their underlying themes have been recurring for centuries. And both story arcs are played out by the same set of characters who—for the time being anyway—are unaware of each other's existence."[44]

Sacrificial violence lies at the heart of divine battles and worldly politics. In both worlds the males are the warriors (even when Rushkoff deploys female characters in this revolutionary struggle, they are merely sexual props). Yet Jake and his student friends fail to recognize the mythological core to their world and to other worlds, and so Isaac appears distant to them, as does Abraham. But the hints are there. Jake and his former girlfriend Miriam (actually, "former" is up for debate) listen absent-mindedly to a lecture on Freud and Jung, but the professor's analysis is anything but subtle: "You'll find strikingly **similar** archetypes across the globe and throughout history. They disappear, submerged in what Jung would later call the 'collective unconscious' for **centuries**, even millennia . . . , and then they recur **again**—as if they were there all **along**." On this page of six square panels, we see the professor lecturing along the top two; then the focus shifts to Jake and Miriam discussing fascism within the emotional tones of youthful desire—only in a comic! But the bottom two panels depict a comic book battle between humans and gods, concluding with a vision of Moloch—the very same image of the bull that Isaac and Abraham worshipped on Mount Moriah (19). We all live in a biblical world of sacrificial violence, a story played out in lecture halls, in comic books, in love stories, and in families. It is the same mythological story.

FIG. 62 Jake and father as Isaac and Abraham. From *Testament: Akedah* by Douglas Rushkoff and Liam Sharp. Copyright © 2006 by Douglas Rushkoff and Liam Sharp.

Where is the offering? Rushkoff believes it is us, always and everywhere. So how do we rewrite and reenvision it?

Akedah is a call to arms—to Jake, Miriam, and the readers who see this violence take place in biblical and modern times. It is a battle among the gods, but it is also our war, our struggle to rescript. This is what the "band of cyber-alchemist revolutionaries" take on in this comic. Even Jake's father recognizes how his mentor appropriated his own technology to track American citizens and to subsume them under a hegemonic world currency. Like the biblical Abraham who sacrificed the ram instead of his son Isaac, the father injects their dog Bucky with the tracing potion instead of his son (I didn't make this up). The two-page spread graphically depicts this interweaving of biblical and modern narratives, but in both depictions it is the gods who battle to manipulate the human story. On the verso (left) side of the page Moloch and Melchizedek (the stand-in for the Hebrew God in *Akedah*) battle each other as Astarte, the blue, bare-chested female goddess of sexuality and war, looks on from afar (see fig. 63). The arms of Moloch and Melchizedek dip below to influence Abraham, and just as Abraham is about to sacrifice Isaac to Moloch, the breath of Melchizedek wraps around and holds his arm above Isaac, preventing the boy's sacrifice. The lamb appears, and on the recto page Melchizedek takes over with an altogether different demand: "Do not sacrifice your children to Moloch's fire. Make a different offering to me" (31). Rushkoff generally follows Kant here in his reading of Genesis 22: the voice Abraham hears in Genesis 22:1 ("Take your son") is not the same divine voice he hears later in this chapter; Moloch demands child sacrifice, but the Hebrew God requires something else (for both, nonhuman animals have little value). But Moloch's and Melchizedek's arms also project upward to the modern Abraham and Isaac and thereby reproduce their feud in every generation. Here we see Melchizedek altering Alan's resolve so that he injects Bucky rather than his son Jake.[45] Moloch, beaten once again by his adversary, complains almost childishly that "it isn't right" (31). He reiterates his protest on the very last comic page, upset yet again that the narrative did not conform to destiny (see fig. 64). And here we read of possible revisionary stories. "It doesn't always come out the same way," Astarte tutors. "The story can be changed" (124). This is clever use of the passive voice, for it leaves open who, in the end, will alter the narrative. To this point it has been the gods, but Rushkoff and Sharp *show* readers how to reimagine the stories already written for us. The gods might instead become onlookers to our active revisionary pressures; we can change that passive expression to an active volition. We can bend the eternal battle of the gods to human desires and actions. Although Astarte warns that more wars await them, Alan and Jake now control their own destiny, and their own stories. This is what Rushkoff means when he challenges us "to engage with our foundation myths as participatory narratives, as stories still in the making."[46]

FIG. 63 Gods manipulating human narrative. From *Testament: Akedah* by Douglas Rushkoff and Liam Sharp. Copyright © 2006 by Douglas Rushkoff and Liam Sharp.

FIG. 64 Revisionary pressures against the gods. From *Testament: Akedah* by Douglas Rushkoff and Liam Sharp. Copyright © 2006 by Douglas Rushkoff and Liam Sharp.

But how does Rushkoff imagine rewriting intrinsically violent stories? How do we refigure a world in which gods play with violence? To bring this discussion of *Akedah* to a close, I want to look at two scenes in which gods deploy violent acts to maintain the scripted biblical narrative. Although this comic takes its name from Abraham's call to sacrifice his son, Rushkoff draws from Abraham's broader narrative life, including his relations with Lot and his troubles in Sodom (Genesis 19). The Genesis text describes how two angels visited Lot to warn him of imminent destruction, and as they do so a mob gathers outside Lot's house demanding that he turn over these visitors "so that we may know them." The text implies sexual molestation, and Rushkoff reads this as "ritualized anal rape."[47] Something like this seems to be the case, for Lot suggests the crowd take his two virgin daughters instead (and Lot's Hebrew draws from the same root as the crowd's desire to "know" the men).[48] Sharp depicts bestial, sexualized men and women awaiting Lot's companions, but one of the two angels (who appears as Elijah some pages later) grabs hold of Lot, drags him back inside, and places his hands on the inside frame of the door. With a blue light resonating from his hands and upper body, the angel radiates divine energy. As readers turn the page, they recognize this glow as Melchizedek's power from beyond the frame (45–46). They are still Elijah's hands, but the god empowers them to destroy the rebellious Sodomites outside Lot's house. Filled with divine light arising from inside their now blue bodies, the Sodomites become electrified by a divine energy of destruction. Rushkoff repeats this scene in its modern variant some four pages later, when a mysterious older vagabond takes hold of a live electrical cable to zap street punks who, like their predecessors in Sodom, transform into a charged blue spectacle (50) (see fig. 65). In ancient and in modern times, violence surrounds these revolutionaries: an unrestrained crowd wishes to sexually violate whomever stands before them. But it is not just their violence, for such violations belong to the superheroes as well: Lot appears much like the very crowd from which he flees (as his daughters soon complain, saying to him, "And **now** you think of your family? Father, you offered **us** to them"); Elijah channels God's power not only to annihilate but, as the graphic image portrays, to cause suffering while doing so; and Melchizedek stands apart from this destruction, guiding the violence from above and beyond the narrative frame. We inherit divine violence and appropriate it as our own.

One of the three "core beliefs" Rushkoff outlines in *Nothing Sacred* is something he calls "abstract monotheism." It is a form of iconoclasm in which "God must, ultimately, be a universal and nameless God. The natural result of settling for an abstract and unknowable deity is to then focus, instead, on human beings and life itself as the supremely sacred vessels of existence."[49] Rushkoff materializes this sensibility by deploying Melchizedek, together with Elijah, as God's emissary so that God can remain "abstract and

FIG. 65 The destruction of the Sodomites. From *Testament: Akedah* by Douglas Rushkoff and Liam Sharp. Copyright © 2006 by Douglas Rushkoff and Liam Sharp.

unknowable," unscripted in the image-text comic. But the comic hints, even if abstractly, at divine intervention, whether from apparently "lower" gods such as Melchizedek or equally fierce ones such as Moloch. Even if Rushkoff appeals to some unknown mystical God from beyond, this God either cares nothing for human pain or practices some kind of esoteric detachment from it. Nameless or named, this God too is caught up in religious violence. It is all around us, part of the mythological core embedded in the religious code.

The natural result of such abstraction is not, as Rushkoff claims, to focus on human beings as "the supremely sacred vessels of existence." As this comic has it, the gods and humans play with violence as tools to further narrative ends. These beings—both gods and humans—are not sacred in the sense of being set apart or treated as holy, dedicated, or sanctified. These are violated sacred bodies, if sacred at all. They are toyed with, abused, tortured, and sexualized. How does Rushkoff imagine rewriting stories for sacred persons who violate and are violated, apparently without empathy or physical concern? When violence, even revolutionary, iconoclastic violence, inhabits the lives of those who fail to imagine the suffering of others, what kind of renaissance are we really talking about here? Is violence in the service of a liberatory politics another "core belief" in the Jewish tradition?

Neither Rushkoff nor Sharp pursue these questions in *Akedah*, but they arise nonetheless as readers inevitably revise the script handed over to them. In a two-page spread toward the end of this graphic narrative, Sharp depicts the Dutch industrialist Pierre Fallow (he's the modern idol worshipper who sacrifices to Moloch) on the verso page and the warring gods on the recto side. As Fallow attempts his world takeover through universal currency and technological tracking devices, Sharp depicts him as pulled by competing narrative threads (102) (see fig. 66). Each block is a narrative unit in both biblical and modern times, and when spliced together they create a mythological, narrative unity. Fallow is just the plaything of the gods as they battle each other for possession and dominance. On the recto page, Sharp beautifully inscribes this warfare in the biblical scroll itself, as we literally see the Torah scroll become a comic book creation (see fig. 67). In these scenes, Lord Krishna plays the trickster who speaks truth to power, saying, "In the thick of it, still, my Hebrew friends? Shaping human destiny to your will?" Melchizedek's response comes across as weak apologetic: "We do not fight for ourselves, dear Krishna, but in the name of the one true God" (103). If that is so, then they all seem unconcerned with human suffering and repetitive violence. This is really *their* narrative, not ours. The backdrop to this divine scene makes this clear: behind Krishna stands an endless bookshelf projected beyond the page, and on each shelf lie countless scrolls. There are other stories, but this is the one the gods choose to inhabit. These narratives could be different, could have been chosen otherwise. Yet in this visual portrayal of

FIG. 66 Fallow pulled by competing narratives. From *Testament: Akedah* by Douglas Rushkoff and Liam Sharp. Copyright © 2006 by Douglas Rushkoff and Liam Sharp.

FIG. 67 Gods with Torah scrolls. From *Testament: Akedah* by Douglas Rushkoff and Liam Sharp. Copyright © 2006 by Douglas Rushkoff and Liam Sharp.

FIG. 68 The building blocks of human narratives. From *Testament: Akedah* by Douglas Rushkoff and Liam Sharp. Copyright © 2006 by Douglas Rushkoff and Liam Sharp.

divine violence, there is very little sense that other shelf stories would be any less violent. The visual dynamics on the page suggest this is just one of many Torahs, but they all remain stories of violation. This is not a belief in abstract monotheism but a codified acceptance of religious cruelty.

As readers continue to read this comic story and see how Moloch and Melchizedek battle to configure the narrative blocks of human violence, it's clear that Krishna has it right: Elijah might claim that violence is all for the sake of God's chosen people, but he really enjoys it all coming together (104) (see fig. 68). Sharp has powerfully depicted a divine comedy that, when translated into scripted units, materially transforms into a violent human tragedy. Like Durga enjoying the beheading of Mahisha, Elijah and Melchizedek relish in the violent war games with other gods. They callously abuse their chosen as pawns in a violence without ethical accountability. When violence becomes mundane, as it does here in *Akedah*, there is no reason to believe that those other unread scrolls would enact a different kind of divine/human engagement. These scripts embody mythological forces in which religious violence lies at the core of human and divine experience. One cannot escape this grotesque story but can only rearrange the narrative units. Yet our destiny is even more complicated than this; like Fallow, we are pulled in multiple directions by competing narrative frames, and so the sequential narrative depicted on page 104 is more idol worship than sacred order. The gods don't care, and if I read Rushkoff correctly (however ungenerously), neither should we as cyber-alchemist revolutionaries and superheroes. The scripts will change only because *we* have chosen them—but the violence, and its more troubling code of aggressive human desires, still remains. Rewriting code does not challenge the very nature of code as violent narrative. In the end, Rushkoff has not broken the code; he has only reinscribed it for a future unable to break from its past. Choosing violence is violent all the same, and *Akedah*, however imaginative and comic, is a failure of the moral imagination to move beyond the violence of self-formation.

"The Coyote Gospel" (1988)

The British comic writer Grant Morrison tells the story of receiving a call from DC Comics in which they ask him to bring back some of their old superheroes. Morrison had been rethinking the superhero genre since Frank Miller's *Batman: The Dark Knight Returns* (1986) and Alan Moore's *Watchmen* (1986), but he had to quickly prepare for the interview. As he tells it, "On the nail-biting train journey south to the London meeting, I worked up a four-issue miniseries pitch for Animal Man, an obscure superhero from the sixties."[50] Morrison had seen the animal rights documentary *The Animals Film* and was now a converted vegetarian. He was drawn to Animal Man's sensory empathy to wildlife and his superhero ability to absorb the powers of nearby animals. *Animal Man* would have an extended run even after Morrison retired from writing it, but the most famous of issues proved to be his mesmerizing account in the fifth volume, "The Coyote Gospel."[51] The superhero Animal Man actually takes on a limited but very important role in Crafty the coyote's story about unending ontological violence; Crafty continually dies a brutal death only to be resurrected—until the very end. There is much to work through before we get there, however. Animal Man, for his part, appears on the volume's splash page, although Morrison subverts the expectation that he will become the comic's focus. Lying flat out on the road over tire tracks, Animal Man's position mirrors that of Jesus dying on the cross, but we see the artist's hand coloring the yellow suit over his left leg (see fig. 69). This splash image hints at what is to come for Crafty, but the foundational sense of violence and violation—that our lives and deaths are determined elsewhere, that we are the passive receivers of an author's whimsical creation unaffected by the horrors of violence—arises out of this page directly from Morrison's authorial intent: "In *Animal Man* I created, with the help of my artistic collaborator, Chaz Truog, a paper version of myself that could be integrated with the 2-D DC universe. I sent my avatar onto the page surface to meet the Animal Man character and confirm suspicions he'd been having that his life story was being written by some demiurgic Gnostic overlord."[52] Creator gods write our worlds, much like Rushkoff's divinities do in *Testament: Akedah*. But whereas Rushkoff appeals to "cyber-alchemist revolutionaries" to help rewrite stories "still in the making,"[53] Morrison denies such a renaissance of human creative desire. As Morrison sees this, "It was the violated superhero finally confronting the voyeuristic reader—I wanted the superhero to face up to us."[54] We *see* violence enacted, and we are held accountable as passive observers to sadistic cruelty.

"The Coyote Gospel" is the story of Crafty, who plays the role of Wile E. Coyote from the Warner Brothers *Looney Tunes* cartoons featuring Wile E. Coyote and the Road Runner (1949). Readers learn this only when Crafty hands Animal Man "the Gospel according to <u>Crafty</u>" three-quarters of the way through the comic, but Morrison hints at this much earlier ("The Coyote Gospel," 17). The opening pages show Crafty's mutilated body lying dead on the desert road as an eighteen-wheeler approaches. The trucker has picked up a young female hitchhiker, and as they learn each other's life stories, they sing along to The Modern Lovers's catchy tune, "Roadrunner."[55] In that span of dialogue and carpool karaoke, Crafty has come to life again, stands tall, and slowly walks to the other side of the street. But he doesn't make it; the trucker runs him over (again?). As the trucker continues on—"Forget it. Don't look back," says the trucker (3)—we see the coyote, what A. David Lewis calls a

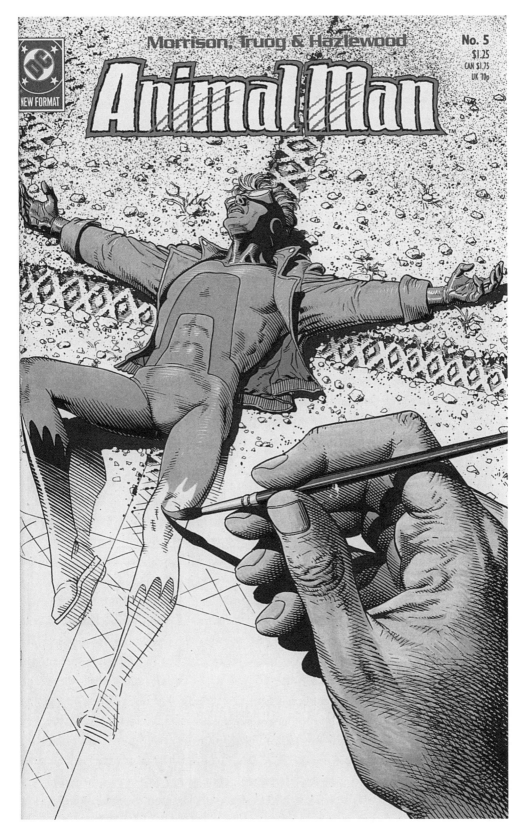

FIG. 69 Cover page of "The Coyote Gospel." From *Animal Man* by Grant Morrison. Copyright © 1991 DC Comics.

"humanoid creature,"[56] slowly recombine his torn limbs and tissues in painful reformations of resurrected flesh (see fig. 70). That opening sequence jarringly transitions to Animal Man's suburban homelife, in which we find him throwing away all the frozen meat—to his wife Ellen's horror, he responds, "Ellen, these are dead *animals*" (8). All this should remind us that violence and death are male domains, here in this volume as well as in previous issues in which Ellen is more the passive observer to Animal Man's heroics. But she is also violated, as good-old-boy hunters callously kill and maim her innocent cats and then turn their violence on her; only her next-door neighbor can save Ellen from rape (*Animal Man* #3). Here in the aforementioned kitchen scene, in which Ellen demands meat for food because, as was clear even earlier, Animal Man earns very little through superhero work, Buddy Baker storms out, seeking solace in his Animal Man suit as he flies away to a place unknown for now (he will soon land next to Crafty). In the meantime, the trucker's life has been ruined since he ran over the desert coyote, and he has committed to killing "the devil" and thus ending his and the world's suffering. This he cannot do until he shoots the "magic bullet" through Crafty's gospel. Crafty is surprised when this happens, and he feels no pain as Animal Man lowers him down to the ground at the crossroads. He finally dies there in the figure of Christ on the cross (22–24). The very last words of this comic—"The End, Folks!" (24)—hearken back to Crafty's *Looney Tunes* roots, but they also witness to Crafty's final end, in which he embraces the peace and quietude of a painless, though clearly still anxious, death.

This summary provides only the background to how Morrison engages religious violence in *Animal Man*. It is there throughout in the language of Christian resurrection and the trucker's sense that the coyote must embody the devil if not Christ. But Morrison's narrative and Truog and Hazlewood's illustrations reveal what resurrection looks like as a violent act of self-formation. The viewer first beholds Crafty's rebirth as a painful fusing of tissues and organs, and Morrison's account is arresting: "The pain is gigantic. A newly activated nervous system is suddenly jammed with frantic signals, like an overworked switchboard. The creature shudders, weeping. Its pelvic girdle fuses along hairline sutures, to cradle rapidly healing organs. A splintered rib, that saws back and forth in one lung, is withdrawn. The thoracic cage locks seamlessly. The lung reinflates. Trembling, the creature rises" (4). In the Christian Gospel accounts, we read of Jesus's death and later resurrection, but we don't *see* it, and we don't know *how* a limp body reenlivens. Recall that even in *Marked*, Ross did not show the resurrected Christ but a forlorn clown in his stead. Here, "the miracle of the resurrection" (4) arises as a painful and violent act of rebirth. Systems are activated, signals jammed, and switchboards are working overtime to reenergize a dead body. Bones are fused, sutured, and healed or, if too deformed and splintered, taken out altogether, like Adam's rib.

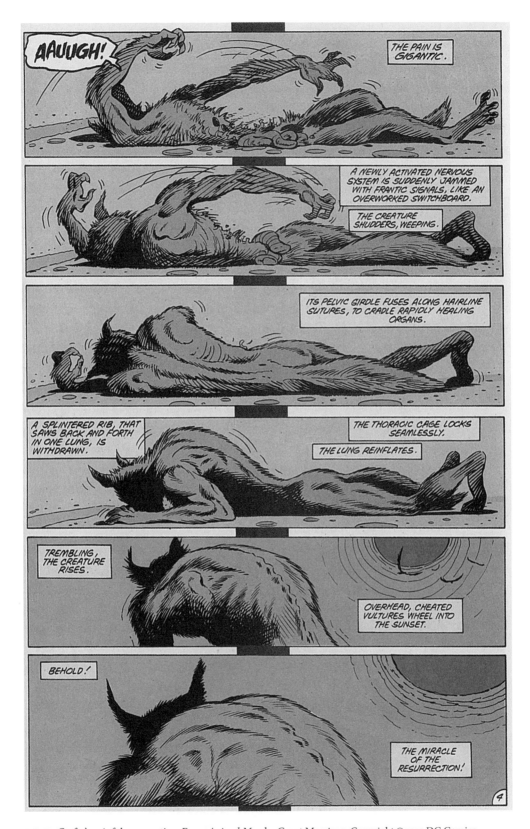

FIG. 70 Crafty's painful resurrection. From *Animal Man* by Grant Morrison. Copyright © 1991 DC Comics.

I put all this in the passive voice because Crafty is powerless as this unfolds: this all happens *to* him. He can only wait for the miracle to end, weeping, trembling, and shuddering as he must once again accept the pain of continual death and rebirth. What kind of miracle is this? It appears barbaric, cruel, and perhaps even sadistic as Crafty suffers again and again. Morrison, Truog, and Hazlewood reveal how violence constitutes rebirth—the miracle cheats not only vultures, now deprived of their sustenance, but also Crafty, who knows the pain and suffering of resurrection. Violence happens to him; it becomes who he is in reliving the ordeal once more. The miracle of resurrection defines Crafty as an animal in perpetual pain.

Chuck Jones, the animation director for the Coyote and Road Runner cartoons, once listed nine "golden rules" for the series. They range from the cartoon's setting (always in the southwest American desert) to the use of Acme products, but the first, second, and ninth rules address violence directly: The Road Runner cannot harm the coyote except by going "beep-beep" (rule number one); no outside force can harm the coyote, only his own ineptitude or the failure of the Acme products (rule number two); and the coyote is always more humiliated than harmed by his failures (rule number nine).[57] None of these rules apply to Crafty in *Animal Man*, which is clear when the trucker attempts to kill this humanoid creature. Returning to Death Valley and the scene of his accident about one year "after he saw the **devil** on the highway" (10), the trucker confronts Crafty again as the animal sits quietly overlooking a desert canyon. The trucker's hands tremble as he raises his loaded rifle ("Why won't they stop?"), and Crafty turns only moments before the bullet pierces right through his upper chest. Much of this action occurs in the gutter, so the reader determines how Crafty knows of the trucker's presence and how long this sequence actually lasts. Still, Truog and Hazlewood depict the force and pain of the trucker's onslaught, violating Jones's rules one and two. Even more, this is neither humiliation nor harm but pure brutality. As Morrison puts it, "The first bullet, a semi-jacketed hollow point, shatters the devil's collarbone and smashes its shoulder blade like a china plate" (12) (see fig. 71). The image graphically portrays the bullet's force as it completely slices through Crafty's projected body, blood spurting out with such force that it appears to pull Crafty off the ground. Crafty, clearly hurt but probably not surprised, plunges backward into the ravine, a fall that breaks his spine, crushes his skull, and snaps both his legs. When he finally hits bottom, he does so "blind and quadriplegic." Even the trucker knows Crafty still lives, suggesting that this may not have been his first attempt at killing the devil. So he dislodges a large boulder, and as Crafty's "ruptured optic nerves reconnect," he looks up only to be crushed again by a series of cascading stones. This too, the trucker understands, is not enough. The violence is unending, repetitive, and horrific, and readers passively watch this violence even as they

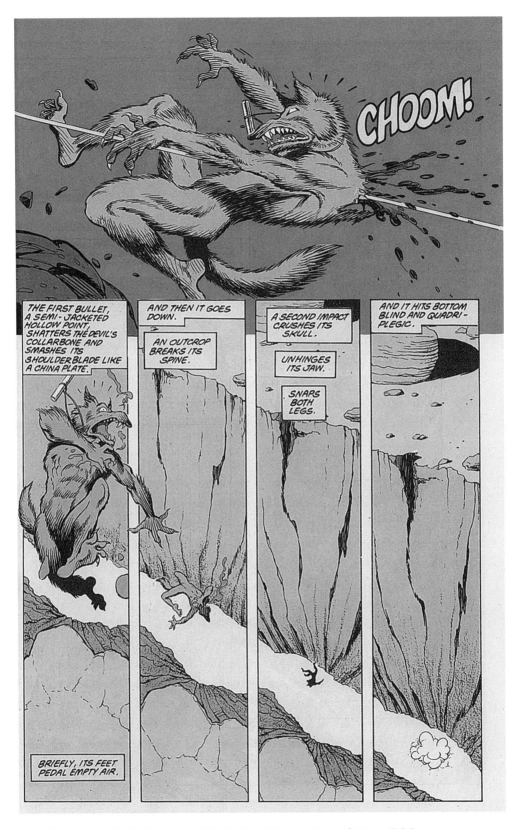

FIG. 71 Trucker shoots Crafty. From *Animal Man* by Grant Morrison. Copyright © 1991 DC Comics.

actively create it in the gutter. When Crafty escapes those heavy boulders to face the trucker once again, he trips over a trigger wire, blowing himself into pieces as the bomb explodes, and this time Morrison describes him as monstrous: "The devil reeks of purgatory, of the inferno. It fixes him [the trucker] with eyes that are glazed like pots of a kiln. And then it lurches past, growing a foot as it goes" (16). The grotesque, the freakish, and the glazed look of an animal subjected to perpetual suffering: here Crafty truly becomes the humanoid creature who eludes definitional certainty. Monstrous beings expose the limits of being human, and in so doing they reveal the moral limits of witnessing violence.

The gospel according to Crafty is a text about witnessing violence and the cruelty inflicted on bodies desiring to escape the brutal cycle of inflicted pain. As Crafty re-forms and the burning fires begin to recede, he finally encounters Animal Man, who has just landed next to the trucker's off-road vehicle (see fig. 72). Morrison and his team thoughtfully visualized this scene to show how Crafty had been waiting for Animal Man all along by the canyon. The trucker had interrupted Crafty's patient watch for the superhero who might end the suffering. Buddy Baker is surprised by Crafty's appearance, though, and apparently loses his superhero capacity to empathize with this fellow animal creature—yet another indication that Crafty plays the monstrous hybrid who defies clear articulation. Crafty hands Animal Man a scroll that Morrison identifies as Crafty's gospel, but Baker does not know what it is. Truog and Hazlewood stage this image of transfer, in which this holy text moves from Crafty to Animal Man, to mirror Michelangelo's *Creation of Adam* painting on the ceiling of the Sistine Chapel (1508–1512). Crafty's hand points in the direction of Animal Man's hand, just as Adam leans forward toward his maker. But here Crafty is the creator not of Baker but of the gospel text—he has given birth to a new beginning, with the hope that it will shatter this unending cycle of violence. A. David Lewis calls this kind of sacred writing a "fictoscripture," a form of "real-world scripture recognizable to the reader" yet invented within the comic text.[58] We know it to be a sacred text, as scroll and as religious creation, but Animal Man remains perplexed. Morrison utilizes what Elizabeth Coody labels the "page-turn reveal," which is when a comic uses the bottom panel to tease a reader into anticipating what will appear on the next page.[59] This is most effective when the reader must actually turn the page, but Morrison wishes to directly connect Animal Man's reading of the gospel with the comic rendition of it; he situates the reader to see what Animal Man sees by portraying the scroll in comic form on the very next page. We imagine that Animal Man reads a comic book as we do, for we have taken on Animal Man's point of view. The *Animal Man* comic depicts the gospel according to Crafty as graphic novel (see fig. 73).

FIG. 72 Crafty delivers his gospel. From *Animal Man* by Grant Morrison. Copyright © 1991 DC Comics.

FIG. 73 Cartoon rendition of Crafty's gospel. From *Animal Man* by Grant Morrison. Copyright © 1991 DC Comics.

This comic narrative within the *Animal Man* comic changes tone and color to better appeal to the alternative reality of *Looney Tunes*. It depicts a time when no one can remember "when beast was not set against beast in an endless round of <u>violence</u> and <u>cruelty</u>" (18). Like Crafty in *Animal Man*, these animals continually undergo a brutal cycle of manipulation and torture. Only Crafty, now portrayed as Wile E. Coyote (and lighting a cannon fuse made by Ajax rather than by Acme), finally challenges this "futile brutality of existence." He walks intractably to a Willy Wonka–type elevator that leads him "into the presence of <u>God</u>" (19) (see fig. 74). Whereas Truog and Hazlewood had situated the reader to see from Animal Man's point of view, they now position the reader as God looking out from his regal chair and awaiting Crafty's challenge. This male God is the comic artist who has painted a stream of red blood leading Crafty to his throne. As comic artist and author, God need not hear from Crafty at all, for he understands Crafty's protest and judges that he "must be punished for this rebellion against my will" (19). Scared, Crafty will accept divine punishment as long as it will "bring peace to the world" (20) (see fig. 75). It's unclear which world Crafty references here, and Morrison cleverly moves Crafty and his readers between multiple realities. Morrison sought to push the superhero genre beyond "grids and imposed structures," wishing to imagine a new kind of "realism": "What *was* the proven tangible reality of comic-book superheroes? What was a superhero, really? What was the exchange—the relationship—between our real world and their visual universes?"[60] In *Animal Man* there are multiple printed universes and multiple realities: Crafty's cartoon life as Wile E. Coyote; the world of Animal Man, the trucker, and monstrous Crafty; and finally, this life in "heaven" with the "demiurgic Gnostic overlord." The reader in some ways constitutes a fourth reality, with the godlike ability to witness all three visual worlds. We see violence enacted in all of them, and the gutter draws us into that cyclical frame. Like the beasts in *Looney Tunes*, we are trapped in a continual spiral of violence not of our own making.

The artist-god is a merciful one and so acquiesces to Crafty's request, but only if he bears the suffering for others "in the hell above," which readers now understand as Animal Man's world. Crafty is thrown into that world through bloodied paint strokes, returning to life—"And Crafty was given new <u>Flesh</u> and new <u>Blood</u>" (20)—as the trucker arrives on the scene to continue "the futile brutality of existence." The challenger to violence must take on that violence to free the world of that brutality. Which world, though, will be freed: the cartoon world or our world? Crafty suffers so that his cartoon friends can live a life beyond violence. But the artist never promised that the "hell above" would be protected from this savagery, and Truog and Hazlewood never show us a *Looney Tunes* reality liberated from the endless rounds of violence and cruelty.

FIG. 74 Crafty before his author God. From *Animal Man* by Grant Morrison. Copyright © 1991 DC Comics.

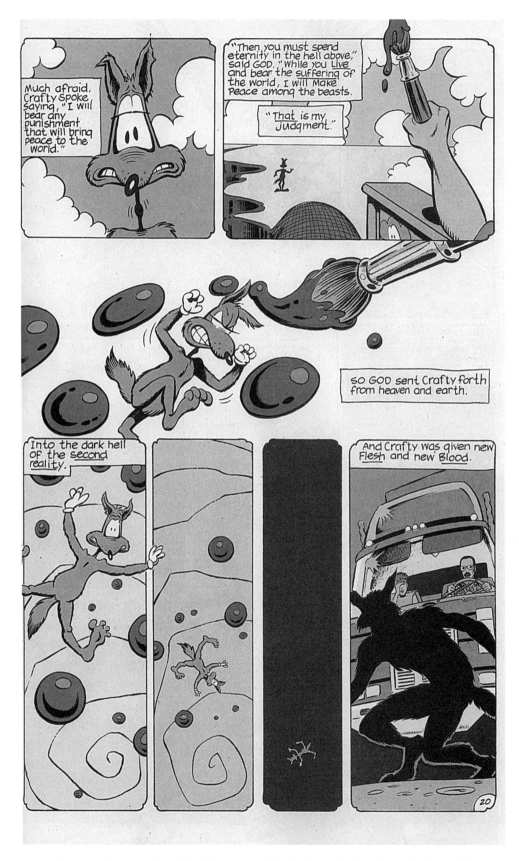

FIG. 75 Becoming Crafty in flesh and blood. From *Animal Man* by Grant Morrison. Copyright © 1991 DC Comics.

All this is both narrated and silenced in the gospel according to Crafty, and this gospel is one that Animal Man cannot read. As the *Animal Man* comic returns to Crafty's violent reality, we see that Crafty never believed in the god-artist and his empty promises, as Crafty offers his gospel to Animal Man in the hope that one day Crafty might "<u>overthrow</u> the tyrant God. And build a <u>better</u> world." Again, we don't know which world Crafty acknowledges here. But his hope is clearly in vain, for as Animal Man opens the scroll he sees only indecipherable hieroglyphics and not the cartoon drawings that the reader had been led to believe were the contents of that gospel scroll. "I'm sorry. . . . I . . . I can't *read* it," Animal Man lets out as he hands the scroll back to Crafty (21). Realities do not slide from one world to the next; what readers *see* is not a text that Animal Man can *read*. The gospel according to Crafty is a cartoon for readers but illegible markings on a page for Animal Man. Violence can be seen, apparently, but not read. In this loss of meaning between image and text we witness Animal Man's loss of empathy for his fellow creatures. He can no longer understand them or their plight. His moral imagination is entirely closed, for his visual world is not theirs, and the demiurgic Gnostic overlord is a cruel trickster god.

Without hope of overthrowing the violence in any world, real or imagined, Crafty's life finally comes to an end (see fig. 76). The magic bullet at the end of the trucker's rifle actually misses its mark. The trucker aims directly for Crafty's head, but he misfires, as the projectile burns a hole through the gospel scroll on its way to Crafty's heart. The trucker believes he has "saved the world" (23), but as he collapses, hand on rifle, it is hard to imagine the cycle of violence actually reversing course. And this is precisely how Morrison and his artists choose to end this comic: as Crafty lies dying on his cross, looking bewildered in his painless death, the artist's brush reappears from above to paint the missing blood surrounding the dying animal (see fig. 77). Violence begets violence as the cycle extends from the barrel of the gun to the artist's brush. This really isn't the end, folks; the tyrant God remains and so does suffering and cruelty. Crafty encounters brutality in every world, and readers witness this savagery enacted on those who challenge and those who do not. This is altogether clear on the comic's last page, which opens with a close-up of Crafty's terrified and anxious look as he awaits death but then recedes as readers take on the tyrant god's point of view. We see Crafty as the artist-god sees Crafty, and in the final panels we are implicated in the physical inking of blood. Truog and Hazlewood have positioned the artist's hand as the reader's own, and so each reader—through the gutter but also inside the panels—becomes the inscriber of violence. This is an inescapable religious violence that marks reality of all kinds—the worlds of the comic book, the artist, and the audience. The silver bullet had to puncture the gospel scroll

FIG. 76 Trucker delivers magic bullet. From *Animal Man* by Grant Morrison. Copyright © 1991 DC Comics.

FIG. 77 Crafty dies on his cross. From *Animal Man* by Grant Morrison. Copyright © 1991 DC Comics.

for it to kill Crafty, because religious violence is constitutive of every reality we know, read, and see.

Conclusion

Douglas Rushkoff believes we can rewrite the scripts designed to violate authentic lives, even if those new scripts reenact the very savagery that has undermined them. He appeals to Judaism's core ideal of social justice, but in a world in which the gods war for our allegiance, overthrowing their tyrannical universe will not happen peacefully. Crafty came to understand this only at the end when he, unlike the trucker, realizes that violence cannot be undone. For Morrison, the tyrannical god is not some writer/artist who scripts our lives from afar. It's the end, folks, because that god is the reader—it is who we are as witnesses to and enactors of violence. Jack Chick accepts that world as a cosmic, religious battle for salvation, because his tracts inscribe violence on others by violating their moral integrity. He defined "real" Islam as an inherently violent religion and Muslims as duped worshippers of a false prophet and an idol god. Those damned to Christian hell were inhuman others, far less monstrous than senseless things outside the borders of human concern. Enacting violence against objectified, inanimate matter, as Chick does in his cartoons, allows him to imagine this violation as an act of Christian charity. But in the saved or damned world of Jack Chick tracts, religious violence is all there is. This is where Rushkoff and Morrison apparently leave us as well.

But Crafty challenges the futile brutality of existence within a world that cannot imagine another kind of reality. That better world, as Morrison makes clear, is illegible, and not only to Animal Man. Yet we can still imagine it and perhaps even see it. The cartoon of Crafty as Wile E. Coyote paints an alternative landscape of creative vision, in which we sit in judgment of Coyote's world and we paint the new blood for Crafty's resurrection. This is not quite Rushkoff's cyber-alchemist revolutionaries who rewrite the code because there is no authentic core to return to and rewrite. There really isn't a better world that we know of. Crafty's challenge to readers, and I take this to be Morrison's provocation as well, is to imagine worlds beyond our imaginations. It is to imagine realities of nonviolence, even though everything we know and read indicates otherwise: "I'm sorry. I can't read it." Those worlds do not exist, either on the comic page or in some other reality. But this is how comics can expand our moral imaginations and our moral universes. We should not be Christian crusaders or hackers of open-source codes; we must become adept at imagining religious worlds no longer imaginable and barely recognizable— beyond the cycles of violence we live in.

Conclusion

The Ethics of Lingering

Comic theorists often compare the virtues of graphic narratives to the drawbacks of film, and Hillary Chute is no exception. The complaint, from Chute and others, often centers on the passivity of watching film in contrast to the activity involved in reading comics. She writes, "When comics evokes the traumatic, the reader engages the form through a participatory mode of agency that film, for instance, structurally eschews."[1] I find this argument to be more a special plea for comics than a critical account of film studies, but Chute draws our attention to a peculiar feature of reading comics, one that I wish to examine in this short concluding chapter. Comic readers determine the pace of their reading in ways quite distinct from viewers engaged in watching a public film or, as Chute reminds us, from people caught up in the speed of our media-rich world: "Joe Sacco calls his work 'slow journalism.' His investment in slowing readers down and asking them to grapple with producing meaning is a deliberate technique positioned against the unremitting speeding up of information that characterizes today's hyperactive media landscape." Sacco's comics are rich in detail and structure, and they are wonderful examples of comics that "slow time and thicken it through the rhythms it establishes in panel size, shape, and arrangement."[2] Comic readers engage in multiple participatory rhythms through linguistic, visual, and structural features of the comic page. Indeed, comic artists manipulate those rhythms, as Steve Ross does in his *Marked* with his "page-turn reveal." Graphic narratives, as material things, demand tactile engagement as much as reflective agency, and they position readers as coproducers of their visual experience. This generative performance takes time—a cultivated sense of dramatic lingering that I have advocated throughout *Drawing on Religion*.

But readers do not have to slow down their rhythmic encounters with graphic narratives; and comic books, as we have seen, often work to increase the pace of visual mediation. Comic use of stereotypes, for one, moves viewers to piece together complicated storylines and character development in order to quickly channel information in meaningful chunks. The gutter between panels often quickens comic time, although readers can just as easily slow down this spatial momentum by lingering in those in-between spaces. Scott McCloud believes that comics ask our minds to become an "in-betweener" by "filling in the gaps between panels as an *animator* might."[3] The implicit psychology here is important: comic readers seek meaningful closure as they seek to tie loose threads together in panel gaps. Stereotyping takes advantage of this psychological need by satisfying our desires for contained meaning, even as it accelerates the pace of unreflective knowledge acquisition. Stereotypes work to short-circuit second-order reflection about the ethical import of comic images and texts.

Drawing on Religion has been a sustained critique of this visual and material quickening. The slow reading that Sacco, Chute, and others defend as a virtue of graphic narratives is a critical feature for expanding our moral imaginations. It is a reflective practice of lingering on and within the page in order to imagine worlds beyond our visual spaces and is thus a conscious refusal to take the stereotypical bait. Comics as lingering texts are pedagogical works that motivate sustained critical engagement with moral visions. McCloud argues that the comic gutter appeals to a reader's desire for closure and meaningful structure. My response is to slow things down, to linger for just a bit in that gutter, to reflect *with* rather than *against* others, and to accept the insecurity and even discomfort of a very different kind of in-between orientation. This reflective mode takes up Robert Orsi's challenge "to set one's own world, one's own particular reality, now understood as one world among many possible other worlds, in relation to this other reality and to learn how to view the two in relation to each other, moving back and forth between two alternative ways of organizing and experiencing reality."[4] This kind of lingering in between requires patience and time, and those with expansive moral imaginations will take hold of that challenge as constitutive of what it means to read comics well.

In these final pages I want to engage Orsi's challenge by re-visioning comics through Jonathan Lear's profoundly moving study *Radical Hope: Ethics in the Face of Cultural Devastation*.[5] Lear offers an account of the Crow leader Plenty Coups, who heroically imagines a world beyond one founded on his tribe's warrior ethic of courage. I want to appropriate this sense of radical hope to think about reading comics beyond the frame, beyond the ethical confines of their graphic rhythms. But I also want to show that this deliberate arresting of pace, this desire to linger, yields distinct readerly pleasures—a kind of luxury that Plenty Coups could not afford but that readers of graphic narratives should enjoy in their reflective stretching of the moral imagination.

Radical Hope is a slow, extended meditation on a puzzling comment by Plenty Coups in the wake of Crow settlement on an American reservation: "But when the buffalo went away the hearts of my people fell to the ground, and they could not lift them up again. After this nothing happened" (*Radical Hope*, 2). What could Plenty Coups possibly mean by this last haunting phrase? Does it suggest that history for the Crow people came to an end? Lear works through various possible meanings, but he settles on the notion that when a way of life breaks down, as it did for the Crow when they could no longer hunt buffalo and live by the warrior codes of bravery, then in some real sense "things would cease to happen." Plenty Coups (1848–1932), a name meaning the counting of many coups or war achievements, was the last great chief of the Crow nation. He recognized only dimly that their way of life would cease with their war of attrition against the Sioux nation and with the white man's encroachment on their lands. The Crow signed a number of treaties with the United States government, first in 1851 and then in 1867 and 1882, with each treaty reducing their land in Montana and Wyoming; they began with thirty-three million acres in 1851 and ended up with two million acres by 1882. Facing starvation and limited resources, the Crow moved to a reservation by 1884 (26–27). When Plenty Coups laments, "After this nothing happened," he means that counting coups—the warrior tradition of bravely staking a claim over an adversary—"makes sense only in the context of a world of intertribal warfare, and once that world breaks down, *nothing* can count as counting coups" (31–32). The planting of a coup-stick as a marker of warrior triumph no longer makes sense when a way of life and a point of view have disappeared.

As a young man, Plenty Coups had a revelatory dream about this impending loss of meaning. He discovered from his oracular vision that he must follow the example of the Chickadee who listens and learns from others to survive. This sense of absorbing knowledge from others in a more reflective, pensive mode opened a way of life far removed from the warrior ethic of the Crow. Lear offers a beautiful reading of what it means for Plenty Coups to imagine a life beyond one's imagination, and it is worth listening to in full:

He has to admit that he has little idea of what is coming—other than a "tremendous storm" that will knock down all the trees but one. The dream did not even explicitly predict that the Crow will survive—though that is how the elders interpreted it. In this way, Plenty Coups can both bear witness to the end of a traditional way of life and commit himself to a good that transcends these finite ethical forms. Precisely because Plenty Coups sees that a traditional way of life is coming to an end, he is in a position to embrace a peculiar form of hopefulness. It is basically the hope for *revival*: for coming back to life in a form that is not yet intelligible. (95)

The hope is that in listening well like the Chickadee, the Crow can survive as a nation in ways unimaginable by those living the traditional life of the warrior. This is not a wistful desire or "mere wish-fulfilling optimism" but a radical hope "directed toward a future goodness that transcends the current ability to understand what it is." This Lear calls an "imaginative excellence" that enabled Plenty Coups to face an unknown future (103, 117, 146).

I want to consider what it would mean to appropriate this imaginative excellence in the reading of comics. Can we think of graphic narratives as oracular dreamscapes that reveal new modes of living well in ways that stretch or radically move beyond our capacity to understand fully what living well might require? Plenty Coups, to be sure, faced the destruction of his people in ways that readers of comics surely do not. But he had to cultivate a capacity to listen well, and comic readers should transpose this aural capacity to a visual one. Seeing graphic narratives well, as I have argued in these pages, is a luxury of a slower temporality in which lingering and engaged reflection frustrate the quickening designs of panel gaps and comic stereotyping. Let us reimagine comics as a Chickadee might, with an eye to new moral worlds barely visible within our moral realms.

Leela Prasad argued that the way we tell stories informs the very ethical richness of our lives. There is a moral aesthetic at play here, as there is in the graphic storytelling of Will Eisner. Although he labeled his own work as graphic narrative in order to convey, and to sell, serious content for an adult readership, Eisner recognized how graphic aesthetics produce moral boundaries. Eisner deploys Hebrew fonts to convey traditional authority, even as he appeals to blatant and problematic stereotypes of the Jewish tenement owner and the sexual but empty allure of the shiksa girlfriend. There are many arresting images in Eisner's *A Contract with God*, but for me none is more so than that graphic novel's splash page (see fig. 4 in chapter 1). On it we see Frimme Hersh bowed low under the heavy burden of God's contract that hovers mightily before the Dropsie tenement, seemingly floating in midair. It appears as an inescapable obligation that forever lingers above a Jewish man who has just recently buried his daughter. Graphic time slows down here, to be sure, for both Frimme and the reader. It is a kind of pacing that directly challenges the stereotypical depictions Eisner uses to quicken the comic narrative thread. But on the splash page Eisner arrests time rather than simply decelerating the pace of it. The splash page reveals a time out-of-time—a moment that hangs around, literally, as Frimme walks home alone but still aimless as the weight of exhaustion and trauma rain down on him. Like Plenty Coups, for Frimme there is nowhere to go after a communal and personal loss. Nothing happens here on this splash page because time has stopped. Eisner requires neither a page-turn reveal nor another panel to move the scene forward. There are no panels and thus no gutters, because the spatial dimensions remove temporality altogether.

There is undoubtedly pain here as Eisner moves readers to linger with Frimme in this timeless space. The interpretive challenge, as I see it in *A Contract with God*, is whether readers can imagine with Frimme a moral universe without contracts, obligations, weighty traditions, or a permanent sense of justice. Frimme tries valiantly to break from his ethical and religious past—selling the synagogue bonds that he does not own, marrying a non-Jewish woman who commands a lighter mode of being to Frimme's darker soul, and becoming a more oppressive landlord even to the poor widow—but he cannot escape the bedrock of divine justice. Eisner draws this as a recursive need, not only for Frimme but also for the young Shloime Khreks, who enters into yet another contract with an uncaring God.

The Chickadee would not have reacted in this way, for Shloime, like Frimme, moved too quickly through this contractual space. In four successive panels, one of the very few pages with distinct borders in this comic, Shloime discovers the Hebrew stone, recognizes it as a contract with God, and immediately resolves to "keep it!" (60). The border panels enact a swift pace, eliciting less reflective awareness than immediate, perhaps even stereotypical, recognition. Yet if Shloime were to hold that stone just for one reflective moment, perhaps turning it over and over as the rabbis suggest we do with words of wisdom, perhaps different temporalities might come into play here in which provocation rather than contractual demand hovers over our moral imaginations. How might Frimme reimagine the hardened contract less as a draining burden and more as an invitational cover? To think differently in these ways is to linger in that in-between challenge of imagining other moral traditions that reposition our own. Eisner offers Shloime and Frimme that reflective time, yet he quickly removes it through the short-circuiting of stereotypical representation.

But readers need not follow Eisner's lead or Frimme's and Shloime's responses. We should take up the challenge to reexamine the weighty contours of religious duties and their pull on us to ground truth and justice. Rather than recognizing divine demands, we might see moments of covenantal play and possibility or even an invitation to engage what justice means on the streets before 55 Dropsie Avenue. I do not mean to suggest that one should simply replace the other; I want instead to think of moving back and forth, as Orsi suggested, between these visions of traditional authority to see what this repositioning can offer reflective souls. The pleasure, as I see this provocation in *A Contract with God*, lies in the taking up of this challenge, not once but continuously, in a time out-of-time. Reflective lingering is good because it allows for comic and serious play. We remain tethered to the burdens of obligation, as Frimme does on this splash page, but we should not dismiss the pleasures of realignment. If we read *A Contract with God* too quickly, taking in the bait of stereotypes and gutters, we abandon the pleasures of reading and seeing "alternative ways of organizing and experiencing reality."

The kind of ethical lingering I am advocating here takes time and patience—it is a luxurious pleasure that only a few of us have or make good use of. At the liberal arts college at which I teach and work, the classroom offers rich pleasures as we take leave of "today's hyperactive media landscape."[6] In the seminar rooms, laboratories, and offices, we cultivate the virtue of concentrated, reflective awareness as we slow down time. The liberal arts college that I imagine and believe in nurtures these spaces in the hope that they generate pleasurable, reflective moments beyond academic borders. The virtues developed in the classroom should engage a broader public and politics as we live in communities that not only survive but also thrive. I recognize that this leisure time is hard to come by, because life's demands can take up all our physical, intellectual, and emotional energy. But we should demand from ourselves, and certainly our leaders, a leisure space to linger in and do the moral work that these comics ask us to do.

This is why I find Allred's *The Golden Plates* such an important text in religious ethics. There is, to be sure, much to criticize in Allred's visual representation of the Book of Mormon—not least the racial depictions of lost souls and the gendered dichotomy of strong masculine leaders and refined feminine enablers. We have seen in this book how comics often work in multiple registers and in dissenting moral visions, and we should criticize those narratives that undermine human flourishing. But Allred's portrayal of Nephi's encounter with Laban (see fig. 26 in chapter 2), a scene that stretches out Nephi's moral dilemma, is a masterful work in graphic aesthetics and gives the lie to Robert Alter's complaint that "the image concretizes, and thereby constrains, our imagination."[7] If anything, the Book of Mormon constrains while Allred's comic expands our moral universe by slowing down time and *showing* us what moral reflection looks like. In 1 Nephi 4:10, Nephi recognizes how the Spirit moves him to kill Laban, yet he retreats from the commanding voice, admitting, "And I shrunk and would that I might not slay him." But this is not how Allred depicts the biblical scene. He changes those words to read "I can not slay him" and renders an upright, strong, and determined Nephi standing over his drunken enemy.[8] The Mormon text suggests a smallness before the moral weight of divine obligation ("And I shrunk") as Nephi hopes for a quick ethical resolution ("would that I might not"). But Allred's Nephi stands tall with conviction, even as the white ghost of the Spirit hovers over his left shoulder. If we read both texts and images together, as I think we should when encountering graphic narratives of sacred literatures, then *The Golden Plates* works to expand our moral imaginations by situating us in between a structured world of divine command and a human one of moral purpose and responsibility. We cannot escape those boundaries, and Allred, for one, does not ask us to leap beyond the frame. All we can do is linger there in the uncertainty of posture, in the intimations of familial and religious allegiance, and in the loneliness of our moral deliberations. This comic, and this sacred text, demand serious play in which we grapple with hope ("would that I might not") even as we know our moral limits ("I can not slay him"). Nephi does, in the end, take up the sword and kill Laban. He must come to a decision and cannot tarry too long in that in-between space. But *The Golden Plates* shows us what lingering does for and to a soul, and for and to us, as we are pulled in and perhaps even constricted by Allred's visual midrash. Our challenge is to stay and linger in that space so we can imagine other religious worlds of divine command and human responsibility.

Comic readers have come to recognize this in-between world of divine/human encounter as the universe of superheroes. But that universe looks different now, with gods who no longer wear spandex. The heroes encountered in works such as *Ms. Marvel* and *The Lone and Level Sands* mirror our own insecurities, doubts, and troubles. They also look more like a diverse reading public, and they appeal to underrepresented histories and to material, vibrant cultural traditions. Kamala Khan's family home is full of ethnic singularity, and yet it functions like many middle-class New Jersey households. Her story is not so unlike the imagined readership for this comic, as many of the printed responses suggest. Kamala's story begins with an encounter with food as she gazes covetously at the forbidden meat, taking in its pleasurable scent. Her friend Bruno drives Kamala to a decision in mocking tones ("Chow or chow **not**, there is no **smell**"), but in this demand he misses the mark, for Kamala has no desire to eat the bacon. All she craves is its sensual, aromatic pleasures and the imaginative possibilities such smells offer for another kind of life. She will not abandon her Muslim heritage and its foodways, but she can imagine what it is to live without those goods as the aroma of forbidden treats prods her to fantasize about a life not her own. Nakia looks on with exasperation ("Seriously, Kamala, I don't understand why you do this to yourself"[9]) because she misconstrues temptation as bizarrely sadistic. But such flights of fantasy are pleasurable precisely because they open new arenas for moral play—even if those worlds would never become real ones in our own lives. Comic readers want their superheroes to look and act like they do, and this familiarity is important for those written out of traditional superhero narratives. But it is just as important that superheroes remain other to our moral universes to better reveal the insularity of our ethical frames. The trace of aromatic bacon, that symbolic "infidel meat," situates Kamala within two competing worlds as she lingers in between her Pakistani-Muslim home and the superhero call to responsible citizenship. That is, in my opinion, a good place for a teenager like Kamala to hang out.

When comic theorists talk about dwelling in those in-between spaces known as gutters, they focus on the empty spaces between panels. These are the places where readers make stories out of visual narratives and the places where readers hang out and create meaning. But comic artists deploy multiple strategies to cajole active reading, and the work we do in the gutter—in McCloud's memorable phrasing, "To kill a man between panels is to condemn him to a thousand deaths"[10]—does not limit our imaginative faculties. Craig Thompson's final image in *Blankets* is one large panel, within which we see Craig gazing upward toward the snowflakes as they swirl, to my eye, upward still beyond the trees (see fig. 49 in chapter 4). Thompson draws the tree limbs to follow Craig's upward gaze, and so the entire movement within the panel stretches beyond the panel borders themselves. With this arresting image on the verso side and only a blank white canvas to confront it on the recto side, Thompson motivates a seeing beyond the panel and the book to infinite, experiential possibilities. But these opportunities are not endless; they are momentary escapes to an unknown contingency. The textual buildup to this last image ensures that at some point one returns to a bounded life: "How satisfying it is to leave a mark on a blank surface. To make a map of my movement—no matter how temporary."[11] This desire for marking unnamed futures is something like what Plenty Coups faced when confronted with cultural loss. The recognized boundaries no longer hold, and one gazes into an unfamiliar destiny. But reaching beyond, or in Craig's moment, stretching further to that beyond, does not dissolve borders so much as reconfigure them in some uncharted form. Plenty Coups too requires a map to chart his future, but he must listen well like the Chickadee to outline an unrecognizable life. That kind of openness can be terrifying and induce a paralysis of our moral faculties. But there are also distinct pleasures to be gained by taking up, however temporarily, the posture of Craig's upward gaze. To imagine worlds beyond our imagination does not mean we leave our worlds, but it does mean we dwell in a kind of vertical limbo where mapping the moral terrain is, just for a moment, suspended in time.

We do violence to ourselves and to others when we move too quickly to secure meaning within the borders of our ethical frames. This is but one way to understand Jack Chick comics, for in their formulaic dismissal of religious and cultural differences, they advance a uniform and constricted version of Christian belief and charity. But this is also how stereotypes function within comics, because they too quicken the pace of identification within recognizable frames of reference. We do not linger when confronting stereotypes; we swiftly move past them, assured by their cultural familiarity. Even Douglas Rushkoff appeals to the familiar technology of coding and digital mapping to guide the reinvention of sacred texts. Coding dominates the current marketplace for inventive autonomy, functioning as an image of ultimate, creative power; we can reinvent the basic structures of our lives and so become "cyber-alchemist revolutionaries"[12] in the pursuit of untrammeled freedom. But the trope of coding also reveals the anxiety of encryption: perhaps there are secrets we will never recover, immune as they are to our technological powers. But for both Rushkoff and Chick, there are no enigmas to leave unresolved or mysteries better left alone. Theirs is a visual and narrative violence of revelatory truth in which certainty overcomes the unease of a far more volatile drifting among moral universes. This wandering is not aimless, I want to emphasize, because it does require the moral fortitude to listen well, like the Chickadee, and hear echoes of distant but unknown shores. But if we face these shores with the zeal of religious truth or the code of revolutionary fervor, then we do violence to our imaginative capacities to eavesdrop on intimations beyond the frame. Neither technology nor the Christian Gospel should crush our imaginative faculties.

Comics, I submit, encourage us to hear those moral vibrations, and we need not become superheroes to do this ethical work. But we also know how comics frustrate that exposure and actively discourage the kind of engaged moral lingering I advance in these pages. Let us commit ourselves to becoming active readers who recognize these double movements in graphic narratives. The comics discussed in *Drawing on Religion* train us to see and read in these ways. They are pedagogical texts in ethical development. The in-between stance of lingering between a familiar world and a barely discernible one is unsettling, to be sure, and at some point we must inhabit a place and take a stand. But let us resolve to not settle down too quickly and so enjoy the pleasures of reading and imagining beyond the frames of our moral lives.

Notes

Introduction

1. "Charlie Hebdo Attack," BBC News.
2. Eck, *Darsan.*
3. Morgan, *Visual Piety;* and Morgan, *Sacred Gaze.*
4. Gateward and Jennings, *The Blacker the Ink,* 2.
5. Eisner, *Graphic Storytelling and Visual Narrative,* 11.
6. McCloud, *Understanding Comics,* 30.
7. Eisner, *Graphic Storytelling and Visual Narrative,* 11.
8. Eisner, *Fagin the Jew,* 3–4.
9. Dauber, "Comic Books, Tragic Stories," 277–304.
10. Oksman, *"How Come Boys Get to Keep Their Noses?"*
11. Ibid., 24.
12. Ibid., 63.
13. Gardner, "Same Difference," 132–47.
14. Chute and Jagoda, *Comics and Media;* McCloud, *Understanding Comics,* esp. chap. 3.
15. Spiegelman, *Complete Maus,* 133.
16. McCloud, *Understanding Comics,* 9, 73.
17. Freedberg, *Power of Images,* xxii.
18. McCloud, *Understanding Comics,* 49. McCloud alludes here to Marshall McLuhan's famous work *Understanding Media.*
19. Varnum and Gibbons, *Language of Comics,* xi.
20. Groensteen, *System of Comics,* 6.
21. Varnum and Gibbons, *Language of Comics,* xiii.
22. Gabilliet, *Of Comics and Men,* xii–xvii, 3–4.
23. Wright, *Comic Book Nation,* 2–3; Gabilliet, *Of Comics and Men,* xviii, 13–14.
24. Groensteen, *System of Comics,* 11–12.
25. For an informative cultural history of comics and their relation to the American film industry, see Gardner, *Projections.*
26. Groensteen, *System of Comics,* 45, 61.
27. Chute and Jagoda, *Comics and Media,* 5.
28. Orsi, "Snakes Alive," 98–118, esp. 115.
29. Taussig, *I Swear I Saw This,* 70.
30. Ibid., 16, 20, 70, 100.
31. Ibid., 23–24.
32. Gamzou and Koltun-Fromm, *Comics and Sacred Texts,* 213.
33. Kwa, "Common Place," 232–48, esp. 234.
34. To be fair, not all of the graphic narratives discussed in this book are American texts—some have been translated and adapted for a North American audience.
35. Alter, "Scripture Picture."
36. Garrett, *Holy Superheroes!*
37. Narayan, "How Native Is a 'Native' Anthropologist?," 671–86.
38. Assmann, "Mosaic Distinction," 48–67, especially p. 50; see also Assmann, *Moses the Egyptian.*
39. Lear, *Radical Hope.*

Chapter 1

1. Orsi, "Crossing the Line," 40, 58.
2. Ibid., 52–56.
3. Orsi, *Between Heaven and Earth,* 4.
4. Prasad, *Poetics of Conduct,* 6–7, 16.
5. Much of what I add here about Eisner's background and the summary of *Contract with God* can be found in Koltun-Fromm, "Imagining the Jewish God in Comics," 369–401.
6. Dauber, "Comic Books, Tragic Stories," 285.
7. Eisner, *Contract with God,* 8, 25, 52.
8. Eisner, *Comics and Sequential Art,* 26–38.
9. Roth, "Drawing Contracts," 44–62, esp. 46.
10. Eisner, *Contract with God,* 61.
11. Eisner, *Fagin the Jew,* 3–4.

12. See Mann, *1491*, p. 282 for his thoughtful account of Indians as "suspended in time."

13. Eisner, *Contract with God*, 32.

14. Spiegelman, *Complete Maus*, 258–59.

15. Ibid., 133.

16. Hirsch, *Family Frames*, 25.

17. Eisner, *Graphic Storytelling and Visual Narrative*, 14.

18. Eisner, *Contract with God*, 39–41.

19. Among Yezierska's most powerful stories of immigrant Jewish life is her book *How I Found America*; on her love affair with John Dewey, see Dearborn, *Love in the Promised Land*.

20. Eisner, *Comics and Sequential Art*, 4.

21. McCloud, *Understanding Comics*, 94–117.

22. Kaplan, "Will Eisner," 269–80.

23. Vakil and Vakil, *40 Sufi Comics*, 8.

24. Ibid., 22.

25. Ibid., 67–68.

26. Barthes, *Camera Lucida*, 92.

27. Tabachnick, *Quest for Jewish Belief and Identity*, 9–13.

28. Silberschein, introduction to *Megillat Esther*.

29. Waldman, "Comix, Judaism, and Me," ix. For biographical background, see Herschthal, "JT Waldman, 33."

30. Waldman, *Megillat Esther*, 163.

31. Tabachnick, *Quest for Jewish Belief and Identity*, 13.

32. Silberschein, introduction to *Megillat Esther*.

33. Much of this discussion up to this point was taken from my previous work on Waldman. See Koltun-Fromm, "Imagining the Jewish God in Comics," 380–83.

34. Spiegelman, *Complete Maus*, 201.

35. A good deal of this analysis of *Habibi* has been taken, with some rethinking, from Backus and Koltun-Fromm, "Writing the Sacred in Craig Thompson's *Habibi*," 5–24.

36. Burton, *Arabian Nights*.

37. Damluji, "Can the Subaltern Draw."

38. Creswell, "Graphic Novel as Orientalist Mash-Up."

39. Damluji, "Can the Subaltern Draw."

40. Elias, *Aisha's Cushion*, 268–69.

41. Silverman, "Arabic Writing and the Occult," 19.

42. Zadeh, "Touching and Ingesting," 443–66, esp. 464.

43. Silverman, "Arabic Writing and the Occult," 20.

44. Barthes, *Camera Lucida*, 57–59.

45. For a thoughtful theological reading of this experiential encounter, and one that subtends my own analysis here, see Marion's account of the idol and icon in *Crossing of the Visible*.

Chapter 2

1. Burke and Lebrón-Rivera, "Transferring Biblical Narrative to Graphic Novel."

2. Stern, "Midrash and Midrashic Interpretation," 1863–75.

3. Schachter, *Image, Action, and Idea in Contemporary Jewish Art*, 106.

4. Auerbach, *Mimesis*.

5. Alter, "Scripture Picture."

6. Mitchell and Spiegelman, "Public Conversation," 20–35.

7. Crumb, *Book of Genesis Illustrated*, introduction.

8. Conan, "R. Crumb Illustrates the Bible."

9. Sattler, "Crumb's Limited Literalism."

10. Dupertuis, "Translating the Bible into Pictures," 271–89, esp. 271–76. See also Dupertuis's excellent essay, "Comic Book Bibles," 159–78.

11. Alter, "Scripture Picture"; and Anderson, "The Bible, Rated R."

12. Harvey, "R. C. Harvey on R. Crumb's *The Book of Genesis*."

13. See Conan, "R. Crumb Illustrates the Bible."

14. Jolly, "Interpretive Treatments of Genesis in Comics," 333–43.

15. Tabachnick, *Quest for Jewish Belief and Identity*, 15.

16. Crumb, *Book of Genesis Illustrated*, introduction.

17. See http://www.biblestudytools.com/kjv/genesis/passage/?q=genesis+5:1-2.

18. Alter, *Five Books of Moses*, 34.

19. Ibid., 35.

20. In his interview with Conan on *Talk of the Nation*, Crumb admits to using the Jewish Publication Society translation in addition to Alter's translation and the King James Version. The Jewish Publication Society translation of Genesis

5:1–2 reads: "This is the record of Adam's line.—When God created man, He made him in the likeness of God; male and female He created them. And when they were created, He blessed them and called them Man." See Conan, "R. Crumb Illustrates the Bible"; and *Tanakh*.

21. Mitchell, *Iconology*, 46.
22. Kant, *Conflict of the Faculties*, 115.
23. Conan, "R. Crumb Illustrates the Bible."
24. For a wonderful overview and account of these midrashic readings, see Spiegel, *Last Trial*. See also Levenson, *Death and Resurrection of the Beloved Son*; and Levenson, *Inheriting Abraham*.
25. Allred, *Golden Plates Volume One*, inside jacket cover.
26. Arnold, "R. Crumb Speaks."
27. Allred, *Golden Plates Volume One*, inside jacket cover.
28. Allred, *Golden Plates Volume One*, chap. 1.
29. Harris and Bringhurst, *Mormon Church and Blacks*, 1–5.
30. Bushman, *Contemporary Mormonism*, 92.
31. "Race and the Priesthood."
32. Stewart, *Mormonism and the Negro*.
33. Harris and Bringhurst, *Mormon Church and Blacks*, 4.
34. Allred, *Golden Plates Volume Three*, 132–33.
35. Allred, *Golden Plates Volume One*, inside front cover.
36. Allred, *Golden Plates Volume Two*, inside back cover.
37. Coody, "Ending of Mark," 104.
38. Goodacre, "The Angel Is a Clown."
39. *The Bible: Revised Standard Version*.
40. Ross, *Marked*.
41. Ibid.
42. Bogle, *Toms, Coons, Mulattoes, Mammies, and Bucks*, 6.
43. Ross, *Marked*.
44. Coody, "Ending of Mark," 100.
45. Ross, *Marked*.
46. See Chute and Jagoda, *Comics and Media*; and McCloud, *Understanding Comics*.

Chapter 3

1. Cocca, *Superwomen*, 1–6, 12.

2. Siegel, "Happy Anniversary, Superman!" See also Weinstein, *Up, Up, and Oy Vey!*, 23–24.
3. Fingeroth, *Disguised as Clark Kent*, 41–42.
4. Oropeza, "Superhero Myth and the Restoration of Paradise," 5.
5. Moore, *Watchmen*; Miller, *Batman*.
6. Wilson and Alphona, *Ms. Marvel*.
7. Janmohamed, "Hallelujah!"
8. Lewis and Mann, *Lone and Level Sands*.
9. Carpenter, "Superheroes Need Superior Villains," 89–93.
10. Knowles, *Our Gods Wear Spandex*, 16–18.
11. Ibid., 10.
12. Klock, *How to Read Superhero Comics*, 15.
13. Garrett, *Holy Superheroes!*, 22.
14. Ibid., 23, 32.
15. Ibid., 36.
16. For a helpful and succinct account of how ideology and myth work together, see Lincoln, *Gods and Demons*, 1–3.
17. Chakrabarty, *Provincializing Europe*, 107.
18. Hirsch, *Generation of Postmemory*, 82–83.
19. Ibid., 85–86. See also Barthes, *Camera Lucida*.
20. Chakrabarty, *Provincializing Europe*, 112.
21. Orsi, "Snakes Alive," 98–118. Orsi reprinted this article with only minimal changes in his book *Between Heaven and Earth*, chap. 6.
22. Orsi, "Snakes Alive," 100.
23. Prothero, "Belief Unbracketed," 10–11. The winter volume of *Harvard Divinity Bulletin* included Orsi's response to Prothero along with other scholarly voices taking sides in this debate.
24. Orsi, "Snakes Alive," 114.
25. Ibid., 112.
26. Reyns-Chikuma and Lorenz, "Kamala Khan's Superhero Burkini," 63–87, esp. 73.
27. Orsi, *Between Heaven and Earth*.
28. A. David Lewis corrected me on this cultural reference, one confirmed by everyone I work with at Haverford College. Thank you!
29. Wilson and Alphona, *Ms. Marvel*, vol. 1.
30. Ibid.
31. Eisner, *Contract with God*, 38.
32. Wilson and Alphona, *Ms. Marvel*, vol. 1.
33. Hirsch, *Generation of Postmemory*, 85–86.
34. Orsi, "Snakes Alive," 114.

35. Again, I want to thank A. David Lewis for noting this reference.

36. Heschel, *Abraham Geiger and the Jewish Jesus*, 14; and Heschel, "Jewish Studies as Counterhistory," 101–15.

37. Walzer, *Exodus and Revolution*.

38. Geertz, "Thick Description," 3–30, esp. 10.

39. For a helpful analysis and review of notions of tragedy, see Young, *Philosophy of Tragedy*.

40. This comment might suggest that his wife, Nefertari, was not actually possessed in an earlier frame. It could be, however, that even at this moment Ramses cannot recognize his own wife in this way. Very soon, however, Ramses will not be able to hide from even this possession of Nefertari.

41. Orsi, "Snakes Alive," 114.

42. Hirsch, *Generation of Postmemory*, 85–86.

43. Chakrabarty, *Provincializing Europe*, 100–101, 108.

44. Ibid., 113.

Chapter 4

1. Narayan, "How Native Is a 'Native' Anthropologist?," 671–86.

2. Ibid., 671, 676.

3. Appadurai, "Putting Hierarchy in Its Place," 36–49. Quoted in Narayan, "How Native Is a 'Native' Anthropologist?," 676.

4. Narayan, "How Native Is a 'Native' Anthropologist?," 673, 681.

5. Ibid., 673.

6. Thompson, *Blankets*, 137.

7. Green, *Binky Brown Meets the Holy Virgin Mary*.

8. Baetens and Frey, *Graphic Novel*, 61.

9. James, *Varieties of Religious Experience*, 154–57.

10. For a concise history of this reception, see Morgan, *Sacred Gaze*, 250–52; and Morgan, *Visual Piety*, 1–2.

11. Mechanic, "Graphic Novelist Craig Thompson."

12. Sfar, *Rabbi's Cat*, 1.

13. Hochman, "Ineffability of Form," 43–55, esp. 47.

14. Orsi, "Snakes Alive," 112.

15. McCutcheon, "It's a Lie," 720–50.

16. Narayan, "How Native Is a 'Native' Anthropologist?," 678–80.

17. Ibid., 673.

18. Tweed, *Crossing and Dwelling*.

19. Taves, "Negotiating the Boundaries."

Chapter 5

1. Pai, *Tales of Durga*.

2. McLain, *India's Immortal Comic Books*, 98.

3. Wertham, *Seduction of the Innocent*; Beaty, *Fredric Wertham and the Critique of Mass Culture*; Hajdu, *Ten-Cent Plague*, 6, 253–57, 285–91; and Gabilliet, *Of Comics and Men*, 38–43, 215–33. Gabilliet notes that "the first day of the [Senate] hearings coincided with the release of Fredric Wertham's *Seduction of the Innocent*, planned by the publisher accordingly" (223).

4. McLain, *India's Immortal Comic Books*, 111.

5. Ibid.

6. See, for example, Girard, *Violence and the Sacred*.

7. Juergensmeyer, Kitts, and Jerryson, *Oxford Handbook of Religion and Violence*.

8. Baker, *Jew*, 4.

9. Fowler, *World of Jack T. Chick*, 1–2; and Kuersteiner, *Unofficial Guide to the Art of Jack T. Chick*, 7.

10. Fowler, *World of Jack T. Chick*, 1–8.

11. Lund, "A Matter of Saved or Lost," 173–92, esp. 174.

12. Kuersteiner, *Unofficial Guide to the Art of Jack T. Chick*, 175.

13. See http://www.chick.com.

14. Kuersteiner, *Unofficial Guide to the Art of Jack T. Chick*, 14.

15. McCloud, *Understanding Comics*, 39.

16. Orcutt, "Comics and Religion," 93–106, esp. 100.

17. Kuersteiner, *Unofficial Guide to the Art of Jack T. Chick*, 33.

18. Varisco, "Tragedy of a Comic," 207–30.

19. Juergensmeyer, Kitts, and Jerryson, *Oxford Handbook of Religion and Violence*, 2.

20. Fowler, *World of Jack T. Chick*, 19.

21. Lund, "A Matter of Saved or Lost," 174.

22. *The Bible: Revised Standard Version*, 978–79.

23. Rushkoff, *Testament: Akedah*.

24. Morgan, *Sacred Gaze*, 117, 123, and 125.

25. Freedberg, *Power of Images*, 409.

26. http://www.rushkoff.com/about.

27. Rushkoff, *Testament: Akedah*, introduction.

28. Rushkoff, *Nothing Sacred*.

29. Rushkoff, *Testament: Akedah*, introduction.

30. Ibid.

31. Ibid.

32. Rushkoff, *Nothing Sacred*, 3, 36, 84, 111.

33. Rushkoff, *Testament: Akedah*, introduction.

34. Ibid.

35. Rushkoff, *Nothing Sacred*, 17.

36. Rushkoff, *Testament: Akedah*, introduction.

37. Rushkoff, *Nothing Sacred*, 245. Here he writes, "John [*sic*] Levenson's book *The Death and Resurrection of the Beloved Son* offers one of the most insightful and informative perspectives on the practice and idea of child sacrifice in the biblical era."

38. Levenson, *Death and Resurrection of the Beloved Son*, 18.

39. Coody, "Ending of Mark," 98–112, esp. 98.

40. Rushkoff, *Testament: Akedah*, introduction.

41. Coody, "Ending of Mark," 98.

42. Juergensmeyer, Kitts, and Jerryson, *Oxford Handbook of Religion and Violence*, 10–12.

43. Rushkoff, *Testament: Akedah*, introduction.

44. Ibid.

45. I want to thank my Chesick scholar students of 2018 who suggested this reading, which is far more insightful than the one I presented to them in class.

46. Rushkoff, *Testament: Akedah*, introduction.

47. Ibid.

48. *The Holy Scriptures*, Genesis 19:5–8.

49. Rushkoff, *Nothing Sacred*, 14.

50. Morrison, *Supergods*, 217.

51. Morrison (with artists Truog and Hazlewood), "Coyote Gospel."

52. Morrison, *Supergods*, 219.

53. Rushkoff, *Testament: Akedah*, introduction.

54. Morrison, *Supergods*, 219.

55. I suggest listening to it here: https://genius.com/The-modern-lovers-road runner-lyrics.

56. Lewis, "Seven Traits," 56–71, esp. 67.

57. "Chuck Jones' 9 Golden Rules." Thanks to my colleague John Muse for directing me to this website.

58. Lewis, "Seven Traits," 57.

59. Coody, "Ending of Mark," 98.

60. Morrison, *Supergods*, 218.

Conclusion

1. Chute, *Disaster Drawn*, 37.

2. Ibid.

3. McCloud, *Understanding Comics*, 88.

4. Orsi, "Snakes Alive," 114.

5. Lear, *Radical Hope*.

6. Chute, *Disaster Drawn*, 37.

7. Alter, "Scripture Picture."

8. I want to thank Adrian Soto Soto, a student in my "Reading Comics and Religion" class, for noting this discrepancy.

9. Wilson and Alphona, *Ms. Marvel*.

10. McCloud, *Understanding Comics*, 69.

11. Thompson, *Blankets*, 581–82.

12. Rushkoff, *Testament: Akedah*, introduction.

Bibliography

Allred, Michael. *The Golden Plates Volume One: The Sword of Laban and the Tree of Life*. Lakeside, OR: AAA POP, 2004.

———. *The Golden Plates Volume Two: The Liahona and the Promised Land*. Lakeside, OR: AAA POP, 2005.

———. *The Golden Plates Volume Three: The Lord of the Vineyard and Discovering Zarahemla*. Lakeside, OR: AAA POP, 2005.

Alter, Robert. *The Five Books of Moses: A Translation with Commentary*. New York: Norton, 2004.

———. "Scripture Picture." *New Republic*, October 19, 2009. http://www.newrepublic.com/article/books-and-arts/scripture-picture.

Anderson, Gary A. "The Bible, Rated R." *First Things*, February 2010. http://www.firstthings.com/article/2010/02/the-bible-rated-r.

Appadurai, Arjun. "Putting Hierarchy in Its Place." *Cultural Anthropology* 3 (1988): 36–49.

Arnold, Andrew. "R. Crumb Speaks." *Time Magazine*, April 29, 2005. http://content.time.com/time/arts/article/0,8599,1055105,00.html.

Assmann, Jan. "The Mosaic Distinction: Israel, Egypt, and the Invention of Paganism." *Representations* 56 (1996): 48–67.

———. *Moses the Egyptian: The Memory of Egypt in Western Monotheism*. Cambridge: Harvard University Press, 1997.

Auerbach, Erich. *Mimesis: The Representation of Reality in Western Literature*. Princeton: Princeton University Press, 1953.

Backus, Madeline, and Ken Koltun-Fromm. "Writing the Sacred in Craig Thompson's *Habibi*." In *Comics and Sacred Texts: Reimagining Religion and Graphic Narratives*, edited by Assaf Gamzou and Ken Koltun-Fromm, 5–24. Jackson: University Press of Mississippi, 2018.

Baetens, Jan, and Hugo Frey. *The Graphic Novel: An Introduction*. New York: Cambridge University Press, 2015.

Baker, Cynthia. *Jew*. New Brunswick: Rutgers University Press, 2016.

Barthes, Roland. *Camera Lucida: Reflections on Photography*. New York: Hill and Wang, 1981.

Baskind, Samantha, and Ranen Omer-Sherman, eds. *The Jewish Graphic Novel: Critical Approaches*. New Brunswick: Rutgers University Press, 2010.

Beaty, Bart. *Fredric Wertham and the Critique of Mass Culture*. Jackson: University Press of Mississippi, 2005.

The Bible: Revised Standard Version. New York: American Bible Society, 1973.

Bogle, Donald. *Toms, Coons, Mulattoes, Mammies, and Bucks: An Interpretive History of Blacks in American Films*. New York: Bloomsbury Academic, 1973.

Burke, David G., and Lydia Lebrón-Rivera. "Transferring Biblical Narrative to Graphic Novel." *SBL Forum*, April 2004. https://www.sbl-site.org/publications/article.aspx?articleId=249.

Burton, Richard. *The Arabian Nights: Tales from a Thousand and One Nights*. Translated by Richard Burton. New York: Modern Library, 2004.

Bushman, Claudia L. *Contemporary Mormonism: Latter-Day Saints in Modern America*. Westport, CT: Praeger, 2006.

Carpenter, Stanford W. "Superheroes Need Superior Villains." In *What Is a Superhero?*, edited by Robin S. Rosenberg and Peter Coogan, 89–93. New York: Oxford University Press, 2013.

Chakrabarty, Dipesh. *Provincializing Europe: Postcolonial Thought and Historical Difference*. Princeton: Princeton University Press, 2009.

"Charlie Hebdo Attack: Three Days of Terror."
BBC News, January 14, 2015. http://www
.bbc.com/news/world-europe-30708237.

"Chuck Jones' 9 Golden Rules for the Coyote
and the Road Runner." Twisted Sifter,
March 9, 2015. http://twistedsifter.com
/2015/03/chuck-jones-9-golden-rules-for
-coyote-and-road-runner.

Chute, Hillary L. *Disaster Drawn: Visual
Witness, Comics, and Documentary Form.*
Cambridge: Harvard University Press,
2016.

Chute, Hillary L., and Patrick Jagoda, eds.
*Comics and Media: A Special Issue of
"Critical Inquiry."* Chicago: University of
Chicago Press, 2014.

Cocca, Carolyn. *Superwomen: Gender, Power,
and Representation.* Reprint edition. New
York: Bloomsbury Academic, 2016.

Conan, Neal. "'Genesis': R. Crumb Illustrates
the Bible." *Talk of the Nation*, November
2, 2009. http://www.npr.org/2009/11/02
/120022241/genesis-r-crumb-illustrates
-the-bible.

Coody, Elizabeth Rae. "The Ending of Mark as
a Page-Turn Reveal." In *Comics and
Sacred Texts: Reimagining Religion and
Graphic Narratives*, edited by Assaf
Gamzou and Ken Koltun-Fromm,
98–112. Jackson: University Press of
Mississippi, 2018.

Creswell, Robyn. "The Graphic Novel as
Orientalist Mash-Up." *New York Times*,
October 14, 2011. http://www.nytimes
.com/2011/10/16/books/review/habibi
-written-and-illustrated-by-craig-thomp
son-book-review.html?pagewanted=all&
_r=1.

Crumb, R. *The Book of Genesis Illustrated.* New
York: Norton, 2009.

Damluji, Nadim. "Can the Subaltern Draw:
The Spectre of Orientalism in Craig
Thompson's *Habibi.*" *Hooded Utilitarian*,
October 4, 2011. http://www.hoodedutili
tarian.com/2011/10/can-the-subaltern
-draw-the-spectre-of-orientalism-in
-craig-thompsons-habibi.

Dauber, Jeremy. "Comic Books, Tragic Stories:
Will Eisner's American Jewish History."
AJS Review 30, no. 2 (2006): 277–304.

Dearborn, Mary. *Love in the Promised Land:
The Story of Anzia Yezierska and John
Dewey.* New York: The Free Press, 1988.

Dupertuis, Rubén. "Comic Book Bibles:
Translation and the Politics of
Interpretation." In *The Bible in the Public
Square: Its Enduring Influence in
American Life*, edited by Mark A.
Chancey, Carol Meyers, and Eric M.
Meyers, 159–78. Atlanta: SBL Press, 2014.

———. "Translating the Bible into Pictures." In
*Text, Image, and Otherness in Children's
Bibles: What Is in the Picture?*, edited by
Caroline Vander Stichele and Hugh S.
Pyper, 271–89. Atlanta: SBL Press, 2012.

Eck, Diana. *Darsan: Seeing the Divine Image in
India.* New York: Columbia University
Press, 1998.

Eisner, Will. *Comics and Sequential Art:
Principles and Practices from the
Legendary Cartoonist.* New York: Norton,
2008.

———. *A Contract with God.* New York:
Norton, 2006.

———. *Fagin the Jew.* New York: Doubleday,
2003.

———. *Graphic Storytelling and Visual
Narrative.* New York: Norton, 1996.

Elias, Jamal J. *Aisha's Cushion: Religious Art,
Perception, and Practice in Islam.*
Cambridge: Harvard University Press,
2012.

Fingeroth, Danny. *Disguised as Clark Kent:
Jews, Comics, and the Creation of the
Superhero.* New York: Continuum, 2007.

Fowler, Robert B. *The World of Jack T. Chick.*
San Francisco: Last Gasp of San
Francisco, 2001.

Freedberg, David. *The Power of Images: Studies
in the History and Theory of Response.*
Chicago: University of Chicago Press,
1989.

Gabilliet, Jean-Paul. *Of Comics and Men: A
Cultural History of American Comic
Books.* Jackson: University Press of
Mississippi, 2010.

Gamzou, Assaf, and Ken Koltun-Fromm, eds.
*Comics and Sacred Texts: Reimagining
Religion and Graphic Narratives.* Jackson:
University Press of Mississippi, 2018.

Gardner, Jared. *Projections: Comics and the
History of Twenty-First-Century
Storytelling.* Stanford: Stanford University
Press, 2012.

———. "Same Difference: Graphic Alterity in
the Work of Gene Luen Yang, Adrian

Tomine, and Derek Kirk Kim." In *Multicultural Comics: From Zap to Blue Beetle*, edited by Frederick Luis Aldama, 132–47. Austin: University of Texas Press, 2010.

Garrett, Greg. *Holy Superheroes! Exploring the Sacred in Comics, Graphic Novels, and Film*. Louisville, KY: Westminster John Knox Press, 2008.

Gateward, Frances, and John Jennings, eds. *The Blacker the Ink: Constructions of Black Identity in Comics and Sequential Art*. New Brunswick: Rutgers University Press, 2015.

Geertz, Clifford. "Thick Description: Toward an Interpretive Theory of Culture." In *The Interpretation of Cultures*, 3–30. New York: Basic Books, 1973.

Girard, René. *Violence and the Sacred*. Baltimore: Johns Hopkins University Press, 1977.

Goodacre, Mark. "The Angel Is a Clown: First Graphic Novel Based on a Gospel Captures Vivid Power of Mark." *NT Blog*, November 10, 2005. http://ntweblog .blogspot.com/2005/11/graphic-novel -based-on-marks-gospel.html.

Green, Justin. *Binky Brown Meets the Holy Virgin Mary*. San Francisco: McSweeney's Books, 2009.

Groensteen, Thierry. *The System of Comics*. Translated by Bart Beaty and Nick Nguyen. Jackson: University Press of Mississippi, 2007.

Hajdu, David. *The Ten-Cent Plague: The Great Comic-Book Scare and How It Changed America*. New York: Farrar, Straus and Giroux, 2008.

Harris, Matthew L., and Newell G. Bringhurst, eds. *The Mormon Church and Blacks*. Urbana: University of Illinois Press, 2015.

Harvey, R. C. "R. C. Harvey on R. Crumb's *The Book of Genesis*." *Comics Journal*, February 16, 2010. http://classic.tcj.com /alternative/r-c-harvey-on-r-crumb%E2 %80%99s-the-book-of-genesis.

Herschthal, Eric. "JT Waldman, 33: The Talmudist of Comic Books." *New York Jewish Week*, June 15, 2010. http://www .thejewishweek.com/special_sections /36_under_36/jt_waldman_33.

Heschel, Susannah. *Abraham Geiger and the Jewish Jesus*. Chicago: University of Chicago Press, 1998.

———. "Jewish Studies as Counterhistory." In *Insider/Outsider: American Jews and Multiculturalism*, edited by David Biale, Michael Galchinsky, and Susannah Heschel, 101–15. Berkeley: University of California Press, 1998.

Hirsch, Marianne. *Family Frames: Photography, Narrative and Postmemory*. Cambridge: Harvard University Press, 1997.

———. *The Generation of Postmemory: Writing and Visual Culture After the Holocaust*. New York: Columbia University Press, 2012.

Hochman, Leah. "The Ineffability of Form: Speaking and Seeing the Sacred in *Tina's Mouth* and *The Rabbi's Cat*." In *Comics and Sacred Texts: Reimaging Religion and Graphic Narratives*, edited by Assaf Gamzou and Ken Koltun-Fromm, 35–41. Jackson: University Press of Mississippi, 2018.

The Holy Scriptures. Jerusalem: Koren, 1989.

James, William. *The Varieties of Religious Experience*. New York: Penguin Books, 1982.

Janmohamed, Shelina. "Hallelujah! Even Muslim Women Can Now Be Superheroes." *The Telegraph*, November 6, 2013. http://www.telegraph.co.uk /women/womens-life/10430505/Even -Muslim-women-can-be-superheroes. -Hallelujah.html.

Jolly, Don. "Interpretive Treatments of Genesis in Comics: R. Crumb and Dave Sim." *Journal of Religion and Popular Culture* 25, no. 3 (Fall 2013): 333–43.

Juergensmeyer, Mark, Margo Kitts, and Michael Jerryson, eds. *The Oxford Handbook of Religion and Violence*. Oxford: Oxford University Press, 2013.

Kant, Immanuel. *The Conflict of the Faculties*. Translated by Mary J. Gregor. Lincoln: University of Nebraska Press, 1979.

Kaplan, Leonard V. "Will Eisner: Master of Graphic Wisdom." In *Comics and Sacred Texts: Reimagining Religion and Graphic Narratives*, edited by Assaf Gamzou and Ken Koltun-Fromm, 269–80. Jackson: University Press of Mississippi, 2018.

Klock, Geoff. *How to Read Superhero Comics and Why*. New York: Continuum, 2006.

Knowles, Christopher. *Our Gods Wear Spandex: The Secret History of Comic Book Heroes*. San Francisco: Weiser Books, 2007.

Koltun-Fromm, Ken. "Imagining the Jewish God in Comics." In *Imagining the Jewish God*, edited by Leonard Kaplan and Ken Koltun-Fromm, 369–401. Lanham, MD: Lexington Books, 2016.

Kuersteiner, Kurt. *The Unofficial Guide to the Art of Jack T. Chick: Chick Tracts, Crusader Comics, and Battle Cry Newspapers*. Atglen, PA: Schiffer, 2004.

Kwa, Shiamin. "The Common Place: The Poetics of the Pedestrian in Kevin Huizenga's Walkin'." In *Comics and Sacred Texts: Reimagining Religion and Graphic Narratives*, edited by Assaf Gamzou and Ken Koltun-Fromm, 232–48. Jackson: University Press of Mississippi, 2018.

Lear, Jonathan. *Radical Hope: Ethics in the Face of Cultural Devastation*. Cambridge: Harvard University Press, 2006.

Levenson, Jon D. *The Death and Resurrection of the Beloved Son: The Transformation of Child Sacrifice in Judaism and Christianity*. New Haven: Yale University Press, 1993.

———. *Inheriting Abraham: The Legacy of the Patriarch in Judaism, Christianity, and Islam*. Princeton: Princeton University Press, 2012.

Lewis, A. David. "The Seven Traits of Fictoscripture and the Wormhole Sacred." In *Comics and Sacred Texts: Reimagining Religion and Graphic Narratives*, edited by Assaf Gamzou and Ken Koltun-Fromm, 56–71. Jackson: University Press of Mississippi, 2018.

Lewis, A. David, and Martin Lund, eds. *Muslim Superheroes: Comics, Islam, and Representation*. Boston: Ilex Foundation, 2017.

Lewis, A. David, and Marvin Perry Mann. *The Lone and Level Sands*. Fort Lee, NJ: ASP Comics, 2005.

Lincoln, Bruce. *Gods and Demons, Priests and Scholars: Critical Explorations in the History of Religions*. Chicago: University of Chicago Press, 2012.

Lund, Martin. "'A Matter of Saved or Lost': Difference, Salvation, and Subjection in Chick Tracts." In *Comics and Power: Representing and Questioning Culture, Subjects and Communities*, edited by Rikke Platz Cortsen, Erin La Cour, and Anne Magnussen, 173–92. Newcastle upon Tyne, UK: Cambridge Scholars, 2015.

Mann, Charles. *1491: New Revelations of the Americas Before Columbus*. New York: Vintage Books, 2005.

Marion, Jean-Luc. *The Crossing of the Visible*. Stanford: Stanford University Press, 2004.

McCloud, Scott. *Understanding Comics: The Invisible Art*. New York: HarperCollins, 1993.

McCutcheon, Russell T. "'It's a Lie. There's No Truth in It! It's a Sin!': On the Limits of the Humanistic Study of Religion and the Costs of Saving Others from Themselves." *Journal of the American Academy of Religion* 74, no. 3 (September 2006): 720–50.

McLain, Karline. *India's Immortal Comic Books: Gods, Kings, and Other Heroes*. Bloomington: Indiana University Press, 2009.

McLuhan, Marshall. *Understanding Media: The Extensions of Man*. Edited by W. Terrence Gordon. Critical edition. Corte Madera, CA: Gingko Press, 2003.

Mechanic, Michael. "Graphic Novelist Craig Thompson on Parental Censorship, Leaving Christianity, and His Epic, 'Habibi.'" *Mother Jones*, October 2011. https://www.motherjones.com/media /2011/09/craig-thompson-blankets-habibi -interview.

Miller, Frank. *Batman: The Dark Knight Returns*. New York: DC Comics, 1986.

Mitchell, W. J. T. *Iconology: Image, Text, Ideology*. Chicago: University of Chicago Press, 1986.

Mitchell, W. J. T., and Art Spiegelman. "Public Conversation: What the %$&# Happened to Comics?" In *Comics and Media: A Special Issue of "Critical Inquiry,"* edited by Hillary L. Chute and Patrick Jagoda, 20–35. Chicago: University of Chicago Press, 2014.

Moore, Alan. *Watchmen*. New York: DC Comics, 1986.

Morgan, David. *The Sacred Gaze: Religious Visual Culture in Theory and Practice*. Berkeley: University of California Press, 2005.

———. *Visual Piety: A History and Theory of Popular Religious Images*. Berkeley: University of California Press, 1998.

Morrison, Grant. "The Coyote Gospel." In *Animal Man #5*. New York: DC Comics, 1988.

———. *Supergods: What Masked Vigilantes, Miraculous Mutants, and a Sun God from Smallville Can Teach Us About Being Human*. New York: Spiegel & Grau, 2012.

Narayan, Kirin. "How Native Is a 'Native' Anthropologist?" *American Anthropologist* 95, no. 3 (September 1993): 671–86.

Oksman, Tahneer. *"How Come Boys Get to Keep Their Noses?": Women and Jewish American Identity in Contemporary Graphic Memoirs*. New York: Columbia University Press, 2016.

Orcutt, Darby. "Comics and Religion: Theoretical Connections." In *Graven Images: Religion in Comic Books and Graphic Novels*, edited by A. David Lewis and Christine Hoff Kraemer, 93–106. New York: Continuum, 2010.

Oropeza, B. J., "Introduction: Superhero Myth and the Restoration of Paradise." In *The Gospel According to Superheroes: Religion and Popular Culture*, edited by B. J. Oropeza, 5–10. New York: Peter Lang, 2005.

Orsi, Robert A. *Between Heaven and Earth: The Religious Worlds People Make and the Scholars Who Study Them*. Princeton: Princeton University Press, 2005.

———. "Introduction: Crossing the Line." In *Gods of the City: Religion and the American Urban Landscape*, edited by Robert A. Orsi, 1–78. Bloomington: Indiana University Press, 1999.

———. "Snakes Alive: Resituating the Moral in the Study of Religion." In *Women, Gender, Religion: A Reader*, edited by Elizabeth A. Castelli, 98–118. New York: Palgrave, 2001.

Pai, Anant, ed. *Tales of Durga: Tales of the Mother Goddess*. Mumbai: Amar Chitra Katha Pvt, 1978.

Prasad, Leela. *Poetics of Conduct: Oral Narrative and Moral Being in a South Indian Town*. New York: Columbia University Press, 2007.

Prothero, Stephen. "Belief Unbracketed." *Harvard Divinity Bulletin* 32, no. 3 (Fall 2004): 10–11.

"Race and the Priesthood." The Church of Jesus Christ of Latter-Day Saints, December 2013. https://www.lds.org /topics/race-and-the-priesthood?lang= eng.

Reyns-Chikuma, Chris, and Désirée Lorenz. "Kamala Khan's Superhero Burkini: Negotiating an Autonomous Position Between Patriarchal Islamism, French Secularism, and Feminism." In *Muslim Superheroes: Comics, Islam, and Representation*, edited by A. David Lewis and Martin Lund, 63–87. Boston: Ilex Foundation, 2017.

Rosenberg, Robin S., and Peter Coogan, eds. *What Is a Superhero?* New York: Oxford University Press, 2013.

Ross, Steve. *Marked*. New York: Seabury Books, 2005.

Roth, Laurence. "Drawing Contracts: Will Eisner's Legacy." In *Graven Images: Religion in Comic Books and Graphic Novels*, edited by A. David Lewis and Christine Hoff Kraemer, 44–62. New York: Continuum, 2010.

Rushkoff, Douglas. *Nothing Sacred: The Truth About Judaism*. New York: Crown, 2003.

———. *Testament: Akedah*. New York: DC Comics, 2006.

Sattler, Peter. "Crumb's Limited Literalism: Seeing and Not Seeing in Genesis." *Hooded Utilitarian*, August 20, 2010. http://www.hoodedutilitarian.com/2010 /08/crumbs-limited-literalism.

Schachter, Ben. *Image, Action, and Idea in Contemporary Jewish Art*. University Park: The Pennsylvania State University Press, 2017.

Sfar, Joann. *The Rabbi's Cat*. New York: Pantheon Books, 2005.

Siegel, Jerry. "Happy Anniversary, Superman!" N.d. http://www.fortress.net.nu/siegel .php.

Silberschein, Moshe M. Introduction to *Megillat Esther*, by J. T. Waldman.

Philadelphia: The Jewish Publication Society, 2005.

Silverman, Raymond. "Arabic Writing and the Occult." In *Brocade of the Pen: The Art of Islamic Writing*, edited by Carrol Garrett Fisher and Ulku Bates, 19–30. East Lansing: Michigan State University Kresge Art, 1991.

Spiegel, Shalom. *The Last Trial: On the Legends and Lore of the Command to Abraham to Offer Isaac as a Sacrifice*. Translated by Judah Goldin. Woodstock, VT: Jewish Lights, 1993.

Spiegelman, Art. *The Complete Maus*. New York: Pantheon, 2011.

Stern, David. "Midrash and Midrashic Interpretation." In *The Jewish Study Bible*, edited by Adele Berlin and Marc Zvi Brettler, 1863–75. Oxford: Oxford University Press, 2004.

Stewart, John J. *Mormonism and the Negro*. Orem, UT: Community Press, 1960.

Tabachnick, Stephen E. *The Quest for Jewish Belief and Identity in the Graphic Novel*. Tuscaloosa: University of Alabama Press, 2014.

Tanakh. Philadelphia: The Jewish Publication Society, 1985.

Taussig, Michael. *I Swear I Saw This: Drawings in Fieldwork Notebooks, Namely My Own*. Chicago: University of Chicago Press, 2011.

Taves, Ann. "Negotiating the Boundaries in Theological and Religious Studies." Paper from Open Convocation, Graduate Theological Union, September 21, 2005. https://www.gtu.edu/news-events/events /lecture-address/convocation/negotiating -the-boundaries-in-theological-and-reli gious-studies.

Thompson, Craig. *Blankets*. Marietta, GA: Top Shelf Productions, 2003.

———. *Habibi*. New York: Pantheon Books, 2011.

Tweed, Thomas. *Crossing and Dwelling: A Theory of Religion*. Cambridge: Harvard University Press, 2006.

Vakil, Mohammed Ali, and Mohammad Arif Vakil. *40 Sufi Comics*. Self-published, CreateSpace, 2011.

Varisco, Daniel Martin. "The Tragedy of a Comic: Fundamentalists Crusading Against Fundamentalists." *Contemporary Islam* 1, no. 3 (2007): 207–30.

Varnum, Robin, and Christina T. Gibbons, eds. *The Language of Comics: Word and Image*. Jackson: University Press of Mississippi, 2001.

Waldman, J. T. "Comix, Judaism, and Me." In *The Jewish Graphic Novel: Critical Approaches*, edited by Samantha Baskind and Ranen Omer-Sherman, ix–xiii. New Brunswick: Rutgers University Press, 2010.

———. *Megillat Esther*. Philadelphia: The Jewish Publication Society, 2005.

Walzer, Michael. *Exodus and Revolution*. New York: Basic Books, 1985.

Weinstein, Simcha. *Up, Up, and Oy Vey! How Jewish History, Culture, and Values Shaped the Comic Book Superhero*. Baltimore: Leviathan Press, 2006.

Wertham, Fredric. *Seduction of the Innocent*. New York: Rinehart, 1954.

Wilson, G. Willow, and Adrian Alphona. *Ms. Marvel: No Normal*. New York: Marvel Worldwide, 2014.

Wright, Bradford W. *Comic Book Nation: The Transformation of Youth Culture in America*. Baltimore: Johns Hopkins University Press, 2001.

Yezierska, Anzia. *How I Found America*. New York: Persea Books, 1985.

Young, Julian. *The Philosophy of Tragedy: From Plato to Žižek*. New York: Cambridge University Press, 2013.

Zadeh, Travis. "Touching and Ingesting: Early Debates of the Material Qur'an." *American Oriental Society* 129, no. 3 (September 2009): 443–66.

Index

Italicized page references indicate illustrations. Endnotes are referenced with "n" followed by the endnote number.